Darknet

Hollywood's War against
the Digital Generation

J.D. LASICA

WILEY

John Wiley & Sons, Inc.

Published by John Wiley & Sons, Inc., Hoboken, New Jersey
Published simultaneously in Canada

Design and composition by Navta Associates, Inc.

For general information about our other products and services, please contact our Customer Care Department within the United States at (800) 762-2974, outside the United States at (317) 572-3993 or fax (317) 572-4002.

Wiley also publishes its books in a variety of electronic formats. Some content that appears in print may not be available in electronic books. For more information about Wiley products, visit our web site at www.wiley.com.

Library of Congress Cataloging-in-Publication Data:

Lasica, J.D., date.
    Darknet : Hollywood's war against the digital generation / J.D. Lasica.
      p.   cm.
    Includes bibliographical references and index.
    ISBN-13 978-0-471-68334-6 (paper)
    ISBN-10 0-471-68334-5 (paper)
    1. Internet—Social aspects—United States. 2. Digital media—Social aspects—United States. 3. Intellectual property—Social aspects—United States. 4. Freedom of expression—United States. 5. Creation (Literary, artistic, etc.)—Social aspects—United States. I. Title : Hollywood's war against the digital generation. II. Title: Darknet : Hollywood's war against the digital generation. III. Title.
    HN90.I56.L37   2005
    302.23'1—dc22   2004018704

Printed in the United States of America

10 9 8 7 6 5 4 3 2 1

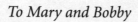

To Mary and Bobby

Contents

Foreword

If you look at my earlier books, *Tools for Thought*, *Virtual Reality*, and *The Virtual Community*, you might notice that there are more quotes, and longer quotes, than in my most recent book, *Smart Mobs*. The explanation for this is that "fair use"—the fundamental scholarly tradition of building upon the (accurately attributed) work of others—has been chipped away by large "content owners." Publishing used to be a more genteel enterprise, with a great deal of slack granted in the service of culture. As long as we used quotation marks and/or block quotes and/or italics and attributed each quote to its author in a standard footnote and/or bibliography, authors were free to make our cases by referring to the work of others. The rule of thumb was that if the quote was under 500 words, explicit permission was not required.

However, when I wrote those previous books, publishing was a very different enterprise. For example, I could have proposed my book to Random House, Knopf, Doubleday, Dell, or Bantam. Today, *all* those publishers are part of Bertelsmann. Publishers are no longer solely in the business of producing books; they are profit centers for large entertainment companies. And those companies protect their property through threat of lawsuit, at the expense of fair use. My editor for *Smart Mobs* told me that I had to obtain written permission for every quote over 250 words. Although there was no case law about this, my publisher's lawyers didn't want to court intimidation by the legal departments of the companies that owned other publishers.

If you can afford an assistant, writing a dozen or a hundred permissions letters isn't a problem, and for the most part, you won't have to pay a large amount of permissions costs. However, the problem is a larger one. First, it's just one early restriction of fair use in publishing. Since publishers have given up without a fight, what is to keep large-content owners from pressing forward in future years, requiring all authors to obtain and pay for permissions for *all* quotes? Second, it isn't limited to publishing. If you want to make an independent film these days, you better not do it on a shoestring. Every brand, every poster, every possible copyrighted image in the background of your film now requires permission—which is not always granted, nor are those that are granted always affordable. The situation is already out of control and getting worse.

This is no longer a matter that concerns only authors, filmmakers, or other "professionals," for we are all members of the media now. It has taken a decade for people to accept the notion that every computer desktop, and now every pocket and camera phone, is a global printing press, broadcast station, and organizing tool. The early years of the World Wide Web marked a historic shift of power from big institutions to individuals, from those who horde information and ideas to those who want to share them.

No wonder the media powers are in a froth about the Internet.

Now the next phase of digital transformation lies before us, one that involves democratized media, peer-to-peer networks, collaborative tools, social software, and the ubiquitous computing of camera phones; mobile devices; and cheap, tiny chips embedded into our stuff. The outcome of this next phase of the disruptive Internet is much less certain, as battles rage over control of the social, economic, and political regimes that these new technologies will make possible.

How we resolve this culture war will have far-reaching consequences for all of us. Five or ten years from now, who will be able to create and share media—individuals, or only powerful interests? When hundreds of millions of people walk down the street carrying connected, always-on devices hundreds of times more powerful than today's computers, what will they be allowed to do?

These decisions, being made today in Washington and in private industry forums, could shape digital culture for generations to come. The battles really boil down to a simple choice: whether we want to be users or consumers.

In one vision, individuals will be free to create and distribute movie shorts, personal musical works, and homemade video, occasionally borrowing bits and pieces from the culture around them. Individuals, acting as personal media networks, will build on earlier works to create and distribute compelling digital stories, true-life dramas, fan fiction, pieced-together television shows, modded computer games, and rich virtual worlds. Some users will go further, creating not just new content but also entirely new forms of media.

The second vision, pushed by entertainment interests and their Washington allies, seeks to preserve the status quo—a constricted view of our digital future that relies on formulaic broadcast content sent along one-way pipes to a passive, narcotized audience. Under this regime, consumers will have the power to choose among five hundred brands offered by the same handful of vendors, with little or no power to create their own cultural products.

Like everything in life, the choice between digital society and consumer culture is not an either-or proposition, for on any given day we juggle our roles as content creators and couch potatoes. But increasingly, we resist one-way media. We reject the megaphone of the broadcast era and turn to the many-to-many collaborative strands of the Internet. And as we do—as we grow comfortable in our new roles as publishers, producers, designers, and distributors of media—we begin to bump up against a legislative regime that threatens to lock down our digital freedoms and turn millions of us into felons. That's when the lightbulb goes off and we begin to see the threat posed to innovative grassroots technology.

Some point to our shiny new toys as evidence that all is well. Michael K. Powell, who just recently stepped down as chairman of the Federal Communications Commission, addressed the National Press Club in early 2004. He told the group:

> The visionary sermons of technology futurists seem to have materialized. No longer the stuff of science fiction novels, crystal balls and academic conferences, it is real. . . . Technology is bringing more power to people.
>
> Computing and communication power is coming to people because the forces of silicon chips, massive storage, and speedy connections to the Internet are combining to produce smaller and more powerful devices that can rest in our hands, rather than in the hands of large centralized institutions.
>
> It boggles the mind to see the fantastic products available to us today. A simple survey suffices to make the point: Digital cameras

and photo printers have moved the dark room into the home. Music players, like the iPod, have taken the rows of CDs out of a music store and placed them in your pocket. Personal Video Recorders, like TiVo, have given us more control of what we watch and when. We want movie theaters in our family rooms. GPS satellite receivers come on farm tractors. DVD players let us watch high-quality movies almost anywhere—just look through the back windows of the minivans pulling out of your neighborhood on Saturday morning and you can catch up on the full season of *SpongeBob SquarePants*.

It is not that we have access to electronics that is earth shattering, it is that we have access to pocket super computers that not long ago would have been the exclusive domain of MIT, NASA, or the phone company. The economics of these mean that they will keep getting more powerful and cheaper, thus the future will stay bright. In short, we are accelerating our ride into the future.

In his speech, Powell overlooked a few things. He neglected to mention the corporate efforts to lock down the Internet and limit the ability of ordinary people to produce cultural works that compete with media conglomerates. He failed to mention Hollywood's attempts to replace the open Net with a secure content-delivery system that resembles television. He didn't mention efforts made to control the flow of information online through a fundamental revision of the PC architecture for the sole purpose of serving the short-term interests of the entertainment industry. He forgot to mention Hollywood's successful efforts—before his own FCC—to impose a tightened regime of control over digital television that strips away rights enjoyed by viewers during the analog era.

When I see my college-age daughter, I think about what kind of media world awaits her. It's imperative that young people who have grown up with the freedom that the PC, the Internet, and the mobile phone granted them won't settle for being put into a passive box.

In *Darknet: Hollywood's War against the Digital Generation*, journalist and open-media advocate J.D. Lasica offers the first comprehensive look at the restrictions being placed on our digital freedoms by the major media powers. He also offers a positive vision of the opportunities open to the people who use tomorrow's technologies—if only fearful entertainment executives and misguided lawmakers would get out of the way.

In less capable hands, this might have been a book about the excesses of copyright law, or about the public policy wars over piracy and file sharing. But the author reaches for something larger: an accessible collection of stories about people whose lives are at the center of this epic struggle over digital culture's future. You don't have to be a technology geek, law student, or policy wonk to keep up with the important issues described in these pages.

Here is why all of this matters profoundly: online and many-to-many technologies can shift the locus of the public sphere from a small number of powerful media owners to entire populations. In the years ahead, Internet-based media will exert more and more influence over what people know and believe, how they interact with each other, and how they stretch communication and entertainment in new, creative directions.

Spread the word—much is at stake. Right now is the time to act intelligently on behalf of our shared future. We can create a world so much richer than the wasteland of today's mass media.

Howard Rheingold
Mill Valley, California

Introduction

DARKNET TELLS THE STORY OF THE DIGITAL MEDIA revolution. The future of movies, music, television, computer games, and the Internet are all on the line in this clash between the irresistible force of technological innovation and the immovable object of the entertainment media powers.

I wrote this book for two reasons: to tell the stories of the strong personalities and colorful characters at ground zero of this momentous battle and to spotlight the threat posed to digital culture.

Darknet will draw you into the secretive world of the movie underground, where bootleggers and pirates run circles around Hollywood and law enforcement. But piracy and file sharing are only subplots. Instead, this book profiles people from the future. To see where society is heading, futurist Watts Wacker once advised, find people from the future and study them. You will meet many people from the future in these pages—early adopters of the digital lifestyle, pioneers of next-generation television, gamemakers creating virtual worlds, all of them wrestling with the law or confronting powerful forces that seek to maintain the status quo.

Darknet goes behind the scenes to pull back the curtain on Hollywood insiders, tech innovators, and digital provocateurs lurking in the darkest corners of cyberspace. You'll meet a Boston pastor who uses illegal clips from Hollywood movies in his Sunday sermons; the double agent who is paid to engage in movie piracy by a large media company; the vice president of the world's largest chipmaker who may have unwittingly run afoul of federal law; the teenage boys who spent seven years refilming *Raiders of the Lost Ark*; the nightclub video jockey who uses dance scenes from old Fred Astaire movies in his routine; the former Byrds singer Roger McGuinn, who is using the Internet to help keep folk music alive; and many others who traverse the fast-changing technological, ethical, and legal landscape of the digital age.

All of these stories—reported here for the first time—speak to how technology is shifting the balance of power between big media and regular people. The rise of "personal media" is throwing the old rules into disarray.

We are no longer couch potatoes absorbing whatever mass media may funnel our way. We produce, publish, reinvent, and share personal media. We make our own movies. We create digital photos, animation, niche news sites, hyperfiction, and online picture albums. We program our personal video recorders so that we watch programming not on the networks' schedule but on our terms. We capture TV shows and stream them from one room to another on home networks. We listen to Web radio or satellite stations that cater to our personalized tastes. We download music from the Net to our MP3 players and burn music to our own CDs. And some of us record music and distribute our works on the Internet.

We make our own media. In many ways, we *are* our own media.

But digital culture faces pushback. Under the banner of fighting piracy and protecting copyright, influential companies are threatening to turn back the clock so that our personal devices become handcuffed, our televisions dumbed down, and our computers hamstrung. This is not a distant threat; it is happening today.

Despite one-dimensional coverage in the mass media, the digital media revolution encompasses much more than piracy or file sharing. I hope to enlarge the debate by bringing into focus some of the important new developments in digital culture: personal media, participatory culture, space shifting, Edge TV, open media, digital rights, and darknets.

Now, about the title. Throughout this book, "darknets" simply refer to underground or private networks where people trade files and communicate anonymously. But I want to suggest two deeper meanings as well.

First, the Darknet is a metaphor for the hidden-away matter of the Web—the burgeoning pool of weblogs, independent sites, and grassroots media well outside the limelight of big media. Collectively, this "long tail," as *Wired* editor-in-chief Chris Anderson put it, far outweighs all the bright material of the commercial Web sites with their seemingly impressive vast swaths of traffic. The dark tail is where the hope and promise of the Web resides.

Second, *Darknet* serves as a warning about a world where digital media become locked down, a future where the network serves not the user but the interests of Hollywood and the record industry. More and more activity on the open Internet will be pushed into the underground if current anti-innovation trends continue.

The next few years will be pivotal. As Joe Kraus of the public interest group DigitalConsumer.org warns, "This battle will affect consumers' rights for the next fifty years."

In this culture war, the major entertainment companies and their political allies are trying to exert control over digital technologies, while users do everything within the law—and sometimes outside the law—to escape those restrictions. The clash, intensifying by the day, is playing out in legislative chambers, courtrooms, and increasingly in the design of the consumer electronic devices, media players, personal computers, and digital television sets coming into our lives.

Only one player's voice has not been heard: yours. The sensible middle ground has been lost in the noise. But now that the battle has reached our living rooms, the public is beginning to stir. What once was an obscure set of public policy discussions may be burgeoning into a populist movement.

I was attracted to this subject from the start, fascinated by the sparks given off by this culture clash. I've spent my career straddling the worlds of both creative professionals and technologists. As a journalist who has covered both entertainment and technology for newspapers and magazines, and later as a member of management in three tech start-ups, I've seen the enormous gulf in worldviews between media people and techies. They don't just talk past each other. They speak different languages.

My friends here in the nation's technology capital (Silicon Valley and the San Francisco Bay Area) immerse themselves in the bleeding edge, working on weblog software, wi-fi, social networks, wikis, e-commerce, personal video recorders, and other cool stuff that will soon become part of our daily lives. Their mantras include user control, flexible systems, and many-to-many media models.

Many of my friends in New York and Los Angeles work in the content community—musicians and artists as well as writers, editors, and managers at national newspapers, magazines, and other media companies. Invariably, those in charge assume a broadcast model of one-to-many, top-down control, with little audience interaction. It's a recipe for friction and customer alienation.

Those two fundamental worldviews animate every aspect of this war of ideas, which pits digital culture (inclusive, participatory, bottom-up) against big media culture (exclusive, controlling, top-down).

I began this undertaking with my own predispositions: I love movies, books, and television shows. I'm also a gizmo freak who loves computers, gadgets, and tech toys. I believe in the traditional principles of copyright—the trade-off in which society grants musicians, writers, filmmakers, and other creative people certain rights and incentives in exchange for public access to their creations. At the end of this journey, my belief in copyright as the bedrock of our culture remains stronger than ever. But it also has become clear that recent excesses in law and private industry have created a new imbalance in the public's digital freedoms that threatens to shackle creative culture.

The two years I spent researching this book took me on a winding road from major media centers to remote hamlets, from the entertainment capitals of New York and Hollywood to the political corridors of Washington, D.C., and from Silicon Valley to tech outposts in Texas and Maine. I interviewed scores of people on all sides of the debate and was struck at how this issue cuts across conventional ideological lines. Progressives worry about corporate interests restricting free expression and chipping away at fair use rights. Conservatives fear that overly restrictive government rules will hamper innovation among entrepreneurial start-ups and harm large companies exposed to frivolous copyright claims by competitors. At the same time, songwriters, producers, and artists of all political stripes fear that their livelihoods may vanish if the Darknet continues to grow.

Other books have tackled this subject through the lens of copyright law. I was more interested in writing about people caught up in the crosscurrents of fundamental cultural change. I've tried to approach the subject with a journalist's eye, though not with the cool detachment of an objective outsider. Although reporting makes up most of this book, you'll also find plenty of opinion. Here's one: I part ways with those who defend unfettered file sharing that leaves artists out in the cold. People who care about the public's right to participate in media culture ought to stand up against misuse and misappropriation of others' creative works. The digital revolution promises so much more than a banal pleasuredome in which people can rip off music tracks or movies.

At the same time, when movie studios and record labels brand a pirate anyone who uses content in unauthorized ways, and when they attempt to lock down content with digital armor in a way that eviscerates traditional fair use rights, they are alienating customers—and pursuing business practices contrary to their long-term interests. They would be much better off devoting more energy to building legal, customer-friendly celestial jukeboxes for movies, music, television, and other media.

We need new rules for the digital age—not the free-for-all goodie bag of Internet piracy, but sensible policies and business models that reward and honor creative people without snuffing out the vibrant interchange of remixing and reinvention at the heart of digital culture. We need to prevent digital pilfering, but we also need to acknowledge that young people who go to movies, listen to music, and play video games approach those media in vastly different ways than did their parents. They expect to be able to interact with media, talk back to it, reshape it in some way. Media need to flow in both directions, not just through Hollywood's one-way pipes. On the Internet, the prime directive is to share experiences. Businesses and laws need to adapt to that new reality.

Darknet raises one central question above all: What kind of media world do we want to live in? The outcome of this protracted struggle will determine how we innovate, educate our children, create and share information, communicate with friends, tell stories, and leave our own marks on the larger culture. Ultimately, the questions raised in this book go to the heart of what kind of society we want to become.

1 The Personal Media Revolution

GROWING UP IN A FLYSPECK TOWN IN SOUTHERN MISSIS-sippi in the early 1980s, ten-year-old Chris Strompolos stared out his bedroom window and dreamed. He fantasized about what it would be like for a whiff of adventure to breeze through his humdrum little burg. On a sticky June afternoon in 1981 he found a vehicle for his wanderlust in the darkness of a local movie theater. He watched, jaw agape, as Harrison Ford outran a rolling boulder, dodged a swarm of blow darts, and dangled over a pit of slithering snakes in *Raiders of the Lost Ark*.

Chris Strompolos was blown away. The movie captured his imagination like nothing he had ever encountered. He thought, *I want to do that.*

And so he did.

Chris first mentioned his outlandish idea to an older kid, Eric Zala, a seventh-grader at their school in Gulfport. Chris did not suggest a quick and easy backyard tribute to *Raiders* that they could pull off on a summer weekend. Oh, no. He proposed shooting a scene-by-scene re-creation of the entire movie. He wanted to create a pull-out-all-the-stops remake of Steven Spielberg's instant blockbuster, which was filmed on a $20 million budget and made $242 million in U.S. movie theaters.

Chris and Eric agreed they would have to cut a few corners, given their somewhat more modest savings account, but, yes, of course they could do it! Eric, a budding cartoonist, began sketching out costumes for each of the characters. Soon a third movie-loving misfit, Jayson Lamb, came on board. Jayson was already heavily into special effects, makeup, puppetry, and lighting. He took charge of the camerawork with a bulky Sony Betamax video camera. Eric created storyboards for each of the movie's 649 scenes. The outgoing, slightly chubby Chris assumed the lead role of Indiana Jones.

The production took on a life of its own. Months passed, then years. On birthdays the boys asked for props and gear: Chris got a bullwhip, Eric a fedora. Jayson bought a VHS camcorder after a summer of delivering pizzas and saving money. Weekends were spent not hitting a baseball or playing a new game called Atari but in memorizing lines, creating plaster face masks, and filming take after take until they knew they nailed a scene exactly right. Nearly seven years later, they wrapped.

The result, according to those who have seen the work—including Harry Knowles, creator of the movie fan site Ain't It Cool News, and *Vanity Fair* writer Jim Windolf—is a filmic tour de force.

In the teenagers' version of *Raiders*, the actors grow older in the span of a few minutes. Voices deepen. Chris sprouts chin whiskers and grows six inches. He gets his first-ever kiss by a girl, captured onscreen. The girl who plays Marion, the Karen Allen character, develops breasts. Over the course of the movie the kids jump through windows; blow up a truck; sew together forty traditional Arab costumes; fill a basement with pet snakes; create giant Egyptian statues; surround Indy with spear-carrying, half-clothed blond warriors; dress up friends as prepubescent Nazis and Himalayan henchmen with glued-on beards; and kill Eric's little brother Kurt over and over again. In one special effect, an actor is shot, and fake blood oozes out of a condom hidden in his shirt. The filmmakers also made some inspired substitutions: a motorboat replaced a plane, Chris's puppy filled in for Marion's pet monkey, downtown Gulfport stood in for Cairo, a dirt mound became the Sahara. But they had done it, a faithful re-creation of the original film: the rolling boulder bearing down on Indy in a cave in Peru (actually, Eric's mom's basement), the live asps (actually, rat snakes and boas), the World War II submarine, the 1936 copy of *Life* magazine, the pulse-racing truck sequence. And everywhere, explosions and fire and flames. (Jayson would later explain how they managed to pull off the pyrotechnics: "I'm like twelve years old and was able to go into a store and buy gunpowder." This was, after all, Mississippi.)

They had a few misadventures, like the time they built a fake boulder in Chris's room and discovered they couldn't get it out the door. Or the time they poured three inches of industrial plaster over Eric's head to make a face mold; when it wouldn't come off, they rushed him to a hospital to remove it in a procedure that cost Eric his eyelashes and half an eyebrow. Or the time they re-created the bar scene in Nepal where the entire set was set ablaze. Eric played a Nepalese villager whose outfit catches fire, and nobody could put it out until Chris resourcefully grabbed a fire extinguisher.

When filming ended and editing was completed at a professional studio, the boys' families staged a world premiere in Gulfport, complete with tuxes and a stretch limo. Almost two hundred friends, family, and cast members turned out to watch the hundred-minute film. But soon their little master-work became all but forgotten as they parted ways and went on to college and careers.

Then, one day in early 2003, it resurfaced. At the New York University film school, which Eric Zala had attended, someone passed along a years-old videotape of the movie to the horror film director Eli Roth. Roth did not know the boys, but he was bowled over by what he saw. He slipped a copy to an executive at DreamWorks, where it quickly found its way into the hands of the master himself. Spielberg watched it—and loved it. Days later, he wrote letters to all three amateur auteurs. "Wanted to write and let you know how impressed I was with your very loving and detailed tribute to our *Raiders of the Lost Ark*. I saw and appreciated the vast amounts of imagination and originality you put into your film. I'll be waiting to see your names one day on the big screen."

Roth also shared a copy of the video with Knowles and Tim League, owner of the Alamo Drafthouse Cinema in Austin, Texas, who were equally impressed. League set aside three days in late May 2003 for the "world premiere" showing of *Raiders of the Lost Ark: The Adaptation*, though before the screening he was careful to sub out the John Williams musical score because of copyright fears. The trailer of Strompolos dodging a giant boulder sparked such interest in the weeks leading up to the event that hundreds of people had to be turned away at the door.

Flying in for the occasion were all three filmmakers: Strompolos, now an independent film producer in Los Angeles; Zala, who works in the video game industry in Florida; and Lamb, an audiovisual technician in Oakland. The three men, now in their early thirties, hadn't seen each other in years, and they were a bit baffled by why anyone would turn out to see their childhood project. To their amazement, the screening was packed to the rafters. The audience watched Chris Strompolos with his wiseacre smirk and rumpled fedora capture the spirit of Indy. They watched, mesmerized, as the kids credibly pulled off one scene after another.

When the credits rolled and the screen went dark, the audience gave them a four-minute standing ovation—almost twenty years to the day after they had shot their first scene.

Knowles wrote on his Web site the next day: "I feel this is the best damn fan film I've ever seen. The love and passion and sacrifice is on every single frame of this thing. . . . This is what fandom to me is about. . . . This is the dream of what films can do. Motivate kids to learn and make it."[1]

Vanity Fair's Windolf agreed: "We have been so entertained for so long that we have, in a way, reached the end of entertainment. An audience jaded by one mega-budget blockbuster after another is all too ready for an action movie made with love instead of money."[2]

It would be wonderful if audiences everywhere could share the love. Only a few hundred people have ever seen *Raiders: The Adaptation*. But the boys are older now and wise to the bare-knuckle realities of federal law. A work that bears "substantial similarity" to the original copyrighted work is punishable by up to a year in prison and a $50,000 fine—even if not a dime changes hands. Happily, Spielberg and Lucasfilm have no intention of pressing charges, but the young men are taking no chances. Strompolos no longer passes out copies of the film to those who want to see it. In fact, he has asked those who do possess copies to return them to him, for fear that the remake will wind up in the Darknet.

As a lark, Strompolos invited Lucasfilm and Spielberg to include their home-brew tribute in the Indiana Jones DVD boxed set that came out in 2003. The studio passed. Lamb then bought an old three-quarter-inch Sony Betamax on eBay so they could digitize hundreds of feet of old outtakes, and in early 2004 a Hollywood producer bought the rights to tell the boys' story. As for showing their *Raiders* homage to others, Strompolos tells me, "We have legal constraints. We can't take advantage of opportunities for theatrical release or home video because the intellectual property doesn't belong to us."[3]

Thus the law gives us the absurdity that you will be able to watch a documentary about the teens' undertaking, but you won't be able to watch *Raiders: The Adaptation* itself. If you want to see our young heroes' handiwork, you'll have to wait until the year 2076, when the original *Raiders* copyright expires (unless Congress extends copyright terms yet again). The boys will be teeing off on their 105th birthdays right about then.

An entertainment consultant who worked as an adviser to Disney management for many years related a meeting he took with executives of another major Hollywood studio in early 2003. As he ruminated on the profound impact that people creating their own media will have on the entertainment giants, the faces around the table grew puzzled.

Finally one of the executives asked, "What did people do before television?"

Well, the consultant said, there were other mass media, like radio.

"Oh, yes, I suppose people listened to the radio."

And before that, people read books.

"Oh, right."

And even before that, people entertained one another.

"How would they do that?" The studio exec seemed genuinely at a loss.

Well, the consultant explained, many years ago people told each other stories, played musical instruments, and sang to one another.

Smiles from the studio people. How quaint.

If I had to bet, the consultant went on, I'd say society is returning to that tradition. The generation of young people now growing up would prefer to watch each other's digital movies—the ones they produce themselves. They would rather experience the worlds they create rather than what Hollywood makes for them.

All the studio people at the table shook their heads. "You're crazy," one said. "No one will turn their backs on Hollywood entertainment."

Inside the Hollywood bubble, it's business as usual. Outside, on the streets, much more interesting things are happening. Kids are taking up digital tools and creating movies and video shorts. Some are remixing big media television shows and movies into fan-style DVD (digital versatile disc) commentaries. Others are creating new musical forms on computers in their bedrooms. While millions sharpen their digital photo techniques, many also have begun using camera phones and mobile devices to post photos or homespun wisdom to a global audience.

The world has changed since Chris Strompolos was ten. What once took seven years to pull off could likely be done in a single summer of youthful exuberance. What once required expensive, bulky equipment and professional editing studios can be done with a palmcorder and desktop computer. As the tools become cheaper and easier to use, the kind of storytelling that infuses *Raiders: The Adaptation*—the grit, the passion, the wide-eyed wonder—is spreading throughout our culture. Such personal works remind us that it is in our nature to tell stories and be creative—instincts that have been too often repressed during the couch potato era of force-fed mass media.

That's not to say that Strompolos and company or other little islands of creativity will give MGM, Disney, or Paramount a run for their money. The motion picture studios, record labels, television networks, book publishers, and makers of video games won't be done in by camcorder-toting teens, Web journal authors, or garage musicians armed with Apple Powerbooks. Make no mistake: personal media will complement, not supplant, the old order of mass media and consumer culture. Most of us will continue to watch entertainment created by professionals working at media companies. High-quality entertainment takes time, talent, effort, and money to pull off.

But that's no longer enough. In ways large and small, individuals have begun bypassing the mass media to create or sample digital music, video diaries, film shorts, weblogs, visually arresting multimedia Web sites—in short, personal media. Sometimes these personal works will be an entirely original creation, borrowing techniques and ideas, perhaps, but no music, video, or photos created by others. At other times these creations will be a collage or hybrid, borrowing bits and pieces of traditional mass media mixed with material supplied by the user or remixed in interesting new ways and transformed into something new.

"People are no longer satisfied with read-only media encapsulated in whatever proprietary formats the entertainment industry sees fit to distribute," Greg Beato writes in his music weblog Soundbitten. "True interactive media isn't just a movie with three alternate endings: it's media that's flexible enough to allow users to do whatever they want with it. Which means copying it at will, using it on different platforms, modifying its contents, combining it with other media, and basically doing anything else that can be done to turn centuries of copyright law on its ear."[4]

Something new is happening. While the pros go about their business, amateurs,[5] and hobbyists experiment with new ways to inform, entertain, and communicate with one another.

Call it personal media, open media, bottom-up media, or home-brew media—it all comes down to people plugging into the larger culture in creative ways. "Today no more than 5 percent of the populace can create. The others watch, listen, read, consume," says Marc Canter, a multimedia pioneer who cofounded the software giant Macromedia. "The new technologies promise to change that, enabling the rest of us to express our creativity. Amateur filmmaking, digital photography, writing in online journals about a topic you know well—all are forms of creativity. All are on the rise."[6] Why is it happening now? Technology is one reason. Personal computers have become so powerful and pervasive (now in two out of three U.S. households) and professional-level software has spread so far and wide that most people now have the tools of digital creativity at their fingertips. Communication is another reason. Smart search engines and community forums let peers collaborate and exchange ideas in ways that were once available only to insiders or those who took expensive training courses.

But there may be a deeper reason for the rise of personal media: a hunger for authenticity in the land, perhaps a Jungian shared memory of a time when stories held power and when creative expression was not reserved for a privileged class.

"If you go back one hundred years, most media were personal media," observes Henry Jenkins of MIT. "The impulse to create stories or make up songs or paint pictures is what culture wants. There was a brief moment in human history where mass culture pushed the other stuff out of the way. Somehow we became convinced that only a few special people have talents or visions worth pursuing. But that moment is ending, and now mass culture and participatory culture have to negotiate their relationship with each other. And that scares the bejesus out of media companies that are still resisting the public's participation in the culture in a more direct way."

A look at the fundamental differences between the two kinds of media foreshadows the battles ahead and hints at the reasons why the major media companies haven't begun to appreciate the shifting sands beneath them.

Old media, born in the industrial age, rely on the economics of conveyor-belt mass production and scarcity of atoms. Broadcast-style media send programming down one-way pipes to a mass audience of consumers, requiring a one-size-fits-all content model catering to mass tastes. Members of the public rarely participate in the media process. Some write letters to the editor. Others might call a TV station when a favorite show gets bumped. But pity the renegade who wants to excerpt material from a song, movie, television show, magazine, or book for use in his or her own work. The game of copyright lawyers, chutes, and ladders makes sure that such a player will rarely reach the finish line.

Add to this equation the disruptive effects of personal media in the information age. While the analog world has long featured a stable landscape of mass media, fixed objects, and predictable atoms, today we swim in a turbulent digital sea of nearly limitless bits. Digital tools now allow people at the edges of the network to create high-quality material, to make as many copies as they like, and to share them worldwide. Hundreds of millions of us are flocking to the Internet as an alternative media source not because it's more authoritative (although it can be), but because we're lured by a medium that allows people like us to become part of the conversation. In this new space, built with two-way pipes, we can choose from not a hundred or two hundred channels but from a million topical niches. Interactivity and personalization are the coins of the realm. In the old paradigm, mass media never let you inside. Conversely, as MIT's Shigeru Miyagawa put it, "In personal media, you are always inside the media, by virtue of being able to control the point of view."[7] Old media demand strict adherence to a rigid, arcane set of laws. By contrast, the rules and social mores surrounding creative reauthoring and sharing in the digital era are still very much in flux.

The differences between personal media and traditional media go even deeper. These are not parallel media universes but worlds that intersect and coexist in the same space. Almost invariably, personal media borrow from popular culture. Mass culture provides the building blocks for the stuff we create. In the emerging digital culture, what we fashion from our own materials and what we borrow from others can sometimes blur. As media become increasingly digital, such remixing becomes the rule rather than the exception.

Take the dance club scene.

On a Saturday night in lower Manhattan, a wiry, brown-haired video jockey outfitted in baggy jeans and a fashionably ill-fitting T-shirt surveys the dance floor of the Roxy nightclub. An ethnically mixed crowd of young hipsters grinds to the drum 'n' bass jungle beat, while those twenty-one and over pool around the bar to buy overpriced drinks. As Asian boys with dreads and young women with peasant tops, Lithium wear, and Kangol hats bop near the raised stage, the VJ tokes on a cigarette and unleashes a big-beat assault over the Phazon sound system. Suddenly a wave of images splashes onto a pair of four-by-six-foot projection screens hovering above the throbbing crowd. For the next three hours, an LCD projector streams kitschy images of our culture. Break dancers from a 1970s flick fill the screens. Sean Connery swaps DNA with a Bond girl. Fred Astaire busts a move, speeding up and slowing down in step with the syncopated tunes.

The footage fascinates. At once endearing and absurdist, it manages to perfectly capture the heart and tempo of this scene. Hands flail in the air, breakers writhe on the floor, and above it all a skinny VJ named Bruno Levy holds forth, fashioning a digital party from disparate bits of sound and scenes, all the while communicating with the clubgoers on an invisible level that elevates the experience to something approaching the mystical. Chalk figures, Japanese anime characters, clips from old TV shows and obscure movies, and the recurring motif of Fred Astaire stutter-stepping in sync with the music—the images flow together in a trippy, free-form visual montage.

Later I ask Levy about the unauthorized use of such Hollywood images. "Oh, what we're doing is completely illegal," he says bluntly. "But so is sampling music, and that's the lifeblood of the club scene."[8]

Levy often pops into Blockbuster and comes out with two or three dozen videos, which he uses to weave a visual cultural montage. "We live in a cut, sample, and paste world," he says. "With today's generation, you sample ideas, you copy and borrow beats and sounds and images, and rehash them into something new and serve them back to the public. The technology has made it so easy to do that now. The creative movements in art and music and culture only work when everyone is copying from each other."

Borrowing from earlier works has always been a time-honored and accepted part of the creative tradition. Every painter learns by emulating the masters. Every musician acquires her own voice and style by first imitating those who came before. Fledgling filmmakers imitate the oeuvre of a Spielberg, Kubrick, Kurosawa, or Cassavetes. The fandom phenomenon celebrates pop culture by appropriating it: young adults publish comic-book fanzines that borrow copyrighted images; on Internet fan fiction sites, viewers write episodes that add new story lines for characters from more than five hundred television shows; amateur video buffs have created more than four hundred homemade versions of *Star Wars* and circulated them online.

Every night, dance club DJs and MCs digitally splice together bootleg remixes of Top Forty hits in remarkable new ways.

"Using the omnipresent sea of symbols, images, sounds and texts as source material, millions of people are laying claim to their cultural inheritance," the *National Post* writes. "Call it postmodern, call it open source, call it rip/mix/burn, the upshot is a culture transformed."[9]

If Bruno Levy and his audiovisual dance club collages stand at the leading edge of a cultural shift in our attitudes toward personal media, middle-class America is not far behind. In the analog world, when we bring home a vinyl album and run our fingers over its grooves or read a book and leaf through its pages, such tactile experiences suggest to us that we own that record or book. And in a real sense we do: we can mark up the book, resell the album, give them to friends, donate them to a library. Today, as digital media begin to stream through our homes, we want to hold on to that tangible relationship. When an article of broadcast media enters our domain, we claim it as our own. The songs on our iPods, the television shows we capture on TiVo, the music videos in our new portable video players, the movies we watch in our DVD collections—we believe that these digital slices of media also belong to us in a real sense.

From there, it is a short leap for people to want to remix songs that we've captured. Many of us will want to swap music videos on our portable video players. We'll want to add "our" video snippets of Brad Pitt or Cameron Diaz to a birthday DVD we're creating for a friend. Some of us may want to send a news clip or recipe from a cooking show across town to a relative—or across the world to a friend.

In short, changes in technology usher in changes in cultural norms. Cultural experts Sheldon Brown and Henry Jenkins are among those who say society is undergoing a remarkable transformation in its approach to media. They suggest that young people in particular are adopting a new set of expectations governing our interactions with media.

Brown, director of the Center for Research in Computing and the Arts at the University of California, San Diego, says the looming cultural war over digital media is the result of an epic transition from one set of societal rules to another. "We're right in the middle of this turmoil today as one kind of culture dies out and gives way to the next, creating a new space." He has seen the changes in attitude firsthand during his classroom instruction over the years.

The graduate students he teaches, the thirty-year-olds, hail from the

Atari generation. They grew up with low-resolution video games and cable TV, and they come from a world where technology was task-specific, Brown says. To this crowd, media are independent of each other. Television, the telephone, the stereo, and the personal computer are considered separate domains.

Brown describes his undergraduate students, the twenty-year-olds, this way: "They're more comfortable with the idea that technology is actively upsetting all of those cultural, social, and technological domains. They get excited about that and dive in and experiment with new ways of communicating, socializing, and sharing information—text-messaging with friends, making dates. But they still think in terms of these separate domains that exist."[10]

When you get to junior high and elementary school students, he says, "It comes as a complete surprise that there's a difference between the computer and the television, that there are different rules governing each. You almost have to explain to them why can't they turn to Channel 3 on the Internet and why can't they Google the TV to find out what's on. It just doesn't make any sense to them that there are these separations and limitations. The younger kids move more fluidly between these different media spaces."

As the digital generation matures, he says, young people won't be satisfied with traditional forms of linear storytelling. Their expectations are bound to alter entertainment as we know it.

"Sometimes I think that 30 years from now it will be funny to think back on these kinds of clean distinctions in media forms, that there are movies and television and video games being separate entities. It's more likely our media experiences will have multiple dimensions simultaneously. It will be more about: Are you engaging this with four other people? Are you looking at this by yourself on your cell phone or in a room 60 feet high? Each medium will be authored with these multiplicities embedded within it."

Brown sees changes in our expectations about media not only in his students but also in his own family. He recalls that when his daughter was four, her first media interfaces came with a computer mouse and interactive learning books, not a television remote control. "She found the remote control very frustrating, because it's connected to this device that doesn't have the viewer at the center. She became upset by the device of the television. The story was exciting and the pictures were nice, but where was the place for her? The only option was to look at something else or turn it off.

"Television never asks you, what do you want to watch now? It just throws stuff out there and you have to figure out how to dodge ads and sift through programming. By contrast, the modern computer interface has been designed around the idea of you telling it what to do next. For young kids, they want and expect things to respond to them. That's why computer games are such a powerful lure. The kids become active participants in the media experience."

Across the continent, you can almost see Henry Jenkins nodding in agreement. The director of MIT's Comparative Media Studies Program and author of nine books on popular culture, Jenkins says that from an early age, children reimagine what you can do with characters and settings from movies and TV. They play video games that permit control over a character within limited boundaries. Newer games allow an even broader range of interactivity and behaviors. When they get online, they can share stories, and children as young as seven are posting to fan fiction sites with simple but interesting stories about Harry Potter and Pokémon.

Jenkins calls Pokémon "the first form of storytelling for a converged media world," sprinkling elements of its universe across the media spectrum. The story can come at you from multiple directions: as a TV series, video games, books, movies, and playing cards. Entertainments like Pokémon or *The Matrix* teach young fans to hunt and gather in their own entertainment experience, he says, letting them drill down to the level of engagement they desire.[11]

When young people get a little older, they might expand their media horizons with a camera or camcorder. "In my early teens I had a Super 8 camera, but if I wanted to show the movies I made, I had to put a sign on the front lawn and a couple of neighbors would take pity on me to watch it in my basement," Jenkins says. "Today, I'm talking to high school kids who have digital cinema sites and have put their films up on the Internet, and their work is being seen all over the world. In some cases they're getting invitations to compete in film festivals."

Jenkins points to his son, now twenty-one, as a child of participatory culture. At age five, the younger Henry started telling stories, which the family would type into the computer, and he drew pictures to illustrate each story. For the next five years, the family printed out little books and sent them to his grandparents during the holidays. Most of his stories were about characters from popular culture. "These stories had two effects," Jenkins says. "One was to encourage him to see the media as something that could be rewritten on your own terms. And the other was to give us an insight into how he was processing the media he was consuming, letting us know his fears and values."

Most parents can relate. My five-year-old son is already directing home movies (I'm the camcorder operator) featuring titanic clashes between heroes and villains. Bobby is big into LEGO, the original "remix" toy, but he draws his iconic figures from mass media and mass merchandising: Power Rangers, TransFormers, Scooby Doo, and the like. Generations ago, children did the same thing with Superman, the Green Hornet, and the Lone Ranger.

"For most of human history, people sat around campfires and told stories about great warriors and cultural heroes," Jenkins says. "In modern times we borrow from television, movies, comic books, and video games. Pop stars and the characters of mass media are the things we have in common regardless of our backgrounds or our local reality." As young people acquire more sophisticated tools, they begin using these cultural touchstones as props in their own works—for example, by grabbing the image or video of a pop star, remaking it with special effects on a computer, and sharing it with friends. Media, after all, exist to be rewritten.

Because these new forms of personal media often include pop culture figures we all can relate to, and because individuals now have the power to distribute media to a global audience, you have a built-in recipe for conflict with the media companies, Jenkins says.

The kids, naturally, come away confused. "They're encouraged to wear corporate logos and brands, and to put them on their backpacks and lockers," he says. "But the minute they put that logo on their Web site, they get a cease-and-desist order. So the media companies are sending profoundly mixed signals."

As more of us create media rather than merely consume it, as more of us turn away from one-way mass media and become immersed in more open media such as the Internet and the virtual worlds of video games, media companies and their allies can respond in one of two ways: resist and place barriers in the way, or bend to the winds of change and embrace the culture of participation.

Hollywood is not known for its warm embrace of change. *Raiders: The Adaptation* has a relatively happy ending in that no one was sued and no cease-and-desist letters were issued (even if the movie itself is now off-limits to the public). But what's most striking about Spielberg's congratulatory letter to the amateur filmmakers is how out of the ordinary it was by Hollywood standards. Threats and confrontation have become the norm in the battle between the entertainment industry and those who make use of their media in unauthorized ways—not only Internet pirates, but also tech innovators, small-business owners, indie record labels, restaurateurs, artists, and regular folk.

Young people especially view intellectual property in a different light than their elders. To many, it's not unusual to see authorship and ownership as a shared, collaborative experience. Remixing and borrowing are native to the culture, and if Bruno Levy did not bother to ask the studios for permission to use their movie clips in his collages, it's because they surely would have said no. (If you have any doubt of this, see chapter 4.)

Today's students see personal media and file sharing as given, even banal, parts of contemporary life. "It's important to understand this as an articulation of their cultural moment," Brown says. "College students today are bombarded with thousands of streams of media information, so their cultural products themselves start to reflect that. They have so many other things dragging on them, screaming at them for attention, whether they're going from the digitally enabled classroom to the broadband-connected dorm room to their color cell phones to their wireless PDAs. So they exercise mastery and control over this media domain in a way that the previous generation did not. They see media as the raw materials out of which they will author their own cultural forms. Instead of fetishizing the record album, as my generation did, they're annoyed by things tied to a physical object. Their attitudes about ownership are changing dramatically and are being shaped by the Internet. Their entertainment centers on collage and meshing music and repurposing media. It's all about mixing, remixing, and re-remixing of these things."

Media companies need to begin catering to this "mix-up culture," Brown says. "The solution isn't to throw college kids in jail for creating online music trading sites, but in creating media forms that have this hybridity built into them, so that the kids can integrate these elements into their own works of personal media." We should begin thinking about how to build online narrative spaces with "enabling hooks" that let us incorporate elements of *The Matrix*, *The Simpsons*, and Jane Austen, he suggests. Instead of buying a DVD of *The Matrix*, we might buy a software engine that creates the character of Morpheus for use in other media.

But that would mean media companies would need to give up some measure of control over their works—a move they have been loath to make.

Jenkins says that media companies aren't prepared for the borrowing and appropriation inherent in participatory culture. "People are making their own versions of popular entertainments, with or without the sanction of media producers. So the question becomes, what will the relationship between those two spaces look like? Will it be an antagonistic one, where those kinds of activities are shut down by legal means and your ability to manipulate content is reined in by technological measures? Or will it be one where there's a greater collaboration between professional and amateur media producers?"

The burden of change does not fall completely on the media companies. Individuals bear a responsibility to set limits on acceptable forms of online behavior. The Internet has not ushered in a new morality, and digital tools will always enable us to go one step farther than we should. At the same time, the mainstream media rarely understand share culture, confusing it with plagiarism and theft. They don't know what to make of kids who mix and match the ideas and images they find in today's culture. The digital generation, meanwhile, looks upon such borrowing, transforming, and sharing as an affirmative, interactive, creative act, akin to artistic license.

The ways in which people appropriate mass media cover a broad spectrum, Jenkins points out, and he draws some sensible lines in our virtual sandbox. He believes the laws should be changed to draw a legal distinction between appropriation by amateurs and appropriation for commercial gain. He would allow the kinds of borrowing and creative remaking that takes place in fan fiction and certain kinds of song sampling. He would allow some kind of celestial jukebox where music or excerpts from other media could be sampled. But he would prohibit the distribution of wholesale works that haven't been altered or remixed by the audience, like the file trading that takes place in the movie underground.

"I think people who care about the public's right to participate in media culture should speak up against forms of media distribution that amount to out-and-out piracy," he says. At the same time, Jenkins and others believe entertainment companies are only hurting themselves when they brand any unauthorized use of their works as piracy.

As more people engage with personal media, obstacles loom. The entertainment companies and their allies on Capitol Hill and in the high-tech sector seem determined to herd us into digital speakeasies, trying to reimpose the old order of top-down media and consumer culture. But participatory culture has no rewind button. People are becoming less tolerant of one-way media. They expect to be able to interact with visuals and songs and games, to manipulate them, and sometimes to share them with others.

Some have gone so far as to suggest we have reached the end of the consumer age. In an essay on his site titled "RIP the Consumer, 1900–1999," the influential new media theorist Clay Shirky wrote dismissively of consumers, "Media is something that is done to them." The Internet has changed the media equation, replacing consumerism with the power of shared connections. "In the age of the Internet, no one is a passive consumer anymore because everyone is a media outlet. . . . There are no more consumers, because in a world where an email address constitutes a media channel, we are all producers now."[12]

Will the new rules being formulated by industry and government help lift us up as partners and collaborators? Or will they attempt to put us in tightly controlled straitjackets, shunting us into virtual shantytowns as their pipes continue to flow in only one direction? The evidence to date is not encouraging.

2 Now Playing

Hollywood vs. the Digital Freedom Fighters

THE ATTORNEYS, BUSINESSPEOPLE, AND ENGINEERS FROM the three industries took their customary seats around the table in a cramped conference room at the Burbank Airport Hilton. Soon to be known as the DVD Copy Control Association, the cross-industry forum was made up of a handful of people who spoke on behalf of the Hollywood studios, the high-tech industry, and the consumer electronics industry.

Months before, at the dawn of the DVD era in 1996, the three groups had wrangled at length before finally agreeing to allow Hollywood movies to play on personal computers in addition to DVD players. Now the studios wanted to enforce their new system of "region coding" around the globe. Like Allied powers carving up Europe and the Middle East as spoils of war, Hollywood moguls had carved the world into six grand regions. To help preserve the system governing movie release dates in foreign markets, the studios believed it necessary to configure all DVD devices so that a DVD sold in the United States (Region 1) would not play in Great Britain (Region 2), Brazil (Region 4), or India (Region 5).

But Hollywood remained unhappy that region coding could be thwarted. In small numbers, movie lovers in Paris, London, and Rome had begun buying the newfangled DVD players and changing the settings to Region 1. In that way they could buy and watch an American DVD long before the foreign version of the same DVD hit their local markets. Desktop and laptop computers were problems, too. Film buffs could pick up a Hollywood DVD during a trip to New York and watch it—sometimes before the film even opened in their own countries—simply by changing the region setting. What to do? How could these rule-breakers be stopped?

The representative from Universal Studios leaned forward. The idea he outlined was simple: place a Global Positioning System satellite chip in every DVD player and computer sold with a DVD drive. Hollywood could then track the location of every individual who uses a DVD player and enforce its rules from the sky.[1]

James M. Burger, a Washington attorney who represents the tech industry, recounted the reaction of the computer and electronics people on the other side of the table to the audacious idea of planting such a James Bond–style tracking device in millions of users' machines.

"We all looked at each other, a little dumbfounded."

"Because of the privacy issues?" I asked.

"Oh, no. Because of the added expense. Do you know how much GPS chips cost back then?"[2]

Eventually the proposal was scrapped and a less costly and intrusive system was agreed upon: a user could change the region code settings on her laptop only so many times before it was locked into one region permanently. (Members of the DVD Copy Control Association now chuckle at that early proposal, saying that lots of freewheeling ideas were floated during these sessions.)

Hollywood has long had a flair for the dramatic—and the imperial. Burger tells of a public hearing held in Washington that illustrates the culture gap between Hollywood and high tech. "One studio executive got up and said, 'People pay for the privilege of watching movies.' Could you imagine a computer executive saying, 'People pay for the privilege of using one of our machines'? He'd be slaughtered. There's sometimes a regal attitude in Hollywood."

The most striking culture gap, however, may be the industries' different attitudes toward change. "We love disruptive technologies," says Intel vice president Donald S. Whiteside. "In Silicon Valley, the only constant is change," adds Joe Kraus, who cofounded the former Excite search engine. "Hollywood has always had a tendency to see change as not desirable, and so they do everything they can to prevent it."

In recent years, the press has framed the conflict between Hollywood and Silicon Valley as a battle about Internet piracy. But piracy is not really the core issue. The studios are chiefly interested in protecting their gleaming new DVD empire. Two technologies enforce Hollywood's business model: encryption (or copy controls), which prevents copying; and region coding, which enables an orderly process for the worldwide release of movies. While copy controls arguably thwart piracy, region coding does nothing to prevent people from redistributing movies onto the Internet. Instead, region coding enables Hollywood's "windowing" process of marching movies from cinemas to home video, pay-per-view, video on demand, cable TV, and network TV in each country.[3] Many Europeans resent having to wait many months after a Hollywood movie is released on DVD in the United States before they can see the movie on DVD in their own countries.[4] A thirty-year-old French programmer living in Ireland who goes by the techie name of >NIL: operates the Pioneer Region Free DVD Firmware site to help those who want to bypass region coding on their DVD players. (You'll find hundreds of such sites on Google and hundreds of region-free DVD players for sale on eBay.) "Being French," he tells me, "I wouldn't mind seeing a revolution occur to shake down this whole monolithic business."

The controversy over Internet piracy is a subplot to a much larger drama. This is a battle about how we may use, own, and share digital media. As more people create personal media and begin to participate in culture, we see backlash from major entertainment companies seeking to control all uses or reuses of their works, even at the expense of citizens' traditional rights.

In this conflict, too often the press has failed to ask hard questions. Will the new wave of restrictions being imposed on law-abiding Americans (described in subsequent chapters) do anything at all to thwart determined pirates? Is the trade-off worth the price? Will home-brew culture be enabled, or will the locks placed on digital devices to prevent piracy also prevent us from adapting media for personal use?

The years-long battle over the proper balance between freedom and lockdown in the digital age shows no signs of abating. While Hollywood and high tech slug it out, the $100 billion consumer electronics industry has remained largely on the sidelines. Despite a few renegades, such as Philips Electronics (headquarters in the Netherlands), Archos (France), Pinnacle (Germany), or start-ups such as the former Diamond Multimedia or Sonicblue, electronics makers have a reputation for being beholden to Big Entertainment. And for good reason: nobody buys a DVD player or big-screen television unless there's killer programming.

By contrast, the giants in the technology industry—which is about ten times bigger than Hollywood—have been less susceptible to the movie industry's entreaties and cajoleries. As a result, high tech has been the public's best friend at the private forums where blueprints for the digital home are drawn up. "We don't just hand over the keys to Hollywood. We negotiate to preserve fair use and customer rights," says Stephen Balogh, an Intel business manager who represented the computer industry at the meeting above.[5]

But increasingly, high tech is becoming a less reliable advocate for the public. Three reasons for that. First, growing media consolidation has muddied the waters. For instance, when it was an electronics company, Sony only had to worry about making cool devices. Now that it owns a major motion picture studio as well as a record label, the company often gives greater priority to protecting copyrighted material rather than delivering a superior customer experience.

Second, Congress sent the message that it would consider imposing government mandates if the tech sector did not assuage the concerns of media companies over digital piracy. Spurred by congressional jawboning and fear of litigation, computer makers lined up behind a "trusted computing initiative" designed in part to lock down devices and prevent people from copying or manipulating entertainment media.

Third, computer companies, seeing slower growth, have begun to invade the home entertainment turf, becoming dependent on Big Entertainment's wares. In 2003 Hewlett-Packard launched 158 consumer products, from cameras to a gadget that converts old VHS tapes into DVDs. Gateway has bet the farm on electronics by branching out into plasma TVs, DVD players, camcorders, and other gear for the digital home. Dell now makes big-screen digital TVs. Microsoft[6] sells a PC-powered digital television and media hub for the living room. Apple sells the world's most popular digital music player, the iPod, and its digital lifestyle software—iTunes, iMovie, iPhoto—have less to do with computing than with creating and managing entertainment. Even cellular giant Nokia has crossed boundaries to make mobile phones that send e-mail, take photos, and play games.

There is an awkward name for this: convergence.

If you enjoy subjecting your children to stories about the good old days, someday you will be able to tell them of a strange time when media existed in separate containers. Television shows were watched only on a TV set. Music was pumped out of a stereo or radio. Hollywood movies debuted only on the silver screen. Home movies were watched (if at all) on a projection screen. Computers were productivity machines. Photos belonged in picture albums or shoeboxes.

All that is changing, thanks to convergence, the dreaded nineties buzzword that is finally becoming a reality. As media transform into series of 1s and 0s—TV shows recorded on digital boxes, ten thousand songs slipped neatly into a shirt pocket—the devices needed to play entertainment are coming to resemble personal computers, complete with chips, hard drives, and connections for networking.

What does this transformation herald? If you hear high tech tell it, convergence means letting all the entertainment gizmos in our homes talk with each other, perhaps commanded by a single all-powerful black box that the tech company places in your living room.

If you listen to big media, you'd think convergence refers to media corporations finding "synergies" and delivering "content" across many divisions. Customers, if considered at all, are looked on as "baby birds with our mouths open, happy to take anything the big media company gives us," as one attendee at last year's Digital Media Summit in New York put it.[7]

But convergence is about more than black boxes, new toys, or the marriage of technology and show biz. True convergence puts a blasting cap to the one-way architecture of top-down media. When media come together in new ways, consumers become producers who want greater ability to participate in media, to reuse it, to design their own experiences. New technologies are changing the balance of power between media companies and their customers so that, for example, computers become not just music and movie playback devices but also photography labs, mini-motion picture studios, and music recording studios.

Genuine convergence happens when people create personal media or capture mass media and personalize it. Meaningful convergence involves the user.

"When media intersect, the public begins to archive, annotate, appropriate, and recirculate media. Each of those steps is empowering to consumers," MIT's Henry Jenkins says. "We're now seeing scorched earth–style warfare between consumers and corporations that continue to resist change. The corporations still control more cards than consumers do. But they control fewer cards concerning how consumers engage media content than they did before the VCR, the photocopier, the Internet, and TiVo."

The media companies and their tech partners don't see it that way.

At the 2004 Consumer Electronics Show in Las Vegas, Carly Fiorina, chief executive of Hewlett-Packard, took the stage and outlined her vision of the digital revolution, an era in which all of us become creators of digital photography, movies, and music. (A year later, she was forced to step down from her post.) "We are all digital revolutionaries now," she proclaimed. In this new era, she said, we rely on technology that is intimate and intuitive, that works when and where and how we want it to work.

But then she surprised many in the crowd by launching a blistering attack on digital piracy[8]: "Just because we can steal music, doesn't mean we should. Just because we can take someone's intellectual property for free, doesn't mean we should. Just because you can do it and not get caught, doesn't mean it's right. It's illegal, it's wrong, and there are things we can do as a technology company to help."

Fiorina held aloft an ultrasleek iPod music player that HP would soon be selling and made a pitch to woo L.A. and New York media execs by announcing that the company would use its $57 billion in market muscle to come down squarely on the side of show biz. "Starting this year, HP will strive to build every one of our consumer devices to respect digital rights. In fact, we are already implementing this commitment in products such as our DVD Movie Writer, which protects digital rights today. If a consumer, for example, tries to copy protected VHS tapes, the DVD Movie Writer has HP-developed technology that won't copy it—instead, it displays a message that states, 'The source content is copyrighted material. Copying is not permitted.' And soon that same kind of technology will be in every one of our products."

It was clear whose "digital rights" HP would now protect: the lock-and-key gang at the major media companies. As for "putting more power in the hands" of "digital revolutionaries," HP will permit you to copy, paste, borrow, remix, and recirculate only the cultural materials not under its digital lock and key. Disagree and you risk being branded a "pirate."

| | |

On the major public policy issues of the digital age, the high-tech industry has splintered into different factions. Some hardware makers such as Intel, for instance, oppose the law that makes picking digital locks a federal crime regardless of the circumstances. Intel also filed a friend-of-the-court brief on behalf of Eric Eldred[9] and fought gallantly in late 2004 against the anti-innovation INDUCE Act. And it hosted a Digital Rights Summit to shine a spotlight on the threats posed to innovation.

Whiteside, Intel's man in Washington, sizes up the struggle over digital technologies this way: "Giving customers the flexibility to make their own music playlists, shoot their own video snippets, and create their own content—that is meeting tremendous resistance from the creative industry because their entire business model is driven off of distributing packaged content in a way that supports their business. So this is going to be a long and contentious battle for years to come."[10]

But some tech companies—particularly software makers—support Hollywood's lockdown agenda. Many tech companies supported anti-innovation laws such as the Digital Millennium Copyright Act as well as government regulations and industry standards that restrict the public's use of electronic media. Other tech companies are happy to build the restrictive digital locks for the entertainment companies. (News Corp. president Peter Chernin entreated the tech crowd at Comdex 2002: Join us and build our watermarking technology and encryption software!)[11]

If high tech cannot always be counted on to defend the interests of a public that increasingly wants to rip, mix, and burn cultural artifacts, who can they trust? The free culture movement.

As the fault lines created by new technologies crystallize, Hollywood and a vanguard of digital enthusiasts are confronting each other in a showdown worthy of *High Noon*. The two camps have come to be personified by two individuals: Jack Valenti and Lawrence Lessig.

Valenti's career is a fabled one. As a lieutenant in the Army Air Corps during World War II, he flew fifty-one combat missions as the pilot of a B-25 attack bomber in Italy. He was in Dallas in the motorcade on November 22, 1963, and "saw that day a brave young president murdered," he says. In the famous photo of Lyndon B. Johnson taking the oath of office aboard *Air Force One*, flanked by a dazed Jacqueline Kennedy, Valenti is stage left. LBJ tabbed him to handle the transition.

Valenti left government service in May 1966 to head the Motion Picture Association of America, the movie studios' trade group. During his remarkable thirty-eight-year tenure, Valenti became a lobbying legend. While Valenti took on reduced duties after grooming his successor, Dan Glickman, in mid-2004, the MPAA remains the House That Jack Built. The ultimate Washington insider, Valenti transformed the MPAA into one of the most muscular legislative powerhouses in the nation's capital. The entertainment industry gives congressional candidates about $25 million per election cycle, not to mention comp tickets that allow Beltway insiders to schmooze with Hollywood stars.[12]

The studios are the forces that guide and direct MPAA policy. With Sony's acquisition of MGM in September 2004, all of the major Hollywood studios are now part of media conglomerates that also own television networks, radio stations, recording labels, and diverse subsidiaries. (When I refer to "Hollywood" in this book, I mean to encompass all these activities, not just the filmmaking apparatus. And it's important to emphasize that Hollywood is no monolith. There are many innovative, forward-looking elements in the new Hollywood that embrace digital culture. The Hollywood in this book's subtitle refers to the change-resistant old Hollywood, which sees the new technologies and the new players on the block as threats to its business models.)

While all of the MPAA's member studios have a say in formulating policy, some are especially vociferous on copyright and piracy issues. "It took me a while to understand that the MPAA represents the viewpoints of the most extreme players," Intel's Balogh says. The major studios can be counted on to fall along a fairly predictable continuum on those issues, with Disney and Twentieth Century–Fox generally staking out the most rigid positions; Universal, MGM, and Paramount steering a middle course; and Sony and Warner Bros. showing the greatest degree of flexibility.

The MPAA achieved a Triple Crown of sorts in 1997–1998 with Congress's passage of three laws. The No Electronic Theft Act subjects individuals to maximum penalties of three years in prison and $250,000 in fines for the reproduction or distribution of copyrighted material over electronic networks. The Sonny Bono Copyright Term Extension Act extended the life span of copyrights by twenty years. The Digital Millennium Copyright Act outlawed any attempt to tamper with copy protection on digital devices. The DMCA and Sonny Bono Act, reviled by much of the digerati, gave rise to the free culture movement.

Valenti has become familiar to many Americans from his appearances onstage at the Academy Awards for the better part of three decades. His best-known accomplishment may be the now-familiar movie rating system of G, PG, PG-13, R, and NC-17,[13] which the motion picture industry instituted in 1968 and which he continues to oversee. Less memorably, he helped devise television's V-chip ratings system in the 1990s.

Now eighty-three, the white-haired Texan with the beetle-brow eyelashes and diminutive frame still has star power. On February 24, 2003, he took the stage at Duke University, taking his "moral imperative" campaign right into the teeth of the opposition: the college campus. Looking fit, poised, and a little imperious, he called on students to lay down the tools of piracy and take up "the old verities . . . words like duty, service, honor, integrity, pity, pride, compassion, sacrifice." In silver-tongued oratory, he said the "migratory magic of digital ones and zeros" had brought about a "collision of values."[14] (Valenti writes his own speeches, but then, no one else could.)

Months later, he tells me he had addressed thirty-five hundred students at eight university campuses during the year. "I believe there is a disengagement by young people about who owns what and why," he says in his familiar, resonant baritone. "They have rationalized, how can it hurt a big movie company if you bring down one movie? But they don't realize that 10 million people are swapping these things."[15]

Valenti, with his easygoing banter and southern gentlemanly charm, seems to enjoy sparring with students over digital piracy. "When I ask them, how many of you believe that what you're doing is wrong, morally and legally, most of their hands go up. But they rationalize it by saying, yes, it is a kind of stealing, but everybody else is doing it, and it costs too much to go to a movie." He has had more success rallying university officials to his cause. At the MPAA's behest, many colleges have adopted codes of conduct that punish students if they download or share copyrighted material.

But Hollywood's antipiracy juggernaut has suffered its share of setbacks. In 1996, the first major skirmish of the digital age occurred when Hollywood and the consumer electronics makers shopped an agreement around Washington that they wanted codified into federal legislation. Among other things, the proposal would have required every computer to scan every file it encountered—every e-mail, document, movie, or piece of music—and look for a code to see whether copying was permitted.

Rhett Dawson, president of a Washington trade association for the computer industry, told the *National Journal* the proposal "was madness" because it would have slowed computer performance by as much as 50 percent, with no benefit to the user and without accomplishing what Hollywood wanted.

In 1998, entertainment companies got nearly everything they wanted from Congress with passage of the harsh DMCA and the twenty-year copyright extension. But in early 2002, Hollywood was back looking for additional legislation and hauled out its big guns for a series of congressional hearings. Disney chief Michael Eisner attacked tech companies for promoting "rip, mix, burn" as a recipe for theft. Time Warner chief Richard Parsons and News Corp. president Peter Chernin spoke darkly of the threat posed by digital piracy and asked Congress to force the tech industry to protect media content from being pilfered. Congress declined to act immediately, but in late 2003 Hollywood persuaded the Federal Communications Commission to adopt a plan that restricts how people may transfer and watch digital television shows. Even that is not enough. Valenti remains disappointed that computers can copy and transfer copyrighted material "without any kind of responsive circuitry in there that could stop piracy." Still, he is heartened by what he has seen of the "trusted computing" effort undertaken by Microsoft and its tech allies to reengineer the PC.

Although it may seem at times as if studio execs long for a Transmooker—the device in *Spy Kids* that shuts down all technology on the planet—Hollywood has a history of assimilating new technologies. Disney, which stands to benefit from wider distribution of its classic children's films, was among the first studios to release movies over home satellite. It pioneered computer animation by partnering with Pixar. On the Web, Disney opened Toontown, the first online virtual world for kids. And it is experimenting with ways to distribute movies digitally.

Valenti, too, is no technophobe. He even owns a TiVo for recording television onto a hard drive. But he says there are limits to what the public should be able to do with movies and TV shows. To that end, the MPAA is working with a dozen technology companies, including Microsoft and IBM, as well as computer scientists at MIT and Caltech, "to try to find the kind of security clothing that we need to put around our movies. . . . Technology is what causes the problem and technology will be the salvation of the problem."

In his scrappy, us-against-them appearances before Congress, Valenti frequently resorts to red meat rhetoric, as when he linked piracy with "terrorism."[16] (My own senator, Diane Feinstein, has become a partisan for Hollywood in these battles, calling file-sharing networks a grave security risk to the nation.) Valenti also sought to stigmatize all peer-to-peer networks as purveyors of piracy and pornography. Thus it should come as no surprise that he is vilified in many quarters of cyberspace. Does it bother him?

"I don't relish it, but I know what I'm doing is right," he says. "I believe in change. Change irrigates every enterprise, and particularly the movie business. So I welcome it, but I want to make sure that thievery is not going to lacerate our future."

A continent away, Lawrence Lessig opens the door to his office at Stanford University. Behind him, stacks of folders totter on a desk next to the Macintosh he used to write *Code*, *The Future of Ideas*, and *Free Culture*, books about the threats posed to freedom and creativity in the digital age.

The towering giant of cyberlaw is wearing a blue cardigan, pale yellow dress shirt unbuttoned at the collar, and black jeans. Wire-rim glasses perch on his pink, compact face. As he talks in measured, soft-spoken tones, one easily imagines a swarm of editorial cartoonists competing to capture the sweep and majesty of his startlingly pronounced forehead once this issue pricks the public's consciousness.

On this day, the forty-two-year-old law professor looks subdued, two weeks after the U.S. Supreme Court dealt him a stinging 7–2 defeat in *Eldred v. Ashcroft*, the most important case of his fabled career. Lessig had invested a considerable amount of emotional capital in the cause of Eric Eldred, a retired computer programmer from New Hampshire who created a Web site of literary works culled from the public domain.[17] Eldred was getting three thousand visits a day from students around the globe seeking out the literature of Nathaniel Hawthorne, Anthony Trollope, and others. Eldred was excited by the prospect of adding works first published in the 1920s: stories by Ernest Hemingway, Ring Lardner, and Virginia Woolf, *The Great Gatsby*, *The Maltese Falcon*, *The Jazz Singer*, *Show Boat*, songs by George Gershwin and Irving Berlin, books by Dr. Seuss, poems by Robert Frost, early stories in *Reader's Digest*, *Time*, and *The New Yorker*. Countless others had similar plans to republish or build on these creative works.

It may surprise you, but you would be infringing on a copyright if you posted half a dozen of your favorite Frost poems or Gershwin lyrics on your Web site. You cannot write a sequel to a Hemingway short story without permission from his heirs. You cannot sample songs by Jimmie Rodgers, the father of country music, who's been dead seventy-one years, without paying a fee to BMG/RCA.[18] You cannot change a word in your local theater company production of the 1927 musical *Show Boat* without getting permission from the copyright holder. You cannot put on a museum exhibit about the Great Depression or the Dust Bowl migration of Okies without tracking down whoever holds the copyright to any photos, video clips, or audio you want to include. By contrast, we all can freely use images of Santa Claus, created by cartoonist Thomas Nast in the late 1800s, only because the jolly old fellow has entered the public domain.

Until recently, copyrights on a work expired fifty years after an author's death (seventy-five years in the case of a corporation). At that point, the work entered the public domain.[19] Once a work passed into this lawyer-free zone, anyone was free to use, remix, update, or redistribute it. But in 1998 Congress stepped in and obliged media interests by extending copyright terms by another twenty years. The Sonny Bono Act prevented an estimated four hundred thousand books, movies, and songs from entering the public domain until 2019—unless Congress extends the limits again, as it has done eleven times in forty years. In January 2003, the Supreme Court expressed doubt on the wisdom of the Bono Act but ruled it was Congress's decision to make.

The *New York Times* editorialized after the ruling, "The court's decision may make constitutional sense, but it does not serve the public well. . . . Artists naturally deserve to hold a property interest in their work, and so do the corporate owners of copyright. But the public has an equally strong interest in seeing copyright lapse after a time, returning works to the public domain—the great democratic seedbed of artistic creation—where they can be used without paying royalties. In effect, the Supreme Court's decision makes it likely that we are seeing the beginning of the end of public domain and the birth of copyright perpetuity."

After the Court's ruling, Lessig recalls, "A lobbyist said to me, 'You know, Larry, all you had on your side was ideals and principles. The other side had all the money in the world. When was the last time ideals and principles beat all the money in the world?"[20]

Yet Lessig fights on. He remains convinced that copyright has strayed dangerously far from its roots. The founders never intended copyright to be a perpetual private property right. Instead, copyright was seen as a way to stimulate artistic creativity for the general public good. It says right there, in black and white, in the Constitution's progress clause: "to promote the Progress of Science and Useful Arts," Congress may grant copyrights for "limited Times."

That careful balancing act has been thrown out of whack in recent years by Congress's catering to special interest groups. While people often think that copyright unambiguously fosters creativity, Lessig says its excesses no longer foster innovation but instead are used by media corporations to hoard ideas and quash creativity.[21] Hollywood is the driving force behind efforts to turn ours into a "permission culture" that inhibits experimentation and novel business models, he says.

One doesn't need to look back to the 1920s to see examples of culture being kept under lock and key. The battles in the digital rights wars are less about the past than the future. The fight has just begun over access to contemporary works.

In the digital age, how will millions of us be able to draw upon and adapt, borrow, sample, and reinterpret the riches of our common culture? When media companies prevent legal uses of their material—such as playing songs or movies on a computer, making backup copies of digital files, or grabbing a single frame of a movie and publishing it on the Web with personalized commentary—what recourse do users have? What are the rules of engagement for the new digital world?

Lessig has considered these matters at length since he first became entranced by the law's collision with new Internet-driven technologies. "The law is just completely screwing it up, so there's a kind of guilty lawyer's conscience here. Someday we'll look back at this extraordinarily crude vision that allowed the courts to regulate speech and creativity in a way we'll find astonishing."

In addition to writing three books about the Internet and cyberlaw, the prodigious law professor also founded the Center for Internet and Society at Stanford, a think tank and law clinic that handles cases involving digital freedom, and he helped launch Creative Commons, an organization that gives creative people flexibility in managing their publishing rights. The son of a steel-fabricating business entrepreneur in Williamsport, Pennsylvania, Lessig came to champion the cause of digital liberty in a roundabout way. He was a delegate to the 1980 Republican National Convention and a self-described "right-wing lunatic"[22] before three years of graduate school at Trinity College in Cambridge, England, changed his outlook. After an uneasy stint as the only liberal clerk for Supreme Court justice Antonin Scalia, he taught at Yale, the University of Chicago, and Harvard before deciding with his wife to head West.

The message he's spreading is simple: Broadcast culture is limiting by nature, while digital tools empower people to participate in their culture—if only the law would get out of the way.

"We've come from a world in which there are a million ways in which to use creative material without ever invoking copyright law," he says. "Read a book, sell it, give it away—those are not fair uses, those are unregulated uses, and copyright law doesn't come into play because there's no copy involved. But on the Internet, everything you do with the book creates a copy. The law, in this crude, formalist way, then says, 'Okay, copyright law gets invoked.' And that means an extraordinary range of ordinary creative activity now must fight off the burdens imposed by the law. The choice before us is how this creative space will be regulated. Will it be regulated and limited by copyright law, or will it be treated in a more balanced way that copyright law has traditionally tried to foster, by securing commercial return while allowing lots of space for creative use?"

Lessig, who has made pessimism his personal brand, fears that the media Godzillas will trample the Internet through a combination of bad laws and restrictive copy protection. He realized before anyone else that code becomes a kind of private law whenever media companies lock down their material in digital armor or, worse, try to rearchitect the Internet into an entertainment delivery vehicle.

One challenge is educating Congress about the issue, Lessig says. "Because they don't have firsthand experience with it, members of Congress buy into the argument that this is a debate about stealing intellectual property, when it's really about something else. We are the cut-and-paste culture. The question is whether that should be presumptively legal or illegal. Right now it's presumptively illegal, and that makes no sense. The cut-and-paste way of living is essential to creativity, and it should be a presumptively legal activity. But people who don't spend time touching these digital tools don't have a sense of what we're talking about."

Hollywood and the record companies, he says, continue to treat digital consumers as passive couch potatoes. Instead of letting people borrow from and build on their works, the entertainment companies are relying on one-way pipes to deliver material "wrapped in a container that forbids you from cutting out any parts and mixing it with anything else."

Lessig fears that these digital wrappers, or copy protection systems, "will make a huge chunk of our culture essentially inaccessible within five years." We will no longer be a culture where we can take the Gutenberg Bible off the shelf, open it up, and see what's inside. Instead, "we'll open it up and get a bunch of garbage inside—because the license has expired, the company that built the encryption system is gone, or the software is out of date." Not long ago Lessig tried to retrieve some files he had created in 1990. But the files were encrypted. The company that created the copy protection was gone. He has no way to access his own material. "We can be absolutely certain that a huge chunk of content will be killed just like this. We're essentially burning libraries with encryption."[23]

Over the next few years, as millions of people take up the tools of digital creativity, we will see remarkable uses of personal media. How amazing it would be, Lessig muses, to see the story of a sixteen-year-old high school student fused into an Orwellian nightmare by borrowing bits of the film *1984*. "That type of creative experience should be just as simple as adding song tracks to a home video on your Mac."

And yet, such borrowing may be against the law. Lessig is itching to set up a public exhibit where families could see the new technologies on display in their full rip-mix-burn glory next to two intellectual property attorneys. "As the kids show off their home movies, the lawyers would step in and say, 'This is a violation, and this is a violation, and this is a violation.' At a certain point, the parents and audience members would have a similar reaction: 'This is outrageous! Why is this a crime?'"

He pauses and looks out his office window at a swirl of leaves billowing in the courtyard. "Unless the ordinary person thinks this is crazy—not just intellectuals and academics and the top 5 percent but the population as a whole—until that happens, we're not going to win this battle."

A month later I run into Lessig again, at the South by Southwest Interactive Conference, where the tenth annual running of the geeks is being held in Austin, Texas. During his keynote speech, Lessig wows the crowd with one of his distinctive PowerPoint slide presentations. Jack Valenti's visage looms onscreen, to hisses and boos from the audience. Lessig solemnly intones each word as it appears on-screen—duty, honor, integrity, compassion—in mock tribute to Valenti's "moral imperative" campaign.

The debate over copyright and piracy has been hijacked by the extremes, he tells his captivated audience. The Alls, Lessig says, believe that their rights need to be controlled perfectly. (On cue, Valenti makes another cameo appearance.) The Alls want to build a future Internet where the architecture defaults to a regime of All Rights Reserved. At the other extreme, the Nones believe in total freedom, a No Rights Reserved world. They believe that none of the creative community's rights need to be preserved on the Internet. A few in this crowd probably fit that description: diehard believers in the mantra "Information wants to be free."[24] Finally, there are the Somes, whom Lessig singles out for praise. The Somes are the 85 percent of us in the middle: those who want to protect some of our rights but are happy to share our works with others under some circumstances.

"These people at the extremes, let's let them be unhappy as they lead their extreme lives," he says. "What I want is a space in the middle. Most of us have an attitude that says, 'Here's my content, I created it, but there are lots of ways you can use it that I'm completely okay with.'"

The law has abandoned the reasonable middle by siding with one extreme. Lessig's voice becomes pained as he talks about the "extraordinary frustration" he feels toward his fellow lawyers. "Let me tell you about us. We believe in control. We work for clients who come to us and we create structures of control. It makes us feel we've given our clients something. But control is not the space in which the broadest range of creativity and innovation can flourish. As the lawyers come down to regulate this space to benefit not you generally but a few in particular, you need to stand up and push us out of the room. You need to reclaim this space because we don't belong there."

When he finishes, the crowd rises up as one and roars its approval. Lessig receives the only standing ovation of the three-day conference.

You don't get a membership card when you join the free culture crowd, so defining its scope gets tricky. But there is no question that a digital protest movement has begun to brew, led by technology enthusiasts, educators, librarians, public interest groups, business entrepreneurs, digital storytellers, college students, political activists, and more than a few artists and writers.

The academic wing of the digital rights movement finds its intellectual nexus under the roof of the Berkman Center for Internet & Society at Harvard Law School. Its Internet Law conferences seek to try to restore copyright balance in the digital age. One I-Law lecturer, Yochai Benkler of Yale, told the *New York Times*, "We are at a moment in our history at which the terms of freedom and justice are up for grabs." He points out that every major innovation in the history of communication—the printing press, radio, telephone—was followed by a brief period of openness before the rules of usage were set and alternatives eliminated. "The Internet is in that space right now."[25]

Outside the groves of academe, other forces have gathered in support of the cause.[26] If Lessig is the legal warrior riding to defend the digital homeland from the Visigoths, John Perry Barlow is cyberspace's leading theoretician and spiritual holy man, appearing fleetingly like Gandalf the Grey to issue quasi-mystical, grandiloquent pronouncements equal to Valenti's soaring oratory. A former songwriter for the Grateful Dead, Barlow foresaw the current conflicts surrounding "the problem of digitized property" earlier than anyone, in 1992, when he penned an influential essay that argued, "Intellectual property law cannot be patched, retrofitted, or expanded to contain the gasses of digitized expression."[27]

Barlow, fifty-six, has staked out an absolutist position on Net freedom. While he has backed away from his early calls for cyberspace to be entirely free from the straitjackets imposed by lumbering governments, he remains steadfast in his belief that the Internet is a fundamentally different space and not just another delivery medium to be regulated "like cable, satellite, or United Parcel Service," as Valenti once remarked.[28] Years ago, Barlow told me: "The Net is not a channel. It's the ocean. And that's a vastly different thing." When we spoke recently, he says people still don't grasp the distinction. "The Internet is a whole world where all the existing media—print, audio, video—come together in new ways."

Barlow considers the DMCA "ludicrously misguided," sees digital copy protection as akin to "building fences around tornadoes," and recoils at the notion that "giving someone a copy of a song is a crime." The law and copy protection have combined to stifle not only creative culture but political expression as well. "If you can't quote from television or film or other kinds of moving media with the same ease that you can quote from text, then you're no longer able to express the full range of your political opinions," he says.

We are using shopworn, analog metaphors for sharing information in the digital world, Barlow suggests. "I think it is simply dangerous to think of expression as property. We have the wrong model for moderating its economic flow and for creating wealth from its distribution. It's a service, not a good." That's not to say he subscribes to the misplaced notion that all information should be free.[29] He makes clear that no one should profit from others' works or pass them off as his own.

Solutions will emerge to reflect the new digital reality, Barlow says. One answer is to change the business models of entertainment companies to leave behind a market based on scarcity of atoms (where physical goods are finite) and embrace the new digital reality of free-flowing, ubiquitous bits.

By cutting out the middlemen—"the gang of thieves," as he calls the record labels—and using the Net to interact with fans, musicians can make more money by touring and selling their works online than they do now under their record contracts.

File sharing, meanwhile, cannot be stopped, and efforts to criminalize the casual reproduction of copyrighted material will ultimately fail, Barlow predicts. Businesses and the law have not yet come to terms with the desires of the tens of millions of people who now routinely trade files online. He frames this as a conflict between the industrial age and the virtual age[30]—a death match between open and closed systems. Barlow says the Internet represents not just a disruptive technology but also a paradigm shift that demands "the renegotiation of authority." The resulting power clashes will be fierce and last "long beyond our lifetimes."

In 1990, before anyone had heard of the Web, Barlow cofounded the Electronic Frontier Foundation to fight for free speech and privacy rights in cyberspace. The EFF, described as a sort of ACLU for nerds, is now leading the fight in the digital rights wars. Other public interest groups in the fray include Public Knowledge, the Center for Democracy & Technology, Consumers Union, and DigitalConsumer.org.

Among other notable thinkers whose views align with the free culture movement, three should be singled out: Brewster Kahle led the effort to build the Internet Archive, the largest library ever assembled. He is slowly adding television programs, movies, music, books, and other material to the collection. To date, only twenty thousand books have been digitized out of the sixteen million books in the U.S. public domain. Kahle is working to change that. Author Howard Rheingold gets the loudest applause at technology conferences when he extols the value of peer-to-peer networks and lambastes entertainment companies for hindering innovation and preventing users from gaining access to cultural materials. For years, Doc Searls, coauthor of *The Cluetrain Manifesto*, has been evangelizing new business models that make individuals equal partners in the marketplace. He wrote:

The real war here is not between a few producers and its billions of "consumers." It's between two completely different visions of the Net itself. One sees it as a medium—a plumbing system for pumping content from producers to consumers, controlled top to bottom by suppliers. The other sees it as a place where people and companies meet to make culture, do business and share stuff that makes life interesting. . . . One wants to protect it and let it grow. The other wants to manage and exploit it. One expects innovation and market forces to solve the business problems that naturally accompany growth. The other wants government to protect established industries against exactly those kinds of problems—by restricting the very operations of the Net itself, and the devices that allow people to use the Net.[31]

Another veteran of the intellectual property wars, Jordan B. Pollack, addressed the subject at PopTech, an annual gathering of tech and academic luminaries in bucolic Camden, Maine.[32] Pollack, a computer scientist, inventor, and Brandeis University professor, outlined a future in which media companies will stop selling us things and instead sell us licenses. Such a world may present a choice of two extremes: "cyber-fascists" and "cyber-Communists." The former group—made up of entertainment giants, publishing houses, and software companies—will rule this new domain as benevolent media monarchists. As copyright landlords, they will grant us read-once, view-once licenses. The second group consists of hard-core file sharers and some free-software advocates who reject the very notion of intellectual property and want to appropriate and share any digital information freely and infinitely. I've run into such zealots and their brand of digital liberation theology on many occasions. Like Pollack and Lessig, I find this belief system hard to understand and impossible to defend.

Pollack told the crowd that the virtual world is transforming our understanding of property and ownership. When we buy a book, he said, we are really buying three things at once: the information or text; the object that carries the information, such as a hardcover or paperback; and the rights that accompany the purchase. In the digital age, the information is conveyed as bits, the physical container becomes superfluous, and the rights are governed not by fair use law or social custom but under terms set by the copyright owner. What used to be a matter of public policy is now a matter of private contract.

In such a rent-a-bit world, we will increasingly confront license agreements that grant us only temporary, day-to-day use of a product or piece of media and that restrict our rights in other ways. We may download a song or a movie, but it will have an expiration date. We may read an e-book, but we won't be able to cut, paste, or transfer passages. "As the shift from ownership to licensing spreads from software to music, movies, and books, human civilization based on property fundamentally changes," Pollack said. Barlow once put it this way: Wrapping media in newfangled copy protection is about "transforming a market where wine is sold in bottles from which everyone may drink infinitely—as is the case with books—into a market where all wine is sold by the sip. Forever."[33]

You may remember the commercial, a noir meets *Twin Peaks* spot that Qwest Communications ran in 1999. A weary road warrior wanders into a seedy motel lobby in the middle of nowhere and asks the receptionist about amenities. Without glancing up from her book, the ruby-lipped looker describes the motel's sparse accommodations. The man prods further. "What about entertainment?" To his astonishment, she replies, "All rooms have every movie ever made, in every language, anytime, day or night."

Qwest followed up with two similar paeans to a celestial media jukebox, one set in a desolate diner whose jukebox plays "every performance by every artist of every piece of music ever recorded," and a seedy newsstand with "every edition of every book ever published in every language."

It's a stirring vision, and it will happen one day—putting the world's music, movies, television, and books at your fingertips. Think of it: a vast concert hall, movie theater, television studio, library, and museum all rolled into one.

There are three possible ways to build a celestial media jukebox: by using a public library model, a commercial model, or an underground model.

Archivists like Kahle are hard at work on the first. While public libraries contain back issues of print publications stretching back centuries, limitations imposed by law and technology have largely prevented anyone in the public sphere from archiving the bulk of television shows, movies, musical works, or radio programs. But Kahle has begun building the Television Archive, a nonprofit enterprise that in 2001 began capturing twenty stations from around the world, beginning with the aim of giving researchers, historians, and scholars permanent access to news telecasts and other programs. (It's unlikely the public will be able to tune in.) He also established the Movie Archive, in which thirteen hundred copyright-free short films were digitized and placed on the Web. Such efforts to make our visual heritage accessible are praiseworthy, but it appears that few television shows or Hollywood movies will become part of a public video jukebox.

Pollack told *Edge* magazine:

The idea we hear of the big Internet in the sky with all the music we want to listen to, all the books and movies we want to read and watch on demand, all the software games and apps we want to use, sounds real nice, until you realize it isn't a public library, it is a private jukebox. . . . The Celestial Jukebox is [the media companies'] ultimate wish—no fair use, no expiration date, no secondary market, no libraries. A perfectly efficient scheme to collect rent forever, leaving peasants with no possessions but our wages and clothing.[34]

Larry Kenswil, president of the eLabs division of Universal Music, seemed to echo this sentiment in a 2003 *New York Times* article when he said of music fans, "You're not buying music, you're buying a key."[35] It is a world where licensing replaces ownership, where the ether grid of music remains behind a locked door.

Entertainment executives have waxed eloquent about the day when consumers will be able to instantly pull down any song, movie, or other media item from a vast commercial database. The music industry has made the greatest strides toward that vision, with Apple's iTunes finally dragging skeptical record labels into the digital age with a topflight online music store. But even the iTunes store, with more than seven hundred thousand titles, doesn't come close to offering every song ever recorded.[36] For one thing, up to three-quarters of the music released by the major labels is no longer commercially available.[37]

Warren Lieberfarb, the visionary former head of Warner Home Video, thinks it won't be long before we'll be able to purchase and store our own personal collection of movies and transport it from device to device, anywhere within an extended home domain. "It will be locked up so I cannot pass it to someone else, but I can log on and get access to my whole video and music library wherever I am, at any time," he says. "That's a killer application."[38]

Already, fans can load a live recording of a concert they attended onto a cigarette-lighter-size device hanging off a keychain—and then share the footage with friends. In a few years, technology will allow us to carry hundreds of movies or TV shows on a single keychain. But will the media companies and their tech allies really get us there? I'm not so sure.

"There's extremely strong consumer sentiment that we really would like a ubiquitous, always-on worldwide catalog that would let people download any song or piece of media on the planet," says Chris Murray of Consumers

Union. "The problem is that vision just doesn't jibe with the track record of these dinosaurs."[39]

One roadblock is analog business models. An unfettered, user-centric jukebox is a nice idea in the abstract, but media chieftains have shown little appetite for making changes to lucrative business models that depend heavily on the sale of packaged goods such as CDs and DVDs. Also, a celestial jukebox is by definition all-inclusive. Will a band without a major label record contract be able to get into a private jukebox?

A second obstacle is copyright law. A thicket of licensing rights would need to be cleared for every single piece of media. At a Digital Hollywood conference I attended, Karen Randall, general counsel of Universal Studios, bemoaned the long-term contracts signed years ago that prevent Hollywood studios from selling their movies in new digital markets.[40] Older films and television shows face the same problem: nobody really owns the rights to show them over the Internet.

The final obstacle is philosophy: the urge to control. A true celestial jukebox would require a fundamental change in how entertainment companies view their customers. The kinds of digital locks under discussion would not let users rip, mix, burn, or share material from big media. The locks may not let you even retain your original copy. Andrew Setos, vice president of engineering for Fox Corp., says that in a world of keychain media, every time we transfer a movie, it would need to disappear from one device as we move it to a new device.

Many users will rebel at such a hamstrung, compromised commercial jukebox.

And so we are moving toward a dual media reality. On one level, we will see legal, sanctioned, locked-down services that scuttle traditional notions of how we interact with media. Permanent ownership, the ability to loan to others, the right to resell the item later—many of these traditions go out the window. Partly as a reaction to this, we will see the rise of a vast underground media jukebox specializing in outlaw culture. The Darknet jukebox—already well under way—will be run not as a business but as a free, decentralized service, fed and nourished by millions of individuals. In the Darknet, digitized media unavailable through traditional channels will be available hassle-free and on demand. People will use, adapt, reinvent, and share media however and with whomever they choose. All rooms will have every movie ever made in every language, anytime, day or night. And no digital handcuffs in sight.

The Darknet is a relatively new concept. The term was coined in a scientific paper four Microsoft researchers released in November 2002 at a computer conference.[41] The researchers defined darknets as "a collection of networks and technologies used to share digital content." But that's techie talk. They really were referring to the vast, gathering, lawless economy of shared music, movies, television shows, games, software, and porn—a one-touch jukebox that would rival the products and services of the entertainment companies.

The researchers' major conclusion was that media companies ought to use content controls judiciously because users don't like digital locks, somebody will figure out how to pick them, and material will spill into the Darknet despite the best efforts to wall it off. The best way companies can fight Darknet piracy, they said, is by offering affordable, convenient, compelling products and services.[42] In other words, the most effective copy protection system is a great business model.

Soon afterward, the press picked up on the term and began using other definitions. The *New York Times*, for example, described darknets as private, invitation-only cyberclubs or gated communities requiring an access code to enter. At the same time, librarians have used the phrases Dark Web, Invisible Web, and Dark Net to refer to the information such as books and periodicals that reside inside walled-off online databases that are off-limits to search engines and indexing software robots. Others refer to the Dark Net as the world of cybercrime, spammers, terrorists, and other underworld figures who use the Internet to avert the law.

In this book, I use darknets strictly as a catch-all term to refer to networks of people who rely on closed-off social spaces—safe havens in both the virtual and real worlds where there is little or no fear of detection—to share copyrighted digital material with others or to escape the restrictions on digital media imposed by entertainment companies.

The capitalized Darknet refers to these networks in a collective sense. For the most part, the Darknet is simply the underground Internet. But there are many darknets: the millions of users trading files in the shady regions of Usenet and Internet Relay Chat; students who send songs and TV shows to each other using instant messaging services from AOL, Yahoo, and Microsoft; city streets and college campuses where people copy, burn, and share physical media like CDs; and the new breed of encrypted dark networks like Freenet that I report on in chapter 12. (Kazaa, Grokster, BitTorrent, and other aboveground networks won't qualify for Darknet status until they provide users a true measure of anonymity. The copyright cops claim that no one is anonymous on the Internet, but as we'll see, they are blowing smoke.)

Darknets may sound sinister, but their roots can be traced to such all-American activities as trading and dubbing cassette music tapes in the 1960s and 1970s, as well as the computer club boom of the 1980s, when people freely exchanged software on floppy disks, an activity dubbed the "sneakernet." The Microsoft researchers see darknets as falling squarely in the same tradition:

> Students in dorms will establish darknets to share content in their social group. These darknets may be based on simple file sharing, DVD-copying, or may use special application programs or servers: for example, a chat or instant-messenger client enhanced to share content with members of your buddy-list. Each student will be a member of other darknets: for example, their family, various special interest groups, friends from high-school, and colleagues in part-time jobs.

The Darknet is less a place or a thing than an idea. On a mundane level, the Darknet is about getting free stuff. On a deeper level, it's about millions of people engaging in a shared media experience and finding a clandestine way to detour around restrictions imposed by the entertainment industry.

Certainly, much Darknet conduct is illegal. Clearly, many underground activities are ethically dubious or flat-out wrong. But much of it is also understandable, as people look for ways to restore balance to a system that has become stacked against digital culture. My intention is not to glamorize the Darknet or condemn it, but simply to help understand it.

Millions of people prowl the Darknet each day. Its most active participants are made up of Pollack's cyber-Communists and Lessig's fringe of Nones.

What will the Darknet look like tomorrow? Ultimately, its dimensions will be shaped by the actions of entertainment companies and policymakers. If people are prevented by technology or law from being able to control their own media experiences, they will not fall back into passive consumer roles. Instead, they will journey underground. The Darknet may become the last refuge for the digital freedom fighters.

3 Inside the Movie Underground

BRUCE FOREST ROCKS BACK IN HIS OFFICE CHAIR, convulsed in laughter at the amateur who wanted to play movie pirate. He cradles his computer keyboard and taps out another scorching barb to his fellow file traders at the expense of the hapless fellow who had just been arrested for ruining Universal Pictures' summer.

Two weeks before *The Hulk* opened in movie theaters in June 2003, the $150 million motion picture made a premature debut in cyberspace. Universal had sent a VHS tape containing an unfinished version of the film to a New York advertising agency, where an employee lent the tape to a friend, a twenty-four-year-old insurance underwriter from New Jersey who digitized the tape and sent it hurtling into a Darknet movie trading channel. Plainly visible watermarks containing an embedded security tag, which identified its origins, foiled his exploit. The man eventually pleaded guilty to one count of copyright infringement and was sentenced to six months of home confinement and three years of probation.

However you look at it, the affair was a Hulk-size tragicomedy of errors. When the grim-looking work print—which lacked special effects and had an incomplete sound track—was leaked online, negative word of mouth spread fast among ardent fans of the garishly green comic book hero with anger management issues. After a gangbusters opening weekend, the film nose-dived at the box office. The novice pirate's stab at Internet fame was equally short-lived. "His fingerprints were all over it," Forest scoffs. "It was like robbing a bank and giving your driver's license to the teller. The Keystone Kops could have busted him."[1]

The Darknet is no place for rank amateurs. Forest should know. He is a member of six major movie piracy groups. He is also a channel operator on Internet Relay Chat for forty piracy channels. He is in many ways the ultimate digital renegade, the kind of copyright-flouting, authority-taunting Young Turk who gives movie studio titans and record company executives the cold sweats.

Except for one thing: he is being paid to commit piracy by a major media company.

Forest is, in effect, working both sides of the fence. The underground movie groups do not know that he is a full-time consultant for the global entertainment goliath—it would be bad news for Forest (his real name) if his online identities were revealed. In turn, his corporate benefactor allows Forest to ply the piracy coves like a swashbuckling one-man Jolly Roger—swapping movie and music files, building up cred in the seamier corners of the Darknet—as a way to infiltrate and keep tabs on the illegal trading networks.

"I guess you can call me a true double agent," says Forest, outfitted in jeans, casual nylon shirt, and tan socks. He stretches out his five-foot-eight frame, perches his shoeless feet atop a desk, and runs his fingers through a mop of unkempt brown hair as a one-carat champagne diamond stud earring gleams in his left earlobe, reflecting the cool glow of the computer screens that surround us. "I lead a very comfortable double life."

Forest, in his mid-forties, has become the eyes and ears of an industry that is ramping up plans to make sure Hollywood does not suffer the fate that has befallen the record labels. Ever since Napster, tens of millions of people have joined in a mass pillaging of digital goods that threatens to turn the music industry into a modern-day Carthage. For many members of the digital generation, music has become as free and taken for granted as the air.

Free does not make for a particularly robust business model. Studio executives fear that films may be the next media domino to fall. As Internet connections become lightning-fast, computer hard drives bulk up in size, and compression technologies improve, movies are poised to take center stage in the file-sharing wars.

"We must draw a moral line and reject the notion that it's perfectly acceptable to steal and loot," Valenti of the MPAA says. "Digital thievery cannot be allowed to lacerate the future of America's most extraordinary enterprise, the entertainment industry."

The battle over movie piracy may prove to be even more fierce and intractable as the one being waged in the music world, given Hollywood's formidable firepower on Capitol Hill and its presence in nearly every aspect of our celebrity-infused culture. While no one has yet shown a link between movie file sharing and a loss of revenue at the box office or at the video counter, Hollywood is clearly worried. Forrester Research estimates that one in five teenagers has illegally downloaded a feature film. All told, between 400,000 and 600,000 movies are being illegally traded online every day, studio chieftains have said in congressional testimony. (The estimate is intentionally high, but there's no question that movie file trading is on the upswing, though still at manageable levels.)[2] Some 17 million pirated movie files now float around the Internet, according to research firm BigChampagne, the Nielsens of file trading.

This brings us back to Forest, who seems to be close at hand—like a veritable Forrest Gump—whenever movies and Internet piracy intersect. Forest was the one who came up with Hollywood's estimate of movie piracy levels, a number he devised after staking out the darkened street corners of the movie underground one blockbuster weekend in May 2002—the same weekend CNN shot footage of an anonymous, silhouetted figure downloading *Star Wars: Episode II—Attack of the Clones*. (The masked marauder was Forest.) When five of the major Hollywood studios unveiled Movielink, their Internet film rental service touted as an alternative to piracy, Forest was one of its key architects, and he owns a patent on the technology. Forest has just unveiled a new business model for digital distribution of music and movies (more on that later). And when I wanted to seek out leaders of the movie piracy underground to interview for this article, it was Forest who successfully set the table for me.

"It has taken me years to build up the trust and respect of my peers," he says in a breezy, broadband-fast delivery fashioned during a boyhood on the streets of Forest Hills, Queens. "You can't just show up on a channel and say, 'Hi, I'm new here and I want some of your movies.' They will laugh at you, and then they'll ban you. It's rough frontier justice. You have to earn your way in by offering value to other members in the form of gear or coding talent or access to the newest, coolest material."

Forest acknowledges that in 1997, as he was scratching his way up the piracy hierarchy, he joined his first release group—clusters of individuals who work secretly in teams to illegally distribute digital goods in the Darknet. He started out as a "server," a low-level position he sardonically likens to a Mafia button man. A server is at greatest risk of criminal prosecution because he distributes infringing movie files on an open Internet address. Performing such yeoman work offers advancement in the scene—the name insiders use for those who actively acquire and trade media files. (Not surprisingly, no one in the scene uses the term "pirate" or tosses off the occasional "yo ho ho.")

Forest no longer serves, having parlayed his familiarity with the scene into a lucrative consulting business. "I don't do anything illegal," he tells me on more than one occasion. Yet, to prove his privacy chops and to maintain the trust he has gained in the movie underground, Forest shares with a few of his peers the password to his private server, a secret stash of digital goods accessible only by invitation. When I stop by later, I spy a treasure trove of copyrighted booty: thousands of songs, music videos, movie files, television shows (including every episode of *The Simpsons*), computer games for Microsoft's Xbox, and software programs that fill up two terabytes on his networked hard drives. (Comparisons can be misleading, but the entire Library of Congress is only ten times larger. Forest's two terabytes would fill 1.4 million 3.5-inch floppy disks.) His online hideout includes the *Billboard* Top 100 of every hit song from the past forty-four years and films such as *Spider-man*, *Gangs of New York*, *Gladiator*, *The Godfather II*, and *Austin Powers*.

Take what you want, he offers.

College students who run similar private file-sharing networks have been busted for less, but Forest does not fear the copyright cops. When he negotiated his contract, he insisted on an indemnification clause, a hold-harmless provision that shields him from being prosecuted for downloading pirated movies belonging to the major movie studios. He also consults for the music industry and has been indemnified by the Recording Industry

Association of America. Forest may be a spy, but he is no snitch, and he takes pains to make clear that he will not fink on anyone in the scene.

Those encounters have come in the form of various personas. He maintains multiple identities, from an entry-level server to a powerful and petulant elder statesman, on different IRC channels as a way to expand his sphere of contacts. "I have different personas on every channel, so I have to be careful that I don't blow my cover," he says.

Forest—whose work chiefly centers on film piracy but also covers file trading of television shows, music, and computer games—writes a two-hundred-page report for his corporate client every two weeks in which he outlines his latest findings, charts levels of movie piracy, and suggests strategies to protect the company's intellectual property. He agreed to share the highlights of what he has observed during the three years he has infiltrated the darkest corners of the piracy underworld in return for a pledge to protect his online identities and a disclaimer that Forest's personal views do not necessarily represent those of his employer.

Release groups and the scene have received little attention in the mainstream press for a simple reason: no participant wants to talk about it. Publicity attracts the attention of law enforcement. But the bulletproof Forest has no such reservations. This is the first time he has taken a stranger on a tour of the digital badlands.

Forest begins each morning, espresso in hand, in the home office of his ranch house in suburban Connecticut on a five-acre wooded tract forty-four miles northeast of Manhattan that he and his family share with deer, moose, foxes, coyotes, and a flock of guinea fowl that keep Lyme-carrying ticks under control. The secluded, bucolic town of ten thousand has counted Christopher Walken, Robert Redford, José Feliciano, Erica Jong, and Keith Richards of the Rolling Stones among its residents.

After I arrive at his house during a driving rainstorm, Forest makes me a cup of tea. We wind past the multimedia-rich living room to his subterranean lair, an electric cave where the only sounds come from the hum of small desk fans that cool the banks of thirteen PCs, Macintoshes, and Linux computers. He sinks into an office chair and watches as pastel-colored scrolls of geeky text flit up the screen. He will remain stationed in this high-tech command center until five in the morning. Four cable modem lines connect him to the outside world—a setup, he says, that packs more bandwidth than some Manhattan skyscrapers. On an adjoining workstation, three monitors keep track of his private army of bots and automated programs that prowl the file-trading underworld. He scoots from machine to machine, alternately checking e-mail, monitoring file-trading activity, and scolding Cookie, his high-strung pit bull puppy, for ripping up my magazine and lapping at my cup of tea, which I had idly placed on the floor. "That dog needs a Valium," he says.

As a precautionary measure, Forest always uses a "bounce" to disguise his computer's location. Rather than log onto piracy channels from his home, which would reveal his machine's unique Internet address and approximate physical location, he logs into a shell account through a computer in the Caribbean. If anyone tried to trace his whereabouts, it would suggest that he was sipping mojitos somewhere south of St. Barts.

My notebook brims with questions, but we get to none of them during a full day of show and tell, for as soon as I marvel at one discovery or another, he would pull another trick out of his magic bag and we'd be off and running in an entirely new direction.

Forest has an intriguing background as a music producer—he mixed more than a thousand music tracks and twenty-four platinum albums for Madonna, Whitney Houston, Elton John, Bruce Springsteen, Lou Reed, Robert Palmer, and Rick James, among others—but he rarely speaks now of that past life. He seems most at home when immersed in the Darknet. Most people associate the Internet with the candy-colored playground of the World Wide Web, but millions of others—geeks, college and high school students, hard-core pirates—navigate to other harbors on the Internet. The Darknet is cyberspace's equivalent of Al Capone country, a lawless, ethics-free frontier impervious even to a legion of industry lawyers. The Darknet is where epic battles over copy protection and file sharing will be joined.

Today Forest has arranged for me to interview two leading figures in the Internet movie underground. The ground rules are simple. The interviews will be conducted over Apple's iChat, a software program that allows participants to type messages to one another onscreen. The connection is untraceable, thanks to the bounce they've set up. I can ask anything during two separate chat sessions. They can see me, through a Webcam, but I can't see them. "They want to make sure you're not wearing a uniform," Forest says, only half joking.[3]

The first underground figure I contact takes the name beneaththecobweb. Forest, who has known him for five years, says he is a member of nine movie release groups and heads six of them. As such, he is one of the highest-ranking members of the scene. Forest describes him as a man in his late twenties from a western state. Beneaththecobweb will say only that he is a U.S. citizen and network administrator temporarily living in Western Europe.

"The amazing part of the scene is that it represents an inner circle . . . a place where people in hundreds of different countries connect, and work for a common purpose," beneaththecobweb tells me. The scene is all about giving people of every social class or budget equal access to great music and movies, he maintains. In turn, Hollywood and the music industry will have to "adapt to changing times."

The second figure takes the name Ninja. Forest tells me he is a college student on Long Island and a former high-level Internet pirate who left the scene not long ago after running three movie release groups and one music release group. Ninja says he was primarily drawn to the scene because "I was able to get access to movies just days after they arrived in the theater." He, too, believes Hollywood and the record labels have refused to embrace their online destinies.

For the next three hours I trade messages with the two of them about how the scene operates, while Forest tosses in running color commentary.

When copies of *Finding Nemo*, *Terminator 3*, or other major motion pictures appear on the Internet days or weeks before their theatrical release, it's almost certain that a movie release group was responsible. Although movie groups first appeared in about 1997, the scene got a kick start in late October 1999 when a fifteen-year-old from Norway wrote a few lines of code that made it easy to pluck a Hollywood movie from a copy-protected DVD. A typical release group, bearing names like Flair, Esoteric, or Opium, consists of anywhere from a handful to as many as 30 individuals, with an average membership of 15. Today there are an estimated 140 underground movie groups worldwide, up from 32 in 2002. Other release groups focus on games, software, television shows, even ebooks.

Releasing a movie onto the Internet follows a process that beneaththecobweb likened to a factory assembly line. While decrypting, encoding, and distributing a single movie could be done by a single individual, the chore is sufficiently labor-intensive that it makes more sense to parcel out the duties to a team of specialists. And so an underground cottage industry was born.

To begin the process, release groups usually obtain the movies from a surprising source: Hollywood insiders. A study published by AT&T Labs in

September 2003 found that 77 percent of the illegal movies on file-sharing networks come from people associated with the movie industry.

Films leak into the piracy pipeline in several ways. Most treasured is a copy of a master print obtained during a film's postproduction, when the shooting has been completed and hundreds of employees typically have access to the film master to make edits, adjust colors and sounds, add special effects, and perform other finishing touches. Equally tantalizing for the release groups are "screeners" released on DVD to a select group of viewers before a film opens in theaters. Another source is the pressing plant, where hundreds or thousands of discs with imperfections might be discarded months before a DVD's retail release. A "telesync" is created when a movie theater employee or his friends set up a camcorder on a tripod and videotape the film from the projection room. Most commonly, someone sneaks a camcorder into a theater and aims it at the screen, though such "screen cams" can produce images with jerky movements and shots of the back of patrons' heads. Still, the audio quality can be excellent; pirates can get good sound quality by plugging into jacks designed to help the hearing-impaired. (Not long ago, Los Angeles police arrested two eighteen-year-olds for videotaping *Star Trek: Nemesis* and a twenty-eight-year-old man for videotaping *The Passion of the Christ* in L.A. movie theaters.) The movie studios have lately tried to thwart screen cams by arming movie theater attendants with metal detectors and night-vision goggles to catch video operators in flagrante cinema. Another link in the chain is the video store employee who has access to DVDs after the film's theatrical release but a few days before their release to the public.

Let's follow the trajectory of a typical title through the movie underground. It begins with a *supplier*, usually someone who works at a production studio, DVD pressing plant, video store, or some organization with ties to the motion picture industry. The supplier hands off the unreleased or recently released film—say, a preview DVD of *Mission: Impossible 3*—to a contact in a release group or at a drop site. Next, the file is transported as quickly as possible to a *ripper*, or *cracker*, either by sending the DVD by Federal Express or by allowing the ripper to grab the file from his computer through a virtual private network connection. The ripper's task is to copy the movie's raw video and audio files and strip out any copy protection. Then he or an *encoder* edits out the identifying marks studios insert to track copies and also compresses and optimizes the video file into formats suitable for downloading and viewing on a computer or television screen. Next, a *distributor* places a file on one of thirty or so top-sites—ultrasecure underground digital vaults. From there, *couriers* transfer the file to a lower-level dump site or to high-speed distribution servers (computers configured to share files). These members, skilled programmers who often double as university or corporate network aces, have access to powerful computers with fast Internet connections. "Couriers are the drug mules of the distribution chain," Forest says. The final link in the chain are the *channel operators*, who announce the movie's availability on individual IRC channels like mongers at a fish market, setting off a feeding frenzy. (An estimated fifteen hundred IRC channels are devoted exclusively to movie piracy.) The entire process typically takes two to three days—with handoffs that often cross international borders.

"It's the balance between Europeans, Americans, and Asians that makes it work across different time zones," Ninja says. Forest adds: "I know of one group that has Belgian encoders, U.S. rippers, Asian hard goods people, and Canadian administrators."

Much of this happens in a loose-knit fashion, with individuals working independently—usually late into the night—in cloistered bedrooms, college dorms, and offices rather than a central location. "Very few members have met each other" in person, beneaththecobweb notes. During all of this, *administrators* help the operation run smoothly, buying hardware, network bandwidth, or shell accounts on the computers that distribute the movie. One or two *group leaders* organize the entire enterprise. And then there are the *donators*, generally sympathetic, older benefactors who donate equipment, bandwidth, facilities, or funds to a release group in exchange for membership, community respect, and access to the group's digital spoils at a "leech site."

Forest is a donator, having supplied computers and camcorders to various release groups on his dime. Forest, who must have balls of silicon, deducts all such donations on his income tax return, saying, "I have an honest accountant. He said I can tax-deduct it as a legitimate business expense."

Some groups specialize only in ripping or encoding, while others distribute the title, and still others handle all aspects of a release. Once released, a title filters out into Usenet news groups (go to Google, click on Groups, and you're there) and the Web-based file-sharing services. The movie piracy network might be described best as an inverted pyramid, with a few thousand members of the elite release groups at the top; a wider group of 50,000 to

200,000 users who operate both public and private servers that store the digital goods; another 3.5 million tech-savvy users who swap files on IRC channels, news groups, and public FTP sites; and finally hundreds of millions of people worldwide—perhaps 60 million in the United States—who use peer-to-peer networks such as Kazaa, eDonkey, and iMesh. By the time a movie or song funnels down to the bottom of the pyramid, it may have picked up a virus, or it may be a bogus file. But the material at the very top is gold.

Standing atop the piracy pyramid are the most daring thrill-seekers, the technologically savvy men (and it is an overwhelmingly male enterprise) who seem to share a youthful swagger, a disregard for authority, and a conviction that, as beneaththecobweb says, "everything" should be up on the Internet. Forest assesses the makeup of movie release groups this way: "Most members are guys in their late teens to early twenties. A third are college students, another third are recent graduates living in some rat-hole apartment with a high-speed T1 line, and a third are careerist geeks—typically a young, underpaid network administrator for a university or corporation. But I know one guy in his sixties who does this, and I know a thirteen-year-old in junior high school who's one of the best coders I've ever seen. On the IRC channels you see a lot of adolescent interplay, with guys talking about girls and breast size, but when they start talking technology, they sound like Stephen Hawking."

What motivates these digital anarchists is less a political movement or philosophical cause than a desire to belong to an edgy, secretive, forbidden brotherhood. And while zinging the Hollywood Goliath is satisfying in itself, at its rawest level the scene is a sporting competition where outsize egos clash and compete. Whoever beats the opposing "teams" wins the challenge—and bragging rights. "It becomes a race between fellow groups to try to release the movie first, for scene prestige," Ninja says. "It all comes down to status," Forest confirms.

While some release groups aspire to be swiftest in releasing a title, other groups strive to produce the best-looking digital fare. Two groups with reputations as the "class acts" of the movie underground are Centropy, known for its high-quality releases, and VCD Vault, whose mission is to convert movie classics from the 1940s to 1970s into a downloadable digital format. "There's a concerted effort under way to make available to the public any movie ever made," Forest says, making it sound like the business plan of an Internet start-up. The undertaking even has a code name, the Netflix Project, in honor of the mail-order company with a catalog of twenty-five thousand DVD titles. Dozens of release group members sign up for a Netflix account, which allows them to obtain as many DVDs as they want in a month. "I know people who have ripped fifty movies in a month from Netflix," Forest says. Project members have converted about half of Netflix's titles.

Release group members are well aware that their activities are illegal, and they take pains to hide their identities. But most film crackers, as they are sometimes called, don't consider themselves pirates ("we are not conniving little thieves," beneaththecobweb says), and many are scornful of traffickers in bootleg DVDs and CDs who are in it for the money. "Profiting from a nonprofit scene is ridiculous," says Ninja, who recently moved on to pursue a business career. Commercial piracy typically involves factories in Asia and Eastern Europe stamping out vast numbers of bootleg CDs, DVDs, or VCDs (low-quality video compact discs) that turn up on urban street corners or in the dusky bins of Hong Kong video stores for a fraction of their legitimate price.

By contrast, the release group Centropy publishes this disclaimer on all its movie rips: "Remember: we do this for FUN. We do not make money off this whole business. . . . We do not condone people selling illegal copies of movies for profit. In fact, all of us go to the movies regularly and pay for our tickets just like everyone else. If everyone only watched illegal copies, there would be no money to make new movies."

Similarly, my interview subjects on iChat tell me they continue to buy movie tickets and purchase DVDs of movies they obtained in the Darknet. "I have an evergrowing dvd collection, and i pay for the movies that are worth the money to pay for," beneaththecobweb types. Such sentiments appear to be genuine, if self-serving. Few dispute that a fair number of film buffs watch the free bootleg version rather than pony up for a movie ticket or DVD. Ninja cops to this: "I'm going to admit that the scene can cost the 'real world' some cash." But only inferior films will suffer that fate, he says, while people will continue to flock to see quality pictures.

This brings us to the million-gigabyte question: why do they do it at all, knowing the severe penalties they face if apprehended?

Ninja says some scene members are just out to obtain free movies, while others build up an online reputation that gets them access to games and software applications "that only a rich person could afford." Beneaththecobweb says the camaraderie of the scene is its own reward, and that the authorities would be hard-pressed to catch them because of the extraordinary precautions members take in their interactions online. "Constant paranoia would be putting it lightly," he says. Indeed, he wouldn't name titles his groups have released, although he hinted at *Memento* and blockbusters on the order of *The Lord of the Rings*.

Forest, who races a catamaran on water and a Formula Dodge on land (he has survived two bad accidents), offers this take on the scene's allure: "The little edge of danger involved is kind of cool. People like belonging to a tight-knit community. It just happens to be a community that skirts the law."

Finally, as a monsoon downpour threatens to wash my car away into the dark Connecticut woods, it's time to leave. "I'm shocked they've told you as much as they have," Forest tells me. (For complete transcripts, see Darknet.com.) At the end of our chats, I feel as though I've been on an anthropological expedition to a strange and perplexing land.

Days later, I mention my encounter with the pirates of Darknet to Valenti. If he had the chance, what might he tell a member of the scene? Known for his silver-tongued oratory, Valenti pauses a moment. "I would borrow the words of the attorney Joseph Welch in addressing Senator Joseph McCarthy. 'Sir, have you no shame?' I'd ask the young man, would you go into a Blockbuster store and furtively put a DVD under your jacket and walk out with it? Of course you wouldn't. But you see no harm in putting a movie in your digital hard drive jacket and walking off with that. But don't you know it's wrong? He'll rationalize it, but he knows it's stealing."

Hollywood attributes worldwide losses of $3.5 billion a year to traditional hard-goods piracy (chiefly the aforementioned bootleg DVDs and VCDs) and "untold additional damages" due to Internet piracy. In truth, a firm cost for Internet movie piracy is impossible to come by. Do college students who download movies and watch them in their dorms cost the industry money if they wouldn't pay to see the films in the theater?

The question may be beside the point, according to John G. Malcolm, director of worldwide antipiracy operations for the Motion Picture Association of America, which monitors piracy out of offices in Hong Kong, Brussels, Toronto, and Mexico City. Whether the movie groups realize it or not, commercial pirates in Asia take the pilfered films off the Internet, burn them onto disc, and sell bootleg copies throughout the world, he says. The motion picture industry seized more than 54 million pirate DVDs and VHS tapes worldwide in the past year. "I understand the leaders of encoding groups say they're in it for the challenge and not the money," he says. "But they're very naive to think they don't damage our industry substantially."[4]

Because it is difficult to place a value on movie titles being traded (or, more properly, copied, because the trader doesn't forfeit his version), law enforcement authorities have shown little appetite for investigating copyright violations at the peer-to-peer level, Malcolm says. The FBI has periodically targeted the underground file-trading groups at the top of the piracy pyramid. Federal authorities took out a "warez" group (which stores copyrighted works in secret online locations) and more than thirty piracy hubs in coordinated raids between 2001 and 2004. In each instance, the undercover busts quieted activity in the scene for only a short while before business as usual resumed. Says Malcolm, "Every time law enforcement takes out an encoding group, a new one is there to take its place. It's really quite bizarre."

That sense of exasperation is widely shared by the Hollywood establishment. According to the *Los Angeles Times*, the chiefs of several motion picture studios held an antipiracy summit meeting in Hollywood in late September 2003, during which Valenti pushed for stronger technological measures that would choke off piracy at the source. The studio scions reportedly overruled Valenti and instructed him to begin the groundwork for filing lawsuits against individuals who illegally traffic in copyrighted movie files.

In November 2004, two months after Valenti stepped down from the MPAA's top post, his successor, Dan Glickman, announced plans to begin filing lawsuits against movie file sharers in 2005.

The motion picture industry has taken a multipronged approach to battling piracy: innovation (chiefly in the form of next-generation DVDs, due out in about two years), legislation, regulation (in the form of the FCC's rulings on digital television and the broadcast flag), litigation against file-sharing services, and education. Valenti has spoken at more than a dozen colleges, taking his "moral imperative" campaign right into the teeth of the opposition.

Valenti says he will continue to push for additional measures to "baffle pirates" as he reduces his day-to-day responsibilities at the MPAA. "If

Internet piracy stayed at this level, we could probably survive it, because even with broadband it takes at least an hour to bring down a movie," he said. But technology is not standing still, and so time is of the essence. In the fall of 2003 he visited Caltech, where a media lab technician downloaded a DVD-quality movie in *five seconds*. "I asked, how soon can this be in production in the marketplace, three or four years? He said, no, with the right funding it could be on the market in eighteen months. Well, my face blanched."

The movie industry is not waiting for a supply of silver bullets to arrive as it pursues other, low-tech measures to baffle the pirates. During the 2002 Oscar season, studios sent out tens of thousands of DVDs to members of the Academy of Motion Picture Arts and Sciences as well as to movie critics, writers, and actors during the run-up to the Academy Awards. Months before their DVD release date, pristine copies of *Chicago*, *Gangs of New York*, *Catch Me if You Can*, and *Die Another Day* appeared on the Internet bearing subtitles or leader frames with the introduction "For your consideration." In all, thirty-four of sixty-eight screener titles were pirated, including all top ten nominees.

"The problem has gotten out of hand," Valenti says. "A friend of mine just traveled on a China Airlines flight. For their in-flight movie, they showed a film, and at the bottom it said, 'For your consideration.' It was a pirated screener."

Forest thinks that whatever preventive measures Hollywood takes will fail. Before the 2004 ceremonies, he spotted in the Darknet such Oscar hopefuls as *Master and Commander*, *Cold Mountain*, *Something's Gotta Give*, *House of Sand and Fog*, and Woody Allen's *Anything Else*. In each case, the identifying serial number—inserted by the studios to trace bootlegged copies back to the source—was digitally obliterated.

"Want to see how easy this is?" Forest asks me. He navigates to an underground site and downloads a pirated version of *Kill Bill*. In fewer than ten minutes he has downloaded it to his hard drive and burned it to DVD. We trek upstairs to the multimedia room, where a phalanx of gizmos—TiVo, DVD player, VCR, network hub, broadband router, networked Xbox, and Playstation 2 module—sit atop a fifty-five-inch Toshiba television.

"Here is what Hollywood is up against." He plunks the DVD into the player. Moments later, a screen cam of the Quentin Tarantino revenge flick barrels into action, with the FBI warning surgically excised. Forest's message is this: piracy is no longer the sole province of geeky college students watching on computer monitors. Mainstream Americans now download pirated movies to a hard drive, burn them onto DVDs, and watch them on a living room television, perhaps connected to a dirt-cheap $35 Apex DVD player sold at Wal-Mart. Forest fingers a stack of DVDs, each one holding a pirated film: *The Matrix Reloaded, The Italian Job, The Sum of All Fears, Lizzie McGuire*. He stops *Kill Bill* and cues up *Finding Nemo*. "Look at that—this is the best cam I've ever seen! No jerky camera motion, just a little pixelization, and those colors are vivid. I'm seeing pastels! Absolutely unbelievable." The release group member who copied it from a theater screen used a $10,000 high-end DV camcorder.

This is the point at which the reader might say: vivid pastels or not, I would *never* watch a pirated movie. For now, that is the cultural norm. But would your steadfastness crumble if you saw your neighbor do so? Or your cousin in the country? "I put this to the studios," Forest says. "I live in a rural area. The closest movie theater is eleven miles away. Realistically, my wife and I have two kids and a household of pets and responsibilities, and it's very hard to get a sitter. The studios are providing no legal way for us to see new movies in our home, other than to wait several months and then watch it on pay per view or drive to Blockbuster. It's not good to steal movies, but file sharing is a symptom of people who want their music and movies digitally, and the studios may need to do more."

At Sony Pictures Plaza in Los Angeles, the executives who run Columbia TriStar Home Entertainment say Hollywood has already shifted its business practices to respond to Internet piracy, which they call the most pressing issue facing the home video industry. The company's president, Benjamin S. Feingold, who helped commercialize the DVD format in the late 1990s, points out that consumers typically can rent or buy a video four months after a movie's theatrical release, while not long ago it took six months for a video rental to appear and a full year for a movie to be available for purchase. The studios also load DVDs with lots of extra goodies—interviews, outtakes, discarded scenes, alternate endings—that make Hollywood products more attractive than the pirated versions. The studios, Feingold tells me, are currently focused on making the next generation of DVDs "an even more compelling proposition" while reminding consumers that "downloading movies over the Internet is an illegal activity."[5]

Adrian Alperovich, the company's executive vice president, sees a troubling undercurrent of entitlement, especially among young people. "I have some nieces who download movies over the Internet, and they tell me they never go to the movies anymore. It's the cool new thing—which doesn't make it right." Feingold said such developments cannot be the controlling factor in Hollywood's business plans. "You don't make business decisions relating to movie formats based on piracy rates, you make it around where your real customers are." That continues to be the DVD, which now accounts for 40 percent of the studios' income.

Warren Lieberfarb, the former president of Warner Home Entertainment who is considered the father of the DVD, says Hollywood may need to reconsider its position. "I think the delay periods between theatrical, video, and video on demand need to be condensed even further," he says. "The existing sacred business models may not be sustainable in a digital world."

At the 2004 International Consumer Electronics Show in Las Vegas, RealNetworks chief executive Rob Glaser warned that the film and video industries face a massive increase in Internet bootlegging if they do not begin to offer compelling online services. "The industries aren't moving fast enough to skip over the Napsterization step," he said. "For video to avoid what music went through, it has to get to that critical mass of great services faster than it is doing."[6]

Still, as the saying goes, in Hollywood it's never about the money. It's about *all* the money.

Hollywood is reluctant to make any changes to its business models until it is certain that its bottom line won't suffer. The studios have fallen in love with the DVD, and Feingold said they are looking toward not online downloads but high-definition DVD discs, loaded down with stronger copy protection, that are due out in a year or so. "The best indication of the future is the past, and transactional pay per view is a business that has never achieved any level of prominence vs. prerecorded media. I wouldn't expect that to change."

Forest is among those who would like to see a greater emphasis on online distribution of movies. He is pitching the entertainment industry on a plan of his own. Unlike technologists who speak a different language than the movers and shakers in the movie and music worlds, Forest has the advantage of having walked the walk of a creative artist. Remember Forest's past: originally a DJ at Better Days, an underground nightclub in New York, he went on to become a record producer in London while living in Boy George's old house. During a six-year stretch, Forest produced records that sold a combined 40 million copies. Forest mixed more than a dozen tracks for Elton John and cowrote the song "Understanding Women," from the 1992 album *The One*. At about the same time, he remixed or produced two dozen songs for Boy George, remixed Steve Winwood's "Roll with It," and created a rare remix of the Bee Gees' "You Should Be Dancing." When he married his British-born wife, Mitzi, in London in 1991, their first dance was to a recording made for them by Elton John on piano and sung by Boy George. Forest dusts off his wedding album and shows a photo with his best man, Shep Pettibone (the producer for Madonna who wrote "Vogue"), David Morales (who produced for Mariah Carey), and David Cole (the keyboardist in C+C Music Factory, whom Forest discovered during his club DJ days). After several more years in the music business, he burned out on the cocoonlike aspects of his job and began formulating ideas for changing the model for distribution of digital media.

Forest acknowledges that his new business model will not be *the* answer to piracy, but it could provide a partial solution. He spun the idea into a new private venture, the Jun Group, which he founded with three other partners. Their business plan, with a patent pending, is based on a simple premise: "The problem with the music and movie industries is that their most valuable asset is their most vulnerable asset," Forest says. "Therefore, the distribution has to change." Under this stratagem, instead of fighting the file-sharing services, musicians would embrace the Kazaas of the world as a free promotion vehicle and distribution pipeline to an audience of millions. Bands would bypass the record labels entirely in favor of a corporate sponsor, which would underwrite the recording venture.

In October 2003, the theory went from high concept to real world. Snapple Beverage Group, maker of Yoo-Hoo Chocolate Drink, agreed to finance a five-song release by Kevin Martin (former front man for the rock group Candlebox) and the HiWatts. The initial EP was downloaded more than 3 million times in less than a month, alongside a "Wayne's World"-style home video of the group. After the track is downloaded onto a PC, it displays a message crediting Yoo-Hoo for sponsoring the music. The band hopes to ride the blast of free online publicity to greater ticket sales for its concerts, where it makes the bulk of its money. If Yoo-Hoo sales rise, the band will receive additional remuneration.

The arrangement relies on Jun Group's secret sauce of underground connections to give the file an extra boost in the file-trading netherworld by feeding material into the golden upper tier of the piracy pyramid. The theory is: if you can't beat the pirates, use the pirates. In this case, however, such underground exploits are strictly legal. Forest and his partners have eight other projects in the works. He believes the concept can work with motion pictures—particularly award-winning independent films that don't receive a big push from a major distributor—as well as television shows and games.

Many more such efforts to provide convenient, affordable online delivery of digital media into the home will need to be devised in the coming years if entertainment companies hope to prevent movie and television piracy from becoming mainstream. If innovative new business models catering to an online audience do not materialize, Forest fears the worst. He believes the entertainment industry remains largely under the sway of "people who want a legal or technological solution, when the only lasting solution is cultural. There has got to be a cultural shift. Right now the culture is telling my ten-year-old daughter that music and movies are free. That's wrong. The culture of the average person is becoming, 'I can get this for nothing.'"

In this cultural battle for hearts and minds, the challenges faced in reinventing our approach to piracy and digital media become evident in the Forests' own household, where copyright is a complex subject. Forest owns Microsoft Office, the expensive suite of productivity software. Bliss, his peppy, cherubic daughter, pops into the basement office three times to announce she cannot use Microsoft Word to do her homework because her father has a document open on their home network. Under terms of the software license, only one person may use the program at a time.

On the other hand, Bliss (she was named after the lead character in Isaac Asimov's "Foundation" series) owns an Apple iPod that contains forty songs she downloaded from a file-sharing network. She prizes her little black folder, where she stores the two dozen pirated movies her father has given her, such as *Legally Blonde 2*, which Forest downloaded to look for identifying marks. When I ask Bliss whether she sees anything wrong with downloading MP3s or watching pirated movies before any of her friends can watch the legal version, she looks at me as if I'm from Neptune. "*Nooo*," she says simply and firmly.

Doesn't the great American piracy conversation begin at home?

Forest considers this. As Bliss skips off, he says, "I've discussed it with her. I know it sounds hypocritical, but I get copies of those movies for my work, so why shouldn't she watch them? She's a bright kid, she understands what

I do for a living. As far as the music, I don't condone her pirating material, but that's how kids get their music these days. You think she's going to save up two weeks' allowance to buy one Christina Aguilera CD?" He pauses. "She's much more into clothes and dressing up than she's into computers or collecting songs. She's just a normal all-American kid."

4 When Personal and Mass Media Collide

I FIRST MEET JOE LAMBERT IN THE DIM, TIMEWORN offices of the Center for Digital Storytelling in Berkeley, California. One by one, visitors file in, snag a bagel, and take a seat around a pockmarked mahogany table. We introduce ourselves: an emergency room nurse, a business executive, a college student, a "retired parent," a journalist, and seven others ranging in age from twenty-one to sixty-two. None of us claims to be a filmmaker. But in this room, and in countless others like it around the globe, digital technology is blasting into oblivion the idea that only a special class of professionals can play in the filmmaker's sandbox.

Lambert, boyish and perpetually bemused at age forty-six, is the center's founding director and resident guru. He rises from the chair next to his wife and fellow trainer, Nina Mullen. All of us, he says, have been taught that only the experts can create media, that it is somehow off-limits to hobbyists and amateurs. But the center's message is a simple one: we all have a powerful story to tell. As Lambert puts it, "The twentieth century was about being talked to in the language of film and television. It was about a cynical, commercial-driven media machine filtering what we were allowed to watch. At some point we'll grow tired of watching 'reality TV' and we'll latch onto people's authentic stories of reality. In the new century, all of us get a chance to talk back. We'll be the authors of our own stories." It's a powerful vision, one that has lured this small group from as far away as Toronto. Kiok Gruttend, the Kaiser Permanente nurse, tells us she signed up for the workshop to tell the story of her upbringing in South Korea, of her marriage to a Swiss man, of the frailties of a multicultural family in Marin County. Ruby Wilson signed on to create a piece honoring the life of a ninety-six-year-old friend. And Toronto businessman Don Jones clutches the lyrics of "Moon River" and wistfully recalls how he sang it as a lullaby to soothe his children when they were very young. He wants to create a digital memento, a visual family album.

Participants in the workshop are asked to bring in photos, videos, scrapbooks, heirlooms, emotional touchstones—anything that can convey the essence of the story in a few visual elements. Most often, they raid old photo albums in the attic or garage. Once they arrive, they don't need to go out and shoot footage because they already have a story in hand. "Use what you've got," Lambert tells us. "Find the stories that are already there."[1]

One challenge facing the digital storyteller is to unlearn the intimidating aspects of big media. "We try to discourage the notion that film production is a worrisome, monumental undertaking, dealing with lighting, sound, characters, and setting," Lambert says. "You don't need all the fancy apparatus as long as you have an effective narrative. I don't mean slides of your summer vacation—that's the kind of superficial use of media we all fear. We're looking for something deeper. We're ready for a new sincerity."

A few of us have scribbled out some ideas, and we begin to discuss our rough-hewn scripts in a group setting—a surprisingly positive session that helps us find the stripped-down, emotional center of our stories. Then we learn the basics of multimedia editing software, the key elements of digital storytelling, and the obligations of copyright. While use of Hollywood video snippets or music clips in a personal filmmaking project arguably falls under fair use, the center errs on the side of caution by telling participants they should get clearances from the motion picture studios and music labels before using any copyrighted images or sounds in their work. Called "clearing rights," the process is often more burdensome than creating the movie itself.

During the three-day workshop, our films slowly take shape. By the final day, the dozen participants have fashioned personal, heartfelt film shorts made up of faded photographs, snippets of video, musical scores—and words. The voice-over narration is the key to giving the work heft and resonance. A few will transcend the specific subject matter to take on deeper social significance: statements about family, racial acceptance, generational conflict.

We leave, eager to spread the message of digital creativity to others. Some four thousand students have passed through the doors of the nonprofit Storycenter, as it's called, since its founding a decade ago.[2] Similar projects have now sprung up in more than thirty states, and scenes such as this play out in towns, shopping malls, and classrooms all over America—indeed, all over the world.

Today, the barriers of storage, price, and technical prowess continue to fall, leading to a prairie fire in digital filmmaking that promises to match or outpace the amateur shutterbug movement of the 1960s. Armed with affordable digital camcorders, fast computers, and easy-to-use movie editing software, regular folks can not only videotape a story or record a scene, but also polish their masterpiece with special effects, smooth transitions, and other tricks of the postproduction toolkit. Such moviemaking tools now come preinstalled in millions of Apple computers, and similar wonders are beginning to bust out in the PC marketplace. In just a few years, these video creation techniques will become nearly as commonplace as VCR technology. Americans have snapped up more than 26 million DVD burners and 85 million DVD players, making it easy to share homemade movies with friends and family.

In short, creating digital home movies is fast becoming an everyday middle-class pursuit. That is why 150 Macintosh faithful have paid to hear Lambert and two other speakers bring their evangelical road show to iDay, a day-long seminar in Palo Alto, California, devoted to mastering Apple's digital suite of movie, photo, and music tools.[3] Apple has traditionally been a couple of years ahead of its PC cousins on the multimedia front, and its influence in the creative community is disproportionate to its 3 percent market share: Macs are the computer of choice in film editing suites, sound studios, ad agencies, musicians' mixing rooms, and writers' bedrooms. A few weeks earlier, the company had pushed the envelope again, integrating its digital hub to let users add a favorite band's music as a sound track to movies they create—without forcing you to navigate through the record labels' licensing sawmill—under the theory that fair use covers such personal, noncommercial projects. (Apple also includes a large assortment of copyright-free musical scores.)

A common theme emerges at iDay: users intensely dislike even the limited restrictions imposed on them by the high-tech industry. For example, Apple takes a rigid interpretation of its obligations under the DVD licensing standard, created by the entertainment and tech industries at the birth of the DVD, or digital versatile disc, in 1997. Apple wired its iDVD software so that a user may not capture a still image or moving scene from a DVD—even from a home movie that she has created. (And Apple is considered one of the enlightened companies. At Sony, you can't listen to Epic/Sony's release of Celine Dion's 2002 CD *A New Day Has Come* on a Sony PC because of copy restrictions.) Dozens of other companies are even more restrictive, fearing that cutting-edge innovation runs the risk of a lawsuit from Hollywood.

The common thread is to prevent any use of copyrighted material without authorization. But unauthorized doesn't mean illegal, and equipment manufacturers invite a backlash if they insert mechanisms that prevent people from remixing small pieces of our media culture for personal, noncommercial use to share with others.

Wielding the power of both publishers and mass distributors, the emerging middle-class armies of digital filmmakers will not be content to capture camcorder footage, create a movie, and stash it in the hallway closet. Through our computers and broadband TV sets, and on little silver discs, we'll want to share our experiences. Many of us will videotape, burn, and swap our stories with others. Whether we can tip the balance away from file-infringing bootleggers and toward personal creative works is an open question. But we'll be far poorer if we close the door on the enormous possibilities of a new democratic medium.

Communities of people who share digital stories have already begun to sprout up. Digital Clubhouses have sprung up in New York and Silicon Valley, documenting the stories of World War II veterans, cancer survivors, and other personal accounts. In classrooms in South Dakota, Japan, Brazil, and England, students are taping video exchanges and responding to one another's visual reports. As the technology takes hold, look for hundreds of informal digital movie clubs to dot the landscape, not unlike today's local book clubs. But the greatest digital swap meets will take place in cyberspace—on the Web, through e-mail, and in darknets, thanks to overly rigid copyright laws—as two-way high-speed connections, now in nearly half of U.S. homes, ripple out to the vast majority of households.

"When the creative spirits of the masses are empowered by these new technologies for artistic expression, a million flowers will certainly bloom," Moses Ma wrote in his newsletter the *Pitch*. "These new digi-indy films will most likely be more sensitive to the rhythms of people and the details of day-to-day existence, and thus, will capture the beauty or anguish of life with greater fidelity and cinematic grace."[4]

College students in particular demand more than a top-down, passive consumer experience. They have been reared in the Internet's ethos of interactivity, and they've come to expect the same kind of give-and-take from all their media, whether it consists of camera phones, digital video recorders, or burn-your-own CDs and DVDs. Now that desktop digital media such as photo slide shows and multimedia editing tools are becoming standard parts of the personal computer, students will want to share their creations and discoveries with networks of friends and classmates. Youth culture has always driven cultural innovation, and colleges, with their broadband connections, are the natural breeding grounds for experimentation with digital filmmaking and video file sharing.

But get ready for a surprise: the most enthusiastic users of the new digital moviemaking technology may be the boomer generation. At iDay, for example, a handful of high school and college students turned out, but the vast majority of those in attendance were forty- to sixty-year-olds. Lambert, a late boomer himself, tells me during a break, "We've spent part of our lives in a great deal of introspection, part of the legacy of the Me Generation. And now we're a gray audience with more time and income, but also the thoughtfulness and critical reflection that comes with life experience. The older generation has always sought to pass along the wisdom and life lessons they've acquired over time."

So far, media companies have done little to accommodate the growing personal media movement. Some of Lambert's students who navigated the bureaucratic hoops to get clearances for their home movies obtained permission with relative ease. But many others did not. "There have been occasions where someone is asked to jump over three fences, hurdle four lawyers, and spend tens of thousands of dollars to use a copyrighted excerpt for a little school project," Lambert says. "They wound up using copyright-free music, or using software that lets you emulate the mood of a song, or they just didn't bother clearing the rights for a film they intend to show only to family and friends."

My own experience with the entertainment companies was similar. I contacted seven record labels and seven motion picture studios for permission to use modest snippets as part of a personal home movie. Universal Music, Atlantic Records, Sony Music, EMI, and Artemis Records all declined or ignored my repeated requests. Warner Music and BMG consented.[5]

The movie studios were even more obdurate. MGM and Paramount declined to answer written requests to use short clips from their movies in a home movie project. Twentieth Century-Fox Film Corp. denied my request to use forty-five seconds from the film *Ice Age* for a home movie, writing: "Fox has reviewed your request and does not approve the use of any Fox copyrighted materials." Universal Studios denied my request to use thirty seconds from the film *The Mummy* for inclusion in a home movie my son and I were making about ghosts. Representative Roni Lubliner wrote: "If you want a licensing agreement from us to use the footage, you would be obligated to pay the appropriated license fees which would be $900 for each 15 seconds. If you go through this process, you would be protected against any potential lawsuits. Otherwise, I would recommend that you remove the footage from your DVD."

Warner Bros. responded to my request to use two ten-second snippets from the 1988 film *Daffy Duck's Quackbusters* and a fifteen-second clip from the 1948 film *The Treasure of the Sierra Madre*. Marlene Eastman, director of Clip & Still Licensing, wrote: "Please be advised, Warner Bros. Entertainment Inc. does not wish to license film clips for use in your personal movies. With respect to lifting material from a DVD or VHS, we do not permit anyone to lift material from a film print, DVD or VHS tape, nor do we allow our material to be edited or altered in any way." (A historical footnote: the fifty-seven-year-old *Treasure of the Sierra Madre* is based on a novel by a German anarchist whose point was to satirize the gold fever that Warner now exemplifies.)

The Walt Disney Co. provided the longest explanation in its refusal to let me use thirty seconds from a well-known 1964 film. Stephanie Martinelli, clearance administrator for Disney's Corporate Legal Department, wrote in part: "It is difficult to respond to your request, since we certainly understand your worthwhile intentions. Unfortunately, however, I am afraid we are going to have to deny your request to include footage from MARY POP-PINS in your home video project, as requested. Due to the growing number of requests that we are receiving from individuals, school groups, churches, corporations and other organizations that wish to use clips from our productions as part of their video projects and other similar uses, we have had to establish a general policy of non-cooperation with requests of this nature. Unfortunately, we simply do not have the staff necessary to oversee and review all of the details of each specific request that we receive in order to determine whether the request uses fall within acceptable guidelines or whether talent, music or film clip re-use payments to those featured in the footage and other legal clearances would be necessary to obtain before permission for requests of this nature can be granted." (The studios' responses and the full results of this experiment can be found at Darknet.com.)

When I asked Benjamin S. Feingold, head of Columbia TriStar Home Entertainment, about splicing a few seconds from his company's movie *Rudy* for a personal home movie, he said, "We do have a problem with that. It's intellectual property. There's blood, sweat and tears behind it. Financial remuneration is required [and] to have people cutting and slicing up your products is not fair." (Ironically, Columbia TriStar was the only studio to give permission to use its film clip in a home movie project.)

Jack Valenti, Hollywood's legendary lobbyist, told me that fair use does not apply to personal media projects. "There is no fair use to take something that doesn't belong to you. That's not fair use. If you're a professor in a classroom, you show *Singin' in the Rain* to your class. You can fast forward it, and there's no performance fee for that. That's fair use. People are taking fair use and changing it to unfair use and claiming that it's fair use."

Valenti's comments echo those of other entertainment officials. Hilary Rosen, former chairman of the Recording Industry Association of America, the record labels' trade group, told the U.S. Senate Judiciary Committee in July 2000 that it is not fair use to make a copy of a legally purchased CD to play in your car. Instead, she said "tolerance" on the part of the recording industry was the only thing that deters the labels from taking people to court for their "unauthorized" uses of copyrighted music. This despite a 1992 law in which Congress expressly gave consumers the right to copy music for personal use.[6]

Since Valenti stepped down from his post, has the MPAA shifted its stance? Only modestly. The MPAA announced in November 2004 that it would launch a full-scale barrage of lawsuits against individual file traders, following in the RIAA's footsteps. Days later, Fritz Attaway, the MPAA's executive vice president of government relations, told me that "there is no clear answer to" the question of whether hobbyists may borrow from Hollywood movies. He said certain uses, such as for parody, academic purposes, or critical commentary, may be permissible under the Copyright Act, but "proceed at your own risk" because "it does open a can of worms."[7]

But you won't be able to rip a movie from a DVD to get your snippet, and you can't bypass Macrovision on your VHS recorder, because those actions are proscribed by law. What to do, then? "You can always aim your camcorder at the television set," he suggested. Never mind that almost no one does this. Oh, and don't forget, he added, that many states—including California—have right-of-publicity laws that restrict how performers' images can be used without their permission. Performers have a cause of action if their images are used in a way they don't approve of—even in a home movie project, he suggested. (Going after the perpetrators may not be practicable, but still, the law is the law.)

Whether or not Big Entertainment's lawyers are accurate in offering such a miserly appraisal of fair use—and many legal experts suggest they are mistaken—copyright law needs to be reformed. Millions of individual storytellers don't deserve to be caught up in the elaborate licensing machinery set up by the media companies. When we borrow a few seconds of a movie scene, television show, or musical score for use in a personal, noncommercial home movie, a different yardstick should apply. The authors of the copyright code never imagined a day when millions of us would be publishers, amateur filmmakers, and personal broadcasters, relying on a new cultural dynamic that treats bits and pieces of big media's parallel universe as fuel for our own creations.[8]

Let's be clear: this is not about taking someone's song or movie and redistributing it without permission on a file-sharing network. Lambert is among those who excoriate commercial entities like Kazaa, which build their brands on other people's works to make a handful of people rich. "To me, that's thievery," he says.

But sharing songs or movies without permission is markedly different from works of personal media that remix, reimagine, and reinvent. If little Caitlyn wants to lift the *T. rex* from *Jurassic Park* and have it go after the neighborhood bully in her home movie, well, isn't that the kind of creative energy we should foster?

As Apple CEO Steve Jobs passionately implored from the stage of

Macworld 2003 when showing off the company's suite of movie tools: "You can *make* this stuff. You can make things that are better than what you get out of Hollywood!"

That's what the digital generation expects. In the next few years, as young people snap up camera phones and portable video devices, they'll want to show their friends the latest Alicia Keys or Eminem music video, but they'll also want to show off the home video they just shot, edited, and uploaded—perhaps with Alicia or Eminem making a guest appearance.

Philip Gaines, a multimedia developer in Bellevue, Washington, was such a devoted fan of the sci-fi TV show F*irefly* that he refused to see it vanish into the abyss when Fox canceled the series after a three-month run in 2002. Instead, he spent months, and $700, creating a fan DVD that paid homage to the show.

What inspired him? "First, this was one of the great TV shows of our time, and I wanted to highlight that," he says by phone from his home. "Second, the project served as a digital portfolio that showcased my skills as an editor and writer. And finally, this is a step that advances intellectual discourse among fans. This shouldn't be confined to professors talking about the show in an academic setting. I wanted to bring the discussion out into the open for the rest of us."[9]

The result is *Firefly: A Special Feature*, a charming, quirky, 3½-hour documentary that may well serve as a prototype for similar homespun multimedia efforts. His project probes the deeper textures of the series, laying out the arguments of why it was brilliant, complete with audio commentary interspersed with series clips. Since the project's completion in November 2003, Gaines has given away six hundred copies of his two-DVD set, asking only a $9 donation to cover costs.

The enterprising twenty-nine-year-old began by writing a thirty-thousand-word script, a fusion of wry observations and essays on subjects like irony and violence. Next, he obtained a DVD from a member of a *Firefly* fan site, who downloaded episodes from the Darknet because Fox had not yet released an official home video version. Then he spent eight hours, at $45 an hour, recording the script onto a CD at a local radio station. (He could have bought a digital tape recorder for less.) Finally, he used encryption and decryption tools as well as DVD authoring software to pull together his audio and scenes from the TV series into a forty-part DVD presentation. He encourages recipients to reproduce his digital tribute and offer it to others.

Gaines took a graduate course at the University of Washington that covered fair use and infringement. "I consider what I've done to be fair use, but I'll admit that in using 3½ hours of video I'm entering a seriously gray area," he says. To ward off liability, he did not include any media company's trademarks—"that's where they usually get you," he correctly points out—and he made certain to use no more than a third of any single episode. More important than the legal issues, though, are the practical considerations. The creators of *Firefly* have responded favorably to his do-it-yourself DVD, he says, and "Fox would have no interest in suing an underdog like me who only wants to promote their show."

Gaines's effort mirrors the territory mined by film critic Roger Ebert, who was so enthralled with the 1998 film *Dark City* that he recorded a lengthy commentary that was included in the DVD released by the studio. Few of us have that kind of clout, however. In late 2002, Ebert proposed an alternative way for fans to participate, suggesting the creation of do-it-yourself film commentaries made up of recorded audio tracks that could be traded over the Net and synched up with the movie. Months later, a Web site called DVDTracks.com began doing just that, with scores of people participating in film culture and cementing the rubric that everybody's a critic.

Apparently Gaines is the first to take this idea a step farther. Instead of the clumsy approach of listening to a downloaded audio file while watching a DVD movie on the TV or a computer, he put his commentary right onto a remixed DVD. "The concept of a self-made DVD has gotten the biggest response from people," he says. "They like the idea of regular folks creating parallel media. I think you'll be seeing much more of this. The online environment allows for much faster and more diverse discourse, and it gives people access to media they wouldn't be able to otherwise get."

Before I can ask him about Hollywood's claim that the studios need to sign off on any use of their work, Gaines beats me to the punch. "No matter what Jack Valenti says, they are in a hopeless position if they want to keep people from trying to manipulate their finished product. If they put out a movie, people will take that movie, re-edit it, and re-release it."

Gaines predicts someone will soon take *The Lord of the Rings* trilogy and edit out scenes that he or she believes slow the narrative. It won't be Gaines. "There were three unaired episodes of *Firefly* that I wasn't able to cover in my original project. I'm contemplating using those unaired episodes in a new project and inviting other viewers to submit essays that I could include in a sequel DVD."

An entire conference could be built around the legal issues raised by *Firefly: A Special Feature*. While *Darknet* focuses primarily on the digital media revolution, a word about the law may be in order here.

Siva Vaidhyanathan, director of communication studies at New York University and an author who has written widely on copyright law, says users are within their rights to borrow and remix cultural works—including movies—for private, noncommercial uses. "Jack Valenti may want to wish away fair use. But his position is in direct conflict with more than a century of case law on the matter. And it ignores the specific language of the 1976 Copyright Act, which codified fair use. In the United States, we have a clearly defined tradition of fair use that speaks to the fact that small, private, noncommercial uses of someone else's copyrighted material should be allowed without having to resort to permission seeking or payment.[10]

"If it's fair use for someone to quote a paragraph of my book and use it in another context—let's say, to criticize it or to write a research paper for school—then it must be fair use to use a snippet of a *Star Wars* film to show that Jar-Jar Binks is a racist caricature," he says. "I should not be allowed to veto the use of a small portion of my work and thus prevent a greater social good. Neither should George Lucas. The law does not affect video differently than text, music, or software."

Vaidhyanathan says we should encourage low-cost, potentially critical uses of copyrighted works because education, scholarship, criticism, and new art are all important and underfunded aspects of our cultural lives. "The scary thing about Valenti's comments is that he basically writes American copyright law these days. Congress listens to him and gives him whatever he wants, regardless of whether it's good for America. And federal courts listen to Congress. If Congress would listen to the American people, it would strengthen fair use. Alas, we may be seeing the last days of fair use because Jack Valenti has declared it so."

Yale Law School cyberlaw expert Ernest Miller offers a different take, illustrating the law's devilish complexity—and the unsettled nature of users' rights in the digital age. "The problem is that fair use analysis is incredibly fact-dependent. Even copying a small amount of a copyrighted work as part of another, new work is a violation of copyright," he says. "For example, a few seconds in a videotape where portions of a copyrighted poster can be seen in the background have been found to meet the threshold for infringement. So, although I would argue that such uses are fair uses, the courts might not agree."[11]

Users who record audio of their armchair criticisms (as on DVDTracks) would undoubtedly be protected by fair use, but Miller cautions that the law does not allow you to burn a DVD of an entire Hollywood film overlaid with your commentary. He also points out that any use of DVD ripping software—which breaks the copy protection on a DVD—is a federal crime on its face (see chapter 6). And he notes that George Lucas's production company Lucasfilm threatened to sue any Web site operator who posted a copy of *The Phantom Edit*, created by a fan who edited out twenty minutes of the annoying Jar-Jar Binks from the official version of the 1999 film *Star Wars: Episode I—The Phantom Menace*. (*The Phantom Edit* proved to be extremely popular online, and copies still circulate in the Darknet.)

While sounding a guarded legal note, Miller thinks the issue goes beyond legalisms to social freedoms and cultural values. "People are waking up from their consumerist coma," he says, and Hollywood would benefit from embracing digital tools that allow greater freedoms, such as allowing users to contribute appreciations and commentaries attached to DVDs. "The studios would sell more copies," he argues. "Gaming companies know this already. The makers of games like *Quake* and *Unreal* provide users with the ability to create new levels of play or to introduce new characters, giving rise to entire communities that support such efforts."

Gaines points out that it has become commonplace to include supplementary material on Hollywood DVDs—interviews with everyone from the director right on down to the sound designer and key grip. Why not provide an easy, legal way for fans to provide full commentaries as well?

In mid-2003, journalists Shayne Bowman and Chris Willis wrote a report called "We Media: How Audiences Are Shaping the Future of News and Information" for New Directions for News, a newspaper think tank. Because I was an early proponent of the "participatory journalism" movement, calling on news organizations to bring readers directly into the news process, I was selected to edit the report. The "We Media" study examined how the Internet and digital technologies have turned readers and viewers into hands-on users who expect a two-way dialogue with their media rather than a one-way lecture.

Dan Gillmor, a business columnist for the *San Jose Mercury News* and a leading advocate of participatory journalism, said, "It's about readers participating in the editorial process, and it's long overdue. People at the edges of the network are getting a chance to become more involved in traditional journalism by using many of the same tools of the trade. This is tomorrow's journalism, with professionals and gifted amateurs as partners." Gillmor, who wrote a book about bottom-up journalism called *We the Media*, put his credo into action by publishing all the chapters on his weblog and asking readers to offer feedback. He then went one step farther, quitting his job to work on setting up a participatory journalism enterprise.

The "We Media" report could have easily been broadened to include entertainment as well as news, for the same winds of participatory culture and open media are whipping through all corners of the media world. Karaoke bars, amateur photography, and *American Idol* are just a few examples of a wider social trend whose roots run deep. If many people have not noticed, it's because the changes are seeping unobtrusively into our daily lives, and as they do, the traditional power structures have not come tumbling down. The major media conglomerates and the Hollywood studios will continue to thrive and rake in billions, but rising alongside them is a new kind of bottom-up media, powered by ordinary people.

Certainly we need to keep in mind that not everyone is a born storyteller, musician, or filmmaker. Paul Saffo, director of the Institute for the Future, goes so far as to lament the democratization of the Web because "the majority of people are really boring."[12] Whether or not that's true, it misses the point, which is that creative individuals who are not part of the mass media assembly line now have a way to contribute to our culture—and at least *some* of them are interesting.

Over the years, I've heard from skeptics who argue that news ought to be left strictly to journalism professionals, that movies and television should remain the exclusive province of a trained elite. But the personal media revolution has always been about bringing the public more choices rather than displacing the pros. In the 1980s, desktop tools democratized publishing, unleashing the creativity of millions of amateur editors and designers who began creating professional-quality documents and publications—without hurting traditional magazine titles. Today digital tools and the Internet are again leveling the playing field, enabling grassroots publishers and multimedia artisans to become active participants in the culture. On the Net, the barriers to entry are trivial. We're no longer shut out of media because we can't afford a printing press or a station license. Today our computers are our personal printing presses and recording, TV, and movie studios.

Some of the seeds of the personal media revolution were first sewn by the MIT Media Lab. In 1992, a class assignment—to design a personalized news system for the university's incoming freshmen—evolved into *fish-Wrap*, an online news publication that offered stories based on readers' individual backgrounds and ranked front-page stories collaboratively, based on what other readers liked. Traditionalists hated the idea of personalized news, suggesting that news filtering would isolate us from important world events. I argued in a series of articles that we live in a media-saturated environment where it's impossible to become closed off from the world at large, and that personalized media is not about filtering out but about *funneling in* information we care most deeply about.

Reader interactivity was nice, but the Media Lab went a step farther by turning readers into writers and editors. Its News in the Future program went on to set up community publishing projects in the United States, Finland, Brazil, India, Ireland, Mexico, Thailand, and in more than forty-five hundred high schools in Italy. One of the projects, SilverStringers, began in 1996 when MIT handed three computers, a laptop, digital camera, scanner, color printer, and software to ten volunteers from a senior center in Melrose, Massachusetts, who created their own online newspaper. They continue to publish each month.

"The news consumer is turning into a news provider," Walter Bender, MIT Media Lab associate director, told me in 1999. "It's not that these news consumers will compete with the *New York Times*, but the consumer becomes part of the process of telling stories in a way that enriches the public discourse."[13]

Today user-created content—also called personal media—is no longer the rarity it once was. In a February 2004 report,[14] the Pew Internet & American Life Project found that 44 percent of U.S. Internet users have contributed files and materials or posted comments online, including 21 percent who have posted photos online. Another recent report, from the Committee for Economic Development, a Washington policy group, concluded: "There has been an explosion in the popularity of downloading and transmitting high-value digital content, triggered by the growth of the Internet and the evolution of peer-to-peer systems. At the same time, there is a substantial disconnect between public attitudes toward copyright and the letter of the law."[15]

Examples of personal media swirl all around us. Look at the "blogosphere": the more than 6 million Web journals that offer news, commentary, and reflections about the world, usually through the subjective prism of a single individual. Weblogs offer vibrant, personality-infused, lances-to-the-ready assaults on the status quo—qualities too often missing in corporate media. Blogs attract everyone from teens to senior citizens who offer up rafts of opinion, eyewitness accounts, expert knowledge, and other tidbits. If you dabble in wi-fi, sonnet poetry, wormholes, or copyright abuses, you'll want to go to the fanatics: the bloggers who specialize in these and thousands of other niche subjects. As James Wolcott wrote in *Vanity Fair*, "Blogs have speedily matured into the most vivifying, talent-swapping, socializing breakthrough in popular journalism since the burst of coffeehouse periodicals and political pamphleteering in the 18th century."[16]

Jazzed by a medium that thrives on individual creativity and group participation, I began my first blog in the spring of 2001, with an emphasis on chronicling the rise of personal media and do-it-yourself culture. Today it's no longer a novelty to see individuals offer first-person accounts of news events in text, photos, and video. On 9/11, bloggers posted eyewitness accounts, commentaries, photos, and videos of the tragedy. During the Northeast's blackout in August 2003, people with camera phones posted scenes of New Yorkers coping with the power outage in real time. In Southern California, a blogger relayed eyewitness reports minutes after an elderly driver killed nine pedestrians at a farmers' market. In Tokyo, a news station aired live coverage of a fatal accident from a citizen-reporter who phoned in a report from the scene and shot footage with a video-enabled cell phone. Baghdad resident Salam Pax became a cyberspace celebrity for his reports during and after the Iraq war. Blog readers sent freelance journalist Christopher Allbritton $14,334 to finance his trip to southern Iraq, where he filed reports from his laptop computer via satellite phone as the war began. Readers also sent $4,000 to fund blogger Joshua Marshall's coverage of the 2004 Democratic primaries. Other blogs, such as the Campaign Desk and FactCheck.org, served as watchdogs of both candidates and campaign reporters during the 2004 election.

Blogs captured headlines during the 2004 presidential campaign when several dozen political bloggers covered the Democratic and Republican national conventions. Their highwater mark during the political season came during Memogate, when bloggers debunked the authenticity of documents purporting to fill in the gaps in President George W. Bush's National Guard service record, forcing CBS's *60 Minutes* to disavow its own report.

In the days following the tsunami that devastated regions of South Asia on December 26, 2004, bloggers once again rose to the occasion, serving a key social media role by helping to raise relief funds for the victims, helping family members locate missing loved ones, sharing the anguish and heartache of eyewitnesses, and giving voice to those in the affected areas through first-person narratives, photos, and videos. The interconnectedness of blogs bypasses the walled gardens of traditional media outlets, making the survivors more tangible and making the free flow of information more likely.

A new breed of bloggers called "videobloggers" rose out of nowhere in early 2005 with the first-ever videobloggers conference in New York City. In the years ahead, as video becomes a more central facet of the storytelling process, blogs will serve as a major publishing platform for the distribution of video. When we hunt for a subject in a visual search engine, the video won't be a disembodied stream of bits; it will be tied to a person, company, or organization with a reputation and track record.

Blogs may be the greatest success story of personal media, but they tell only part of the story. In September 2004, a San Francisco bicyclist discovered that his ultratough Kryptonite bike lock could be picked open with a ballpoint pen. He sprang to action, posting his findings on an online forum for bike enthusiasts. His post was read by more than 400,000 people. A video, showing the pen doing the deed, was downloaded more than 3 million times in a few days. Within a week, thousands of the bike locks were returned to the manufacturer, and retailers were clearing their shelves of the product.

A new medium called podcasting began spreading in late 2004. The audio cousin of weblogs enables individuals to Webcast their own do-it-yourself radio shows, with files that could be played on portable players or desktop computers at any time. Early subjects included movie commentary, law, business, comedy, music, gossip, and sex. Best of all, no ads, and the files can be easily captured through RSS feeds. Similarly, a few tireless souls, such as Rob Greenlee and Ken Rutkowski, have become one-man Web radio news networks. Christopher Lydon posts audio interviews with dozens of well-known public figures.

Tens of thousands of people have become consumer reporters on sites like Amazon.com, *Epinions*, and *BabyCenter*, offering firsthand reviews of detective novels, camcorders, breast pumps, and other products and services—reviews that often contain the level of depth and sophistication found in major magazines and newspapers. Sites like Snopes.com offer a reality check for debunking Internet rumors. The Independent Media Center offers news coverage supplied by anyone who wanted to contribute, routing around mainstream news coverage to provide subjective multimedia news takes; more than a hundred Indymedia centers now circle the globe. *Dilbert* cartoonist Scott Adams said in a *Washington Post* chat that he gets much of his best material from reader e-mail, though he complained, "But the lazy %#$*s refuse to draw the comic too, so I have to do that part."

Wikipedia has been an amazing success story. The free-content encyclopedia—where anyone can write or edit an entry—produced more than 1 million articles in under four years. At 127 million words in the English version alone, Wikipedia is larger than any other English-language encyclopedia, including the *Encyclopaedia Britannica*, which weighs in at 55 million words. What's most remarkable is that every word is written by volunteers and no one gets paid for a submission.

MoveOn, a Net-based activist organization with more than 2 million members, played a large role in the 2004 presidential election with its grassroots organizing and media efforts. The group sponsored a contest called "Bush in 30 Seconds," in which 1,500 participants created 30-second political ads that criticized Bush administration policies. Many of the ads were as creative as anything that ever came out of professional ad agencies. As tech publisher Tim O'Reilly pointed out, "the cost of creating TV spots has gone from millions of dollars to near zero."[17] The winning spot, which showed young children working in gritty jobs to pay off the mounting national debt, aired in a dozen key swing states, although CBS banned it from the Super Bowl telecast because of its political advocacy.

While most media empires show little interest in user participation, there are exceptions. Pioneering video producer Steven Rosenbaum told me in 1996, "Viewers want to take control of TV, turn it inside out, and go from being spoon-fed observers to active participants." His *MTV News Unfiltered* put camcorders in the hands of viewers to tell their own stories. For years, National Public Radio has turned over tape recorders to citizens who have created moving examples of first-person journalism. BBC News and online newspapers have begun publishing photos and videos submitted by users. Some mainstream sites have begun to study the success of collaborative operations like *Kuro5hin*, *Metafilter*, *Fark*, and Slashdot.org, a thriving site about technology and current events where users post essays and commentaries and vote to rank others' contributions. *OhmyNews*, a Web publication in South Korea, draws 2 million readers a day. The site's editors post hundreds of stories daily, about four-fifths of them written by a nationwide army of 26,000 housewives, schoolchildren, professors, and assorted citizen-reporters, along with a handful of professional journalists. Considered the country's most influential news site, *OhmyNews* is widely credited with helping Koreans elect a little-known human rights attorney as their new president.

The music field has seen a dramatic drop in the cost of making demo CDs. Thousands of amateur musicians now compose musical works with digital tools and distribute them on peer-to-peer networks. In early 2004, Apple introduced GarageBand, an inexpensive application that lets you create music from scratch or mix your tracks with 1,000 professionally recorded loops, even if you can't read music or play an instrument. Almost immediately, two online communities—MacBand and MacJams—sprung up around the software, letting people work and play collaboratively without having to worry about violating copyrights. Another site, TuneYard, lets people post compositions or listen to others' creations.

The film industry was once all but closed off to amateurs. Then came *The Blair Witch Project*. The independent film, made by five guys in Orlando, Florida, and starring three unknown actors, cost $35,000 to make and earned $250 million at the box office. Since the film debuted at the Sundance Film Festival in 1999, production costs have dropped even lower. *Tarnation*, a documentary shown at Sundance in 2004 and nominated for a Caméra d'Or award at Cannes, was made on a budget of $218.31 and edited on Apple's iMovie. (The total will rise to $400,000 after paying for rights to music and video clips used to illustrate a mood or era.)

Or consider Matt McDermitt, who first picked up a video camera when he was six. With a low-cost Panasonic camcorder, Macintosh computer, Final Cut Pro software, and his natural talent for filmic composition, Matt won several awards for his professional-looking work by the time he was in eighth grade. "Ten years ago, Roger Ebert said that the next Orson Welles will be some kid with a home video camera, and the industry laughed," Moses Ma wrote. "Well, he was right and Matt just might be that kid."[18]

Today, talent and vision—not money and technology—are the only barriers to great filmmaking.

In the literary world, a curious genre known as fan fiction has begun to flourish. Years ago, it existed as a fringe hobby in which friends penned and swapped manuscripts that borrowed heavily from popular culture. But the Internet kick-started the practice, connecting people with others who shared each other's tastes for collaborative writing and instant feedback. Fan fiction sites let users create new story lines involving familiar TV, movie, or book characters. On FanFiction.net, the granddaddy of fan-fiction sites, people have expanded the world of Harry Potter by writing more than seventy-five thousand stories. Fans riff on Scooby Doo, the Monkees, and their favorite characters from *Dawson's Creek*, *CSI: Miami*, and dozens of other shows.[19] The explosion of these part-original, part-borrowed works has set authors of fan fiction against Hollywood studios, TV networks, and book publishers in a battle that pits users' rights against the copyright holders' attempts to control their works. Fan fiction devotees have grown so legion that they even have their own convention, Fanzillacon.

Personal media are rapidly outgrowing their hobbyist roots and blossoming into a mass movement. Although some of my friends have never heard of weblogs or niche news sites, the more tech-savvy of them rely increasingly on grassroots media for news and entertainment. This is no fad but a sea change in how we interact with media.

What I've described is just version 1.0 of the personal media revolution. "It's difficult to figure out where all this is going to wind up," author Gillmor says. "The only thing certain is that we'll never return to the days when people are treated as passive vessels for content delivered by big media through one-way pipes—no matter how disruptive these changes may be for traditional media. We're in for a fascinating ride."

Cheaper, smarter tools have served as personal media's great equalizer, allowing us to make our creative visions real. In a few years, experts predict, faster pipes will turn the Web into a more visual medium. But for creators of personal media, getting from here to there may prove tricky. Almost none of the twenty thousand personal movies made at Joe Lambert's Storycenter are available for public viewing, in part because of concerns about rights clearances. How will our stories proliferate and spread? How will grassroots filmmakers and video hobbyists find their audiences?

How will personal media turn into shared experiences?

5 Code Warriors

'M SITTING IN A CLUTTERED CONFERENCE ROOM IN THE headquarters of DivXNetworks in San Diego. Two of the company's top managers and I are kicking back, watching scenes from the Vin Diesel flame fest *XXX* on a twenty-seven-inch TV screen. As Diesel improbably maneuvers his motorcycle through one fireball after another, the stereo sound booms and the special effects crackle with eye-popping intensity. But we're not watching a DVD, we're watching a live video stream over the Internet.

This is supposed to be impossible.

Video is a notoriously voracious medium, demanding lots of bandwidth. A television show or movie can take many hours to transfer over a high-speed cable or DSL line. If you order a movie over the Internet from Hollywood's Movielink, you generally have to wait a long time before you can watch a single frame. Researchers are devising next-generation

Internet pipes that will be a hundred times zippier, but such efforts are years distant.

There's another way to transfer video over the Net with no lag time: instead of fattening the pipes, squeeze the content.

It's a formula that has already wrought revolutionary changes in music: file sharing and portable music players would be fringe pastimes rather than mainstream activities today without MP3 compression technology. A typical seventy-four-minute compact music disc contains 650 megabytes, a size that would take hours to transfer over high-speed data lines. But MP3 squeezes a music file to an eleventh its original size; a song squeezed this way takes only a couple of minutes to download and still sounds pretty good to most listeners. With my iPod, I carry a thousand songs in my pocket.

Entertainment people work themselves into a froth about the Internet's role as an infringement pipeline, but few of them fully appreciate that the real agent of change in home entertainment is the codec. Invisible to the end user, the unheralded codec is a little piece of software used by media players to <u>co</u>mpress and <u>deco</u>mpress audio and video. You rarely hear about them, but codecs are the lifeblood of digital media. MP3, MPEG-2, and AAC (Dolby Labs' Advanced Audio Codec that Apple uses for songs sold in its iTunes store) are all examples of codecs. MPEG-2, introduced in 1994, reduces video files to about 3 percent of their original size. As a result, we can watch Hollywood movies on DVD, digital cable and satellite operators like DirecTV can squeeze hundreds of channels onto their signals, and a new generation of gadgets like digital camcorders and TiVo has been born. When you watch *Law and Order* or a Hollywood movie on your TV, you probably have a codec to thank.

Having sent the music business on its ear, codecs are about to rock Hollywood's world. Jordan Greenhall grasped that insight when he was just two years out of Harvard Law School. Vice president at a music start-up called MP3.com, Greenhall began considering the next wave of disruptive homebrew media. "What would be the video side of the MP3 revolution?" he recalls thinking. "How could digital video—Internet video—really take off, with people taking control of their own media?"[1]

One day in late 1999, Greenhall was prowling an IRC channel in the Darknet, downloaded a movie, and began watching it on his PC. What he saw astounded him. He could scarcely believe that in twenty minutes he was able to pull down an entire DVD-quality movie from the Internet. That told him that his vision was not only realistic but also within immediate reach.

Until then, video on the Web consisted of ugly, jerky, postage-stamp-size images that almost no one wanted to watch. Here was a technology that allowed viewers to quickly access and watch a movie over a broadband connection at a high level of quality on a full-size screen. This was Internet video's holy grail.

Greenhall, who had left MP3.com, began a Darknet hunt to learn the identity of the coder or coders who had pulled this off. He spent weeks using back-channel contacts, offering assurances that he was a businessman and not a digital bounty hunter. He learned that the coder behind the hack was a furtive figure, or composite of several programmers, named Gej. Through IRC chat, he managed to contact Gej and discussed the technical, economic, and political merits of joining forces and forming a video compression company. After many weeks, he learned Gej's true identity: Jerome Rota, a twenty-seven-year-old French graphic artist and movie buff. By that time Greenhall had begun meeting with technology experts and financiers. Lee Gomes, a *Wall Street Journal* reporter, learned of the venture and began working on a story that would give the tech start-up national exposure and instant credibility. Greenhall bought Rota a plane ticket, and the French programmer left his home in the Riviera, flew to Los Angeles, met with the reporter, and signed with the fledgling enterprise.

Rota's original software—the codec that caught Greenhall's eye—was a hack born out of frustration with Microsoft. Rota had created an artistic portfolio and résumé with Windows Media software, but when Microsoft released an upgrade, it would no longer open. Rota got mad. He took matters into his own hands, rewrote the code so it would work with all sorts of computer file formats, and released it into the Darknet. "It took a week to set the information free," he says. The pirate code exploded in popularity on underground IRC channels, for this was the first time people could get their hands on an easy-to-use technology that would let them pass around high-quality video on the Internet. Rota named his pirate code DivX ;-) in a sardonic reference to DivX, or Digital Video Express, an obtuse technology backed by most of the major Hollywood studios as an alternative to the new DVD format. It is little remembered today that in the mid-1990s, most studios fought the DVD and tried to derail its introduction. Only Warner and Sony pushed the DVD, which offered a packaged product similar to books and CDs that movie lovers could own, collect, and resell.

By contrast, Disney, Fox, Universal Pictures, and DreamWorks supported Digital Video Express's pay-per-view scheme. Digital Video Express required special modem-equipped machines that phoned in to a central computer for authorization each time someone wanted to watch a movie and imposed a fee for each viewing of a DivX movie disc, which could not play on standard DVD players. Digital Video Express sparked an Internet boycott movement, and even movie critic Roger Ebert complained, "It confuses fans with pirates." Despite Circuit City pumping an estimated $350 million into the effort—including more than $20 million apiece in fees up front to the major studios—the original DivX died, unloved and unmourned, in June 1999 after only nine months and two hundred thousand players sold.

Irony aside, the new DivX would have far more success than its predecessor. Flush with $5.6 million in venture funding, the partners at DivXNetworks hired a small team of world-class video coders and moved them from Italy, Russia, Britain, and China to San Diego. The vision was to make DivX the global standard for digital video by persuading other companies to insert its MPEG-4-based code into set-top boxes, media players, and video cameras. Greenhall and Rota thus set out to transform a burgeoning underground movement into a legitimate, play-by-the-rules enterprise. That meant rewriting Rota's pirate code from the ground up.

As the founders settled into their new roles, Greenhall, a thin, swarthy thirty-two-year-old with clean-cut GQ looks and an expansive, self-assured manner, took the title of CEO. Rota clung to his geek chic persona—owl glasses, shoulder-length hair, shy, awkward manner—and hunkered down at his computer to play with code long into the night. Neither took a private office, preferring to work alongside rank-and-file programmers.

Since its founding, DivXNetworks has grown from five to eighty employees to become a sort of international cabal of film-loving geeks. Renting offices in a flat, squat brick building set back from the road behind a wrought-iron security gate, the company's headquarters is spare and functional: dim fluorescent lights wash down on clusters of workstations, while surfboards line the hallways. Codecs improve as they mature, just as surely as PC processing speeds increase, and the DivX codec now reduces an already compressed MPEG-2 video by another four-fifths, making the file less than 1 percent of its original size. DivX made an early decision to release its software onto the Internet for free. As a result, about 150 million people worldwide are using DivX regularly. The company earns income by charging for its software player, which lets users watch DivX movies on their computers.

But Greenhall and Rota knew all along that the living room, not the home office, was where most of us watch movies. So in 2003, DivX morphed from a software start-up into a consumer electronics technology company. In a series of epiphanies, Greenhall began to understand how critical consumer electronics was to video in almost every respect. Building technology for consumer products, the DivX team soon discovered, was a very different proposition than writing PC software.

"The difference is this," Greenhall says in his bullet-train delivery. "Consumer electronics is about getting technology into an integrated circuit, which means building your technology in a way that's easy to get onto a chip, that works perfectly all the time, and that is not going to require a lot of upgrades. Contrast that with creating software for the PC, where you put it out there and it has just kind of got to work, and you upgrade it later and it's no big deal. To get into consumer electronics chip sets, you literally have to have a completely different culture than a software company. When you're in a chip, it's got to be perfect."

The executive team broke the company into three groups: a software group devoted to Internet content production tools; a consumer electronics hardware group; and a video solutions group that works with cable and satellite operators and content providers like the Hollywood studios. Quickly, the company managed to springboard onto a host of new devices, with scores of companies building DivX into camcorders and other gizmos. For example, Alaska Airlines passes out small video players to passengers during flight, letting them watch a dozen or so movies stored in DivX format. Most significantly, Philips and Samsung are adding DivX to new lines of DVD players. (Until recently, no DVD players let you watch movies encoded in DivX.) DivX takes in $2 for each branded DVD player sold. Greenhall says he expects DivX to be in a majority of all DVD players sold in a few years—not too shabby, considering that more than 20 million units are sold annually just in the United States.

Before the company veered into consumer electronics, the founders had thought that video on demand would be their mainstay, as with the *XXX* trailer I watched. So far it hasn't turned out that way. In his halting English, Rota envisions the day when DivX spurs a new appreciation for experimental movies and film classics, allowing viewers to set themselves free from two hundred channels with nothing on. He says video compression opens new channels and markets for independent producers who no longer have to rely on marketing muscle and retail stores to distribute their works. Content owners can charge fees and set rules so viewers can watch a film for a day, a week, or forever, or pass it along to others. Greenhall hints he would like DivX to become part of a grand video jukebox, offering the breadth of titles available to Netflix's 2 million subscribers, but using the Internet instead of the Post Office for distribution. That way, customers could instantly access any film on demand—say, a Katharine Hepburn romantic comedy or an early Chaplin film. "That would be nirvana," he says.

But nirvana is on hold. In contrast to its booming entry into consumer electronics, DivX has had a tough time persuading the studios to open their vaults, where the treasures reside. The company has shopped its technology around to all the major studios, but Hollywood has not allowed any of its titles to be zapped into customers' home by DivX. This led to Greenhall's second big ah-ha moment: the insight that the digital media revolution would not be led by established media companies.

"The major content companies aren't about innovation. They're about market power," Greenhall says. "They want someone else to go in, innovate a new technology or marketplace, figure it out, make sure it looks viable, and then exert their economies of scale to go in and take it over—to try to control the end game. On the flip side, the major content companies can also be a major blocker. They want to make sure that any market that gets built is ultimately a market that they can move into. So when you go out and try to create a new revolution in media, you have to walk a very fine line between those two points. On the one hand, you can't expect to get the major content providers to endorse you or promote the marketplace that you're developing. At the same time, you can't alienate them or demonize them, because ultimately they could throw down a major blocker."

Despite praise from the MPAA's Jack Valenti, who was impressed with the copy protection safeguards DivX has built into its products, the company has not yet signed any deals with the studios, and so far no studio offers DivX-encoded DVDs.

At an early meeting, Greenhall recalls, "The chief technology officer for a major studio told us, 'You've got some of our folks interested, you've got a lot of visibility. I just want you to know we won't be doing any business with you for years. Maybe something will happen down the road,' which was frank and ultimately true. Not every studio has been that up front, but they've all behaved in the same way. The reality is, no matter how amazing something is, it just takes time for something the size of a studio to even digest it. Also, the more amazing a technology is, the more dangerous it is, and therefore the more they really want to control it."

Video codecs in home entertainment products have become largely a four-way race between DivX, in central casting's role of David, against Microsoft, RealNetworks, and Sony. Seattle's RealNetworks, which remains a dominant media player on PCs, created the Internet's first music player and has moved into some mobile devices, but it has not yet made the difficult leap to the living room. Sony dreams of the day when its PlayStation console will become the hub of the digital lifestyle.

To date, the Hollywood studios have relied on Microsoft's technology to stream movies into PCs in the home office and media centers in the living room. But their efforts have been modest, partly because it's still a small market and partly because the studios have no incentive to disrupt their lucrative home video business. Greenhall says that at a meeting with another major studio, the vice president of strategy told the DivX delegation not to bother comparing their technology with Microsoft's. "It doesn't matter," the studio exec told them. "Hollywood hates Microsoft. We're not going to use Microsoft. We'll play with them and let Microsoft do some stuff, but the No. 1 thing Hollywood hates is a monopoly bigger than we are." That may be so, but the Redmond Goliath has too much influence for Hollywood to long ignore its entreaties.

Can DivX best the big boys? Perhaps. DivX likes to call itself "the MP3 of video," and if Greenhall can realize that ambitious goal, the payoff would be huge: royalties from the device makers and profit sharing with the content companies from home delivery of digital entertainment. Although the earliest adopters of the original open-source DivX codec were pirates who used it illegally to trade movie files in the Darknet, and the earliest content companies to sign up with DivXNetworks were adult entertainment sites that delivered porn on demand, Greenhall figures that's the marketplace in action, where the illicit and the unseemly help kick-start more mainstream, legitimate businesses. The company has signed deals with thirty smaller companies, including indie film distributors and the Jim Henson Co.

But Greenhall sees bigger things on the horizon for codecs' role in the personal media revolution. "These are technologies that can change the cultural balance of power," he says.

Put aside for a moment the fact that right now DivX can deliver a television experience over the Internet that is superior to both broadcast digital cable and digital satellite. Look past the cool applications right around the corner that video compression will bring about: video e-mail, video phone calls, movies on demand.

The real power of the codec lies not in improving the quality of the visual experience in the home, but in bringing an entirely new range of visual experiences to people's doorsteps. When you no longer have the cable or satellite operators controlling what comes through the pipes into your living room, everything changes. Broadcast can deliver a small number of signals to a large number of people, but only the Internet can effectively deliver a large number of signals to a large number of people.

Greenhall sees an imminent, broad-based grassroots video movement taking form. "The question is, how will it happen, who controls it, in what time frame, and what are the economics around it?" He thinks the first step is to build out personal networks, letting people rent a movie or record a television show to watch anywhere: on TV in the family room, upstairs over a home network, on a mobile device, even at a neighbor's house. Once people begin to think of visual material as fluid, their expectations begin to change. It's one thing to watch TV in your home, locked into a schedule set by the networks, he says. "Compare that to being able to choose exactly what you want to watch, when and where you want to watch it, whether it's a fifteen-minute clip on the train during your morning commute or a three-hour block when you want to be absorbed."

That opens up a potentially large market for tailoring material to specific needs. Time shifting with TiVo and personal video recorders has changed our habits, so we watch only programs we want, and "we won't put up with a lot of crap in between," Greenhall says. Still, we're now limited to the mass-appeal shows put out by the broadcast and cable networks. "But if you start layering in the Internet, you can do one-to-one communication. You don't have to get out to an audience of a million in order to be viable, you can get out to an audience of six and be viable, depending on what you want to accomplish. So that signals the ability to deliver very narrowly tailored content out to individuals. People will be able to slice and dice what they consume, and they're increasingly becoming aware that they have the power to control what they watch."

Here is where you ask: who wants to watch amateur video when you can watch *CSI: Miami* or the latest Tom Hanks flick? And that's true, as far as it goes. But the argument goes only so far because, just as each year brings about a new crop of surprising new authors, so we will discover people who have talent with a video camera—especially a high-definition digital camcorder, which can make just about anything look good. If you pack a high-def camcorder, you've got quality in your hands superior to broadcast television and the equivalent of theatrical film. Lots of people will experiment with creating visual media. Much of the new video verité will be bad. But some will be watchable, perhaps even addictive. Where big media will continue to offer polished, mass market shows with linear narrative, high production values, and orchestrated story lines, the video of participatory culture will be marked by the quirky, personal, edgy, raw, unpolished, unscripted, unconventional, hyper-realistic, and genuinely surprising.

"It's no longer a surprise that individuals can create interesting stuff and that you can use the Internet to disseminate and find it," Greenhall says, pointing to film shorts, amateur music, and weblogs. Seven years ago, no one predicted that 2 million amateurs would pick up blog publishing tools and become Internet publishers. Today we live in a new world, one that fully expects a multimedia video movement to arise out of digital culture.

For that to happen, Greenhall says, the early users of personal media need to have "room to breathe" and for the tools to mature. Once the tools become ridiculously easy to use—so that you can videotape your daughter's first steps and zap it off to her grandparents or your family TV set at the click of a button—then it explodes into the mass marketplace.

But the personal media revolution will not just add a new layer of home-brew programming. "The transformation will occur across the entire media landscape, largely driven by the grass roots but affecting every other kind of medium," Greenhall says. He bounces to his feet and begins to scribble diagrams on a whiteboard. "It starts at the bottom, but whether you're talking about Blockbuster-style home video, watching TV, or going to a movie, all of these experiences will also be transformed, because the changes in what people expect from media, and what we can do with media, will be so significant that the fundamentals of television, movies, and home entertainment will also have to change."

Greenhall is in the zone now, the words spilling out like water down a mountain. Look at the last structural shift in the motion picture industry, he says. In the mid-1970s, *Jaws* and then *Star Wars* became mass-market blockbusters that changed Hollywood's market dynamics. Studios became less able to make small movies that achieved only modest success. Soaring production costs and bigger budgets led to greater studio consolidation, which in turn led to fewer films requiring higher returns. As the multiplex soared, independent cinemas died off. Marketing became king, and small, independent studios were pushed to the periphery.

"This new media environment is going to bring about a substantially larger change than what took place in the seventies," he predicts. "It's the butterfly effect. Initially the change will be small. But small changes across entire landscapes grow relatively quickly to become gigantic changes. Just imagine if you were to see three *Blair Witch Project* films every year, three films with a low budget that enjoyed a large success, driven by Internet promotion and distribution. At the same time, you start seeing a 5 percent reduction in the amount of people who attend showings of blockbuster films. Those kind of economics in a very competitive marketplace change the market. Studios will have less ability to make big blockbusters because their return on investment is not as high, and they'll have more incentive to create lower-budget films. A structure that creates $400 million investments in three *Lord of the Rings* movies isn't the right structure to support the creation of thirty *Blair Witch Projects*. So when structures start to change, everything starts changing. All these elements that are creating personal media start pecking away at the fundamentals of the existing structures of television and theatrical and home video, and as a consequence everything will have to morph to create a new structure that will support the new economic reality."

As more people take up the tools of creativity, they will cross wires with the entertainment companies over access to cultural works. Sparks will fly over whether we can borrow short snippets of Hollywood movies for home use. Another battle will take place over whether grassroots media will be allowed to compete with Big Entertainment in America's living rooms. And a third clash will occur over the kind of wholesale movie piracy that Bruce Forest keeps tabs on.

Today movie file trading takes place mostly on campus, where cash-strapped students have time on their hands, access to high-speed networks, and a rich tradition of flouting authority. In the old days, young people swapped bootleg cassette tapes of live performances, sometimes with the encouragement of groups like the Grateful Dead and John Mayer. Later, the same personal file-trading culture gave birth to the sneakernet,[2] the nickname for informal networks of people who use floppy disks to swap data files. Today the sneakernet has evolved, with the CD as the medium of choice for sharing music and sometimes movies. In 2003, the 6 billion blank CDs sold surpassed the number of prerecorded music CDs for the first time.

Will sneakernet-style darknets soon come to a living room near you?

We're about to find out. Here's why: a Hollywood DVD contains 4 to 10 gigabytes of data, too big to be easily transferred or copied. DivX can shrink a movie file to a fraction of that size—size small enough to fit onto a single CD. The online Darknet is rife with such "single CD" DVD rips, and many look amazing. Until now, this has been a niche pastime, because movies squeezed with DivX won't play on DVD players, and who wants to watch movies on a computer? But the market is changing. Millions of machines capable of playing DivX movies are beginning to stream into people's homes, in addition to 60 million Playstation 2 consoles that can play DivX movies with the proper software. (Just as MP3 players cannot tell if a song has been pirated or ripped from a purchased CD, neither can DivX DVD players tell if a movie originated on the Darknet.) Thus the temptation will be great for thousands of tech-savvy folks to crack the protection on a movie, shrink it down with DivX, burn multiple copies on CDs that cost less than a quarter, and pass them out to friends so they can watch in their living rooms in the great tradition of Blockbuster.

"Super DVD players, turbocharged with video compression technology, will offer a ticket to an endless supply of free, cheap, pirated entertainment," a technophile acquaintance who burns movies for his friends claims. "Millions of terabytes of information will change hands this way every week, in offices, schoolyards, and cocktail parties."

Under this scenario, as the mobile Darknet becomes detached from the Internet, movie file sharing would become a rite of social networking, like sharing cocktails. But it strikes me as unlikely that such activity will ever become a mainstream pastime. I suspect that such predictions from movie-loving wireheads arise in part from guilt—and their hopes that wider social acceptance would take the edge off an activity that is ethically murky at best.

The Microsoft researchers who authored the "Darknet" paper made no predictions about how widespread this kind of "small worlds" activity would become, but they said such file sharing can be kept at acceptable levels if entertainment companies offer a compelling market solution.

Many analysts believe movie piracy will never approach the level of file sharing that bedevils the recording industry.

"I think there's a fundamental difference in the way movies and music are consumed, so sharing movies will not become a mainstream phenomenon like audio piracy," says Thomas Adams, a well-regarded home-entertainment analyst whose firm, Adams Media Research, tracks DVD sales and trends. "I just don't buy the idea that better broadband or DivX players in the living room will turn people into thieves." For one thing, we've long had the ability to copy movies for friends with dual-deck VHS recorders, and few people did that. (All VCRs sold after March 2000 contain Macrovision, which prevents flawless copying of a videotape or broadcast show.) But the larger reason, he says, is this: "DVD is the perfect medium for watching a $100 million blockbuster movie. It's convenient, reasonably priced, packs lots of extras, and plays to our basic human nature as hunter-gatherers and collectors of things."

People have also been exposed to that ubiquitous FBI warning at the beginning of videos for years, and they regard movie trading as less defensible than music trading. Significantly, you can experience a movie in a wide variety of convenient and affordable formats: on the silver screen, on DVD or VHS, on TV, pay-per-view, and cable, in flight, and on the computer. (Compare this with the recording industry, where until recently there was only one legal way to obtain music: go to a store and buy a CD or tape.) People know it's expensive to produce a major motion picture. As Jack Valenti likes to point out, only two in ten movies ever make back their costs from domestic theater ticket sales, so the home entertainment market is critical for an industry that spends more than $90 million to make and market a typical release.

Movie piracy will continue to be a fringe activity online, Adams says, and only movie fanatics—less than 1 percent of the population—will actively burn, trade, or give away Hollywood movies on cheap plastic discs.

The evidence suggests he is right. Despite file sharing, movie theater attendance continues to set records. Not since the 1950s have so many movie tickets been sold. Even heavily pirated titles haven't dented Hollywood's profits. *Star Wars: Episode II—Attack of the Clones* and the *Matrix* series were best-selling discs despite massive bootlegging. *Finding Nemo* became the best-selling DVD of all time, in spite of Bruce Forest, file traders, and college students pulling it down from the Darknet for free.

Still, Hollywood remains haunted by the specter of movie piracy. Valenti tells me, "If you can make a perfect copy of a silver plate in front of your home, why would you want to go to Tiffany's to buy one? Anytime you make a perfect copy, why would you want to go to a Blockbuster store and rent or buy that DVD? So if you have 50 million perfect copies and subtract 50 million sales from the Blockbuster-type stores, that's a serious decay."

What proactive steps is Hollywood taking to head off piracy and embrace its digital destiny? So far, not much. Despite Hollywood executives talking a brave game, the studios have devised a series of customer-unfriendly online movie services that the public has greeted with a collective yawn. Movielink, CinemaNow, and the independently owned Starz Ticket all suffer from studio-imposed limitations, such as ticking time bombs in downloaded films (watch them before they self-destruct!) or the inability to watch movies on the living room TV.

The reason for the lack of a serious online strategy is simple: Hollywood's pocketbook isn't hurting so far. The videocassette tape has brought the studios more than $100 billion over its lifetime. The DVD has become the fastest-selling consumer electronics product in history, fueling Hollywood's economic engine by bringing in $17.5 billion in 2003, compared with theater ticket sales of $9.2 billion. Some 53 million homes now have at least one stand-alone DVD player, with Americans snapping them up faster than the cell phone or personal computer when those devices were introduced.

Can Hollywood be satisfied with the immense profits it is reaping from DVD, despite a leaky format that gives individuals greater access to movies than Hollywood wants? It remains to be seen. Studios are eager to roll out a high-definition DVD format with better copy controls so they can "sunset" current DVDs, Feingold said.

But that is just the beginning. Americans will soon pay a high price to soothe the jumpy nerves of studio chiefs.

Public interest groups have begun to rally public attention on the subject. Officials of Public Knowledge say that rights should not be taken away from the public simply because the material is in a digital format.

Chris Murray of Consumers Union says the new generation of digital restrictions being rolled out will hamper the public's ability to use media in ways we've come to expect. The tradition of media openness—being able to buy a book, video, or piece of music and view it any time, lend it to others, dispose of it as you see fit—is giving way to a regime of digital control.

"Up until now, the architecture of innovation has been fairly decentralized," Murray says. "You just plug in your TV set and it works, without getting permission from the power company. The content industry would like to go to a world where every device—your TV, PC, Walkman, or digital VCR—scans every piece of content you play to see if it's legitimate. They are gaining de facto veto power over what new technologies will be permitted. What boggles my mind is that policymakers seem willing to go along with this.

"If consumers lose the ability to do things they're accustomed to doing, I think we'll see marketplace rebellion."

6 Cool Toys Hollywood Wants to Ban

OR YEARS, DAVID CLAYTON TOILED IN THE TRENCHES OF the PC gaming industry, developing computer games that raked in more than $1 billion for his employers. One of his titles, *WCW Wrestling*, brought in $36 million its first weekend on the shelf. On the verge of burnout, Clayton left to consult for Lockheed Martin, designing training applications for the defense contractor. One day he was overlaying text onto a video screen when his mind began free-associating. What if he could create a program that lets a user actively interact with an existing media stream of digital audio and video?[1]

Clayton, a thick-necked, round-faced, solidly built man with thinning dark hair, brainstormed with friends and settled on the idea of interacting with DVDs, a relatively new technology just beginning to catch on with the public. He noticed the emergence of a handful of small companies that were building businesses on the premise that many customers wanted to watch

Hollywood movies at a different rating level than the final cut released by the studios. Was there a market there? How broad was it? He hired a market research firm to find out. To his surprise, 76 percent of respondents across the nation said they wanted to use movie rating controls in their own homes.

Clayton was on to something. He pushed forward, and in 1999 founded Trilogy Studios in Sandy, Utah, on the southeastern fringe of the Great Salt Lake. To almost no one's surprise, the major movie studios sued the twelve-person operation before it celebrated its third birthday. More on that in a moment.

From the outset, Clayton instinctively knew he was lighting a new trail. Since the mid-1990s, stores had offered bowdlerized versions of hit Hollywood films—videotapes with nicks, tucks, and trims to fit someone's idea of squeaky clean entertainment. A few video chains had even sprung up taking the same slice-and-dice approach to Hollywood movies on DVD. Think *Good Will Hunting* minus its 205 curse words, or *Platoon* excised of graphic scenes.

Clayton took a different path. His software let customers watch more than a dozen possible variations of a movie, including the original version. Rent a DVD, plop it into a compatible player, launch the program, choose your comfort level, sit back, and enjoy. Next day, return the DVD to Blockbuster, completely unchanged.

The inspired idea relied on a fundamental principle of the digital age: media are malleable. In a sense, digital media amount to nothing more than electronic Play-Doh. Once digitized, any piece of media becomes a goopy blend of 0's and 1's that could be reshaped at will. Clayton's insight was in seeing that the physical media form—the DVD—could be left unaltered, but the viewing *experience* could be altered to fit viewers' likes and dislikes. His movie filters accomplished that bit of magic.

The company's staff set out to capture and quantify research studies centering on appropriate material for children, adolescents, young adults, and adults, together with existing ratings methods for motion pictures, television, and the Internet. (A rival, ClearPlay, appeared at about the same time and may ultimately prove to have the superior technology.) After developing a frame-accurate decoder that gave pinpoint control over DVD playback, the Trilogy team set about evaluating movies for language, violence, and adult situations, creating ratings levels for different ages. Reviewers began charting movies one at a time, producing digital templates that identify every obscene phrase, blood spatter, or bare midriff in a flick. The first films to pass through the filtering cycle were *The Matrix* and *Saving Private Ryan*.

Then an interesting thing happened. Trilogy's most diehard users began offering their own edits to Hollywood films. In addition to its MovieMask software, the company offered a more powerful DVD authoring tool called Designer, which gave viewers even greater ability to customize a movie to a family's tastes. Soon the majority of the "masks," or templates, offered by Trilogy for new releases began coming from a small but active set of customers who uploaded their film edits to the Trilogy site for review and approval. For example, the amateur editor who created a filter for the R-rated *Matrix Reloaded* created a version equivalent to PG-13 by removing part of the rave scene in Zion and skipping over the sex scene between Neo and Trinity. The technology is so seamless that if you didn't know the scenes were there, you'd never suspect they were deleted.

David and Diana Miller, a couple with five children in Taylorsville, Utah, use Clayton's software to widen their family's viewing choices. Fifteen years ago, when their oldest child, Kristin, arrived, they made a family rule not to watch R-rated movies at home. "You want to feel safe with your kids in front of a screen, not worrying about what's going to show up next," Diana Miller says.[2]

The couple jumped at the chance to use movie filtering when it hit the market, knowing that a lot of R-rated films have a worthy story line or historical lesson to impart. Take *The Green Mile*. "We saw the movie in its R-rated form in the theater," Diana says. "There was no way we could show it at home with the objectionable scenes in it: the inmate in his jail cell spewing a string of obscenities, the prisoner getting fried alive when the execution was carried out the wrong way. But being able to skip over those few seconds didn't take away from the central story and message of the movie, which was wonderful."

The Miller family gathers around the electronic hearth on Saturday nights after Dad hooks up his laptop to the TV set and dials up a rating for language and violence, depending on which of their children are watching. They've watched *Murder by Numbers*, *The Hurricane*, *Ali*, *Three Kings*, *The Mexican*, *We Were Soldiers*, and many other movies. "We have four boys and they were just hounding us to watch *Saving Private Ryan*," Diana says. "For us to customize the setting so that you don't see all the blood, gore, and swearing, it was like Christmas for them."

For its part, Trilogy wanted to be in the software-licensing business, not the movie-editing business. It made repeated overtures to Hollywood to buy or license its digital toys, which would streamline the process of editing movies for airlines and network television.

That led to a fateful meeting in June 2002. The Trilogy team flew to Hollywood for a chance to show off its whiz-bang tools. The demo focused not on Trilogy's skip-and-mute software already on the consumer market but on high-end digital editing software. In a darkened theater, director Rob Reiner, ten other leading filmmakers, and executives from the Directors Guild of America sat and watched the pitch.

The screen filled with Leonardo DiCaprio sketching Kate Winslet's sumptuous seminude figure on her stateroom bed in *Titanic*. Then the scene flashed by again, this time with Winslet wearing a corset and with DiCaprio's sketchpad showing a ruffled bodice in place of a bare breast. Next, real swords morphed into light sabers in *Braveheart* and Reiner's *The Princess Bride*. One of Jack Nicholson's profanity-laced tirades in *A Few Good Men* metamorphosed into milder language. In *The World Is Not Enough*, James Bond's aging Jornada palm device transformed into the current model. In other films, cans of soda and other products were digitally replaced by competitors' products as a Trilogy exec suggested that product placement could become an additional revenue stream for the studios.

When the lights came on, the filmmakers' faces were ashen. "It really did horrify us," says Warren Adler, associate national executive director of the Directors Guild. "Directors put years of their lives in creating a motion picture, and they feel passionately about how their works get presented to the public. There need to be some limits placed on this new technology or it could potentially become very damaging to our craft."

Two months later, the lawsuits started flying. Eight major studios and sixteen filmmakers—including Steven Spielberg, Robert Altman, Steven Soderbergh, and Martin Scorsese—filed suit, claiming that a dozen companies, including Trilogy and ClearPlay, were violating federal copyright and trademark laws by tampering with Hollywood films. (Some journalists, like film critic Roger Ebert, sided with Hollywood. At Sundance in 2003, Ebert came face to face with ClearPlay CEO Bill Aho and called him "a parasite.")

The case brought the issue of disruptive digital technologies to the fore. The crux of the controversy centered on creative control. Once a movie enters a private home, do the studio and filmmaker retain some artistic and legal rights over how you and I may view it?

It's important to draw distinctions between what each of these technologies can do. One approach is to take a movie like *Titanic*, clip out certain scenes or bleep out certain words, and burn a new version onto DVD or VHS. That's done for airline movies and television broadcasts, with a critical difference: the studios have a say in the editing process. Not so in the case of Clean Flicks of Colorado, a video chain operating eighty stores in eighteen states and offering hundreds of sanitized titles. It also does a brisk mail-order business, sending sanitized videos to customers nationwide. In my view, this crosses the line because it permanently alters a creative work for commercial profit without the owner's permission.

A second approach involves an automated filter. Now in 2.5 million homes, TVGuardian from Principle Solutions of Rogers, Arkansas, snoops for foul language on the closed captioning track of a film or TV show and blacks out the viewer's screen for seconds at a time. (Did you know there are forty-one cusswords in *Dr. Dolittle* and eighty-three in *Independence Day*, both rated PG-13?) The result can be jarring and clunky, blacking out the viewer's screen for seconds at a time. Still, some families consider it better than nothing. At Wal-Mart's urging, the Japanese electronics maker Sanyo built the TVGuardian technology into some of its VCRs and DVD players.

A third approach involves software programs that work hand-in-hand with DVD players. ClearPlay, Family Shield, and TVG Vision (the successor to Trilogy) are the main players. These companies don't rent out videos, just the filters used when viewing a DVD.

The good folks at the Directors Guild frown on all of these practices, but they have been particularly critical of the first and third approaches, insisting that films should be viewed as their creators intended. Steven Soderbergh, the Oscar-winning director of *Traffic* and a Directors Guild officer, said in a statement, "We are appalled at the proliferation of companies that bypass the copyright holder and the filmmaker and arbitrarily alter the creative expression and hard work of the many artists involved in filmmaking. It is unconscionable, and unethical, to take someone else's hard work, alter it, and profit from it."

Nonsense, says Clayton, who argues that Hollywood is seeking unprecedented control over how digital media may be watched in the privacy of one's home. He emphasizes that all of the filtering software being sold is *subtractive*—that is, it does nothing but skip and mute legally purchased or rented studio versions of DVD movies (it won't work on pirated versions). He insists that any *additive* technology—the flashy technowizardry of adding clothing or altering scenes—would be done only at a filmmaker's behest. That's a crucial distinction. For example, the producers of the 2002 film *Out of Step* approached Trilogy for some creative digital touch-up. They wanted to distribute the film through a retail channel of conservative Christian bookstores, which asked for a more modest look for the lead actress, Alison Akin Clark. Trilogy complied and clad her in virtuous virtual clothing.

Trilogy also invited the studios to explore the commercial opportunities of altering DVD movies by region. Hollywood divides the world into six regions, and movies are often released with different languages and occasionally different edits to suit local sensibilities. When Disney re-released *Snow White and the Seven Dwarfs* in October 2001, the more significant alterations to the film occurred in other DVD regions. If you watch the movie in Germany, the names of Sleepy, Dopey, Doc, and the other dwarfs are now inscribed on their beds in German. "Regionalizing a film has the potential to bring it closer to the local audience," Clayton says. He maintains that his digital tools can do the job much faster than the techniques used by Hollywood.

It's not hard to imagine a day, a year or two from now, when a parent will be able to type in her children's names and have the words magically appear on those bed stands. Better yet, Mom or Dad could import images of their kids and have them appear in a Hollywood movie, perhaps using a camera plug-in in real time. The technology is here. All that's missing is a studio with imagination and a change in philosophy to bring it to life. If Hollywood sanctions the digital alterations, it's good. If the public does, it's bad—and illegal.

Already, the video game industry has embraced the concept of bringing customers into the creative process. Today you can insert your face over the characters in a video game. Now, imagine the possibilities if your medium is *Alice in Wonderland* and your canvas is digital. Think about the opportunities for cameo roles in bit parts by extras who don't figure prominently in the film's story line. Capture your children's images with a digital camcorder, import them into the movie, and consider how much more captivated they'll be than if it were merely a passive experience.

I mentioned this idea to Benjamin S. Feingold, head of Columbia TriStar Home Entertainment, in his spacious office at Sony Pictures Studios. He waved his hand to dismiss the notion of a greater creative role for customers in DVD movies. "That would be violating our guild contracts," he says.

And yet, innovative uses of new technology were envisioned as part and parcel of the digital movie experience when the DVD standard was created in 1996. Built into the fabric of every DVD is something called seamless branching, which gives viewers the option to watch alternative scenes, directors' interviews, behind-the-scenes outtakes, additional footage not shown in the theatrical release—and anything else the studios could dream up. "The filtering capability is what the movie studios promised consumers when the DVD format was first introduced," Clayton says.

Warren Lieberfarb, the man most responsible for creating the DVD during his years as president of Warner Home Video, thinks the studios ought to fashion a compromise with the DVD software makers—one that respects the artists' expression while recognizing the new digital realities.

"You don't take a paintbrush and add to Picasso's work simply because you can. So I tend to be in the camp of drawing certain limitations on how far you take the capabilities of digitalization," he says. "On the other hand, historically there has been a need in a home environment to be sensitive to the age appropriateness of content with respect to violence and sexuality so that youths do not get access to that material prematurely." The best solution, he says, is for the studios themselves to incorporate different levels of violence, language, and sexuality into new video releases by employing the underused DVD branching technology available to them.

That's precisely what Clayton has been advocating. "As a consumer, I would prefer to have different versions of movies brought to me by Steven Spielberg and Peter Jackson—by the artists and directors themselves— rather than by a third party. We built our tools with the goal of putting them into the hands of the studios." That does not appear to be a likely outcome. Hollywood's visceral opposition to this kind of digital technology runs deep. "We feel very passionate about this," Adler says.

Trilogy also broached the idea of family filters for television programming and was in talks with NBC at one point. But an NBC executive told me he didn't see a big demand by families to tailor shows for violence, language, or adult situations. "This company is not very interested in technology right now. That whole technology thing in the late nineties went much further than it should have. People here felt burned and annoyed, and the feeling now is, when there's a technology that's necessary, we'll know it. Other than that, we don't need it."

By early 2004, the movie studios' lawsuit had claimed one casualty: Trilogy closed its doors and laid off its staff. Hollywood's lawsuit had spooked investors and dried up additional funding, Clayton says.

In most cases, that would have marked the end of the story: another technology start-up brought down by the entertainment industries parachuting in the lawyers. But this story has a different ending, thanks to the intervention of an unlikely rescue party: Wal-Mart.

Where Hollywood saw a violation of its artistic rights, Wal-Mart saw a market opportunity. The beast of Bentonville, Arkansas, has never shied away from imposing its own sense of morality in home entertainment—banning racy magazines from its racks and refusing to carry violent video games or CDs with objectionable lyrics. Now it stepped into the fray by persuading three of its top DVD vendors to include Clayton's technology in millions of new DVD players. Because Clayton had licensed his filtering technology to Trilogy but retained personal ownership over it, he was able to sell the rights to the parent company of TVGuardian, which quickly licensed the movie filters under a new brand, TVG Vision. Plans called for Clayton's movie filters to be included in a quarter of all DVD players sold in the United States, many priced as low as $29.

As industry analyst Richard Doherty said, "We have a director's cut, but we haven't had a family cut." Until now.

The directors take a different view. "Steven Spielberg, Ridley Scott, and others make movies about war with horrifying graphic violence, but that's part of the message they're trying to convey," Adler says. "It makes all the sense in the world for them to say, 'This is not a movie that should be seen by a twelve-year-old.' Other companies shouldn't be able to step in and say, 'I'm going to show you a sanitized version of *Saving Private Ryan*.' We're talking about the integrity of artworks made for adult audiences."

Perhaps. But it's more likely that those viewpoints are holdovers from the analog age and may soon seem as anachronistic as eight-track tapes, troll dolls, and hot tech stocks. We live in a fascinating time, as the analog and digital worlds—and their accompanying cultural sensibilities—bump against each other.

Hollywood studios, filmmakers, and copyright owners have a strong case against third parties that reproduce permanently altered versions of their works. (Frankly, those sanitized, hard-copy videotapes and DVDs also seem like dusky relics of the analog age.) Digital technologies now offer a third way, an approach that empowers the viewer without trampling on artists' rights.

Some critics have berated the DVD software makers and Wal-Mart for cultural censorship. Personal liberty advocates have a built-in distaste for anything that hints of curtailing freedom of expression. But Americans have never embraced the European tradition of "moral rights" that gives artists the right to control their work in perpetuity. In France, for example, an author can force a publisher to stop selling a book he no longer believes in. In the United States, we don't give artists such veto power. We value individual choice, and digital technology gives the user a powerful new locus of control.

Clayton gets it right. "Censorship is one person imposing his standard on everyone else. Choice is about consumers having the right to watch a movie free of material they find objectionable in the privacy of their own homes. We're about offering choice. Choice empowers; censorship is wrong."

Meanwhile, back in Utah, homemaker Diana Miller thinks the film industry has been too dismissive of parents seeking to protect their kids. "Some people in Hollywood have a distorted view of what people want coming into their homes. It's too bad it has come to the point where they're leaning on the crutch of artistic license instead of putting out more family-oriented programs. Moviemakers should be excited by the prospect of whole new audiences they can bring in, instead of complaining that we're infringing on their artistic rights."

Directors, producers, and other traditional power centers need to acknowledge that their creative control does not extend into private living rooms. How we consume fluid digital media, how we interact with it, alter it, and—why not?—star in it, should be solely our choice.

Americans celebrate innovators. It's ingrained in our DNA, this love of progress, this drive to blaze new trails and pursue new ventures. So there's something disconcerting when barriers are placed in innovation's way. Every time federal agencies or the courts prop up analog-era models at the expense of technological progress, we should be skeptical—and recall history. For in case after case, stretching back decades, the entertainment powers have fiercely opposed changes that could disrupt their existing business models, only to discover later that those disruptions proved beneficial.

"In the history of intellectual property," Jim Griffin of Cherry Lane Digital says, "the things we thought would kill us are the things that fed us."

In the early 1900s, publishers of sheet music sued the makers of piano rolls used in player pianos, claiming copyright infringement. The Supreme Court disagreed, and Congress stepped in to fashion a compulsory licensing right that continues to benefit music publishers, who today receive $500 million in royalties a year from recordings and performances.

In the 1920s, vaudeville performers sued Marconi for inventing the radio. They said it would cut into their profits from live performances. Vaudeville died, but radio wasn't the culprit, and many performers made the leap to the new medium.

In 1933, Edwin Armstrong invented FM radio. But the record companies had begun investing heavily in AM and in 1945 persuaded the FCC to move the FM band to a different part of the spectrum, making useless all transmitters and receivers designed by Armstrong over the previous decade. The FCC also limited FM's broadcasting power and banned radio relays from mountaintops so that FM broadcasters had to use expensive cables. In 1954, after a twenty-one-year battle with the media giants, Armstrong jumped to his death from a thirteenth-floor window.[3] Years later, FM dominated the airwaves.

In the late 1940s and early '50s, movie studios treated television as its enemy, fearing the networks would decimate box office receipts. But movie theater attendance has remained robust, and the studios rake in hundreds of millions of dollars from movies on television.

In 1959, publishing interests opposed the first successful photocopier, fearing it would lead to widespread content theft and threaten the book business. Instead, photocopying proved essential to business, and publishing continues to thrive, despite the occasional copyright infringer.

In the late 1970s and early '80s, Universal City Studios and Walt Disney Productions sued Sony, trying to stop the sale of VCRs. Hollywood claimed VCRs violated federal law by letting viewers time-shift programming and build home libraries of videotaped movies without the copyright owners' permission. Jack Valenti famously told Congress in 1982, "The VCR is to the American film producer and the American public as the Boston Strangler is to the woman home alone."[4] A studio attorney told the Supreme Court that VCRs constituted "a billion-dollar industry based on the taking of someone else's property." The studios lost, but it was an exceedingly close call, with Justice Sandra Day O'Connor reportedly switching sides to give Sony a 5–4 victory. Activists hail the 1984 *Betamax* ruling as the Magna Carta of the technology age. But Hollywood is still looking for ways to overturn the decision, even though rentals and sales of VHS tapes and DVDs (a technology that most studios also initially opposed) now make up 63 percent of the movie industry's revenues, far exceeding the 21 percent that comes from theater ticket sales.

In 1998, the recording industry sued to prevent Diamond Multimedia from releasing the world's first portable MP3 player, the Rio, claiming that

MP3 players were piracy devices. The courts disagreed, and today online music stores enjoy a booming business in selling music over the Internet for use in portable players.

In 2001, twenty-eight movie studios and media companies sued Sonicblue for copyright infringement because its ReplayTV players let viewers skip commercials and share shows with a handful of friends, among other things; Sonicblue was forced into bankruptcy two years later, partly because of the litigation.

Today, in speeches and public hearings, media executives bemoan the growing number of CD and DVD burners in personal computers, labeling them piracy tools.

Amir Majidimehr, who runs Microsoft's Windows digital media division, told *Business 2.0* magazine, "The studios care about three things. Piracy, piracy, piracy."[5] Notice what doesn't make the list: the customer experience, convenience, user rights.

The current battles raging between the entertainment industries and today's tech innovators may seem novel because of the technologies involved. But Joe Kraus, founder of DigitalConsumer.org, reminds us, "This is not a new fight. It's another round of a fight that has been raging for a long time. The content industry has a history of trying to control innovation that has fallen outside their control by using the court system and their very effective lobbying in Washington. They're fighting really big on this one because they realize how big the technology shift is that's going on beneath them."

Kraus has the tech credentials to back up his talk. He made millions as one of the six founders of the Excite search engine, and he became so invested in the issue of digital rights that he launched DigitalConsumer.org in March 2002 on the day he testified before the Senate Judiciary Committee on the threat to fair use posed by digital rights management (DRM), a form of content control that sets rules on how people may use a wide range of products.[6] Within months, his advocacy group had signed forty-five thousand members.

Today, companies are making an end run around fair use by increasingly locking down devices and content with encryption, Kraus says. To break the seal is to break federal law. Until recently, the law has permitted the public to use content in ways the copyright owner never authorized. But a company can add encryption to any piece of media and claim that the DMCA has been violated if anyone cracks the copy protection to use the material in a way the maker doesn't want.

Now take another step. Imagine a world in which every digital device—every digital television, every movie player, every music player, every video recorder, every PC, every wireless device—contains Hollywood-approved circuitry or chips that give the entertainment companies full control over how your device may be used. There's no precedent for such a regime of control.

Historically, Kraus points out, unauthorized use has rarely meant unlawful use. A good thing, that "by not having to ask for permission, creative people can come up with unanticipated uses of content and in the process create greater economic value than the content owners ever imagined. MGM didn't come up with the VCR, Sony did. RCA Records didn't come up with the Walkman, Sony did. If the copyright owners had been allowed to control how their content was played or used, we wouldn't have the photocopy machine, the VCR, the MP3 player, the Walkman, cable television, TiVo—all that goes out the window. If you don't allow that kind of tinkering, it stifles a huge amount of innovation. That has enormous implications. It's why I'm passionate about it."

The crowd at Oakland's Black Box spills out the door into a warm summer night. The event, part of the "Illegal Art" exhibit[7] held to dramatize the tightening noose of misapplied copyright laws, features creators of electronica, digital film, and "appropriation-based" art along with leaders of the free culture movement. More than 150 people mill about, from deeply earnest Berkeley activists to nose-ring-clad San Francisco *fashionistas*. A college student lets his black T-shirt speak for many here with its simple sentiment: "Sharing isn't stealing."

Six of us huddle around a television as a scene from *Teletubbies* appears onscreen. But this is not your father's PBS: as morning dawns in Teletubbyland, the sun morphs into the face of George W. Bush and begins shooting death rays at bunnies and wild creatures. In the next video, we see the Little Mermaid, but the animator of this five-minute film short inserted burning skeletons, a menacing cat-faced woman, the ominous sound of a music industry lawyer, and the voice of the Little Mermaid dubbed over the band Negativland's helium-tinged cover of Black Flag's "Gimme Gimme Gimme." Not exactly Disney fare—and this may have been the artist's point.

Here, and at a related show across the bay at the San Francisco Museum of Modern Art Artists Gallery, we see works pushing the edge of cultural expression, pricking our dulled sensibilities. But now large corporations are pushing back. Mattel sued artist Tom Forsythe, who placed Barbie in a blender as a way to expose the efforts to sell "an impossible beauty myth" to children. Playwright Jason Sherman's play *The Message*, about the last years of Marshall McLuhan's life, was set to open in Toronto in fall 2003 but was canceled when McLuhan's family made vague threats about suing for copyright infringement. A court banned a documentary on Karen Carpenter's battle with anorexia from movie theaters because it included music by the Carpenters without authorization; the film portrayed her brother, Richard, in an unflattering light, and he refused to grant the filmmakers permission to use the music. Thus the screening shown tonight is a bootleg. The exhibit also features a CD containing two dozen songs that have been embroiled in legal troubles.

Near the doorway, Richard Prelinger, the silver-haired film archivist who has put twelve hundred public domain films online at the Internet Archive, inspects a Krishna wall mural. The movies he oversees were downloaded about a million times in the past year, but few additional films will be added to the collection over the next twenty years, thanks to the Sonny Bono Act. "Members of the public have no affirmative right to access cultural information," Prelinger tells me. "People need to understand that it's the middlemen—distributors and publishers—who are using copyright laws to clamp down on expression and trying to turn the Internet into a read-only medium. Artists have to organize and stop letting the corporations act on our behalf to impose an all-rights-reserved view of the world. Art has never been about that."

Next, I run into one of the night's speakers, Fred von Lohmann, the ponytailed attorney for the Electronic Frontier Foundation. Whenever the EFF defends a file-sharing network or someone charged with violating the Digital Millennium Copyright Act, the dark-eyed, boundlessly energetic von Lohmann typically appears in court or files briefs. As I peer around the gallery, I tell von Lohmann that while the clampdown on artistic freedoms is important, I suspect many people in my suburban town would find the issues too abstract and removed from their lives. How is middle-class America suffering, as he claims, from the entertainment industries' regime of tightening control?

He begins by mentioning court cases in which musicians have been fined as much as $90,000 and had their albums recalled for failing to secure the proper licensing rights to borrow from earlier works. Since the early

1990s, court rulings have so drastically limited the art of sampling—forcing bands to sometimes pay six figures for a snippet lasting a couple of seconds—that many musical acts have given up on sampling. The hip-hop group Public Enemy never regained its earlier mass appeal after the courts turned sampling into pay to play. Sampling now enjoys its greatest popularity in underground dance clubs.

The court battles over file sharing show no signs of subsiding, with the entertainment industries seeking to shut down Kazaa and other file-trading networks and the recording industry, filing hundreds of lawsuits against individuals who make copyrighted music available to others on peer-to-peer services. (My own view is that Kazaa is largely an outlaw outfit but that not all file-sharing networks are equally culpable.)

"Lawsuits and legislation have become the weapons of choice for dealing with file sharing and cultural recycling," says von Lohmann, wearing a black blazer, jeans, tennies, and EFF cap.

But he says the clampdown on digital culture is taking place not only in the courts but also in neighborhoods, nightclubs, exhibit halls, and homes, where the culture of reinvention is under assault. If the current legal climate had been in place decades ago, all of jazz would have been illegal. Traditions that rely on reworkings of real-world images, such as surrealism, collage, and Pop Art, might have been smothered in the cradle.

Public libraries are another battleground. Librarians are trying to protect the public's access to new books and articles against the efforts by some publishers to push a pay-per-view model so that whenever a reader wants to access information on an electronic device, it becomes a billable event. Many e-books forbid copying or making printouts, even for books in the public domain. Copy protection also impairs a library's ability to archive and preserve materials that may disappear within a few years. Over the long term, such practices could jeopardize the very underpinnings of the free public library system.

Closer to home, the media players and digital devices entering our living rooms are being designed in ways that serve Hollywood at the expense of the public. Von Lohmann predicts we'll soon see personal video recorders that automatically delete recorded shows after a certain amount of time at the copyright holders' behest. "I'll guarantee you that's coming," he says. Hollywood already has the right to begin erasing a digital pay-per-view program from your recording device as soon as ninety minutes after the telecast ends.

Von Lohmann and Kraus both point out that computer companies and consumer electronics companies had long acted as surrogates for the public in these private industry forums. Because the interests of Hollywood, the tech industry, and the CE industry overlapped but did not align completely, the hardware manufacturers could be counted on to fight for consumers' rights. "My, how things have changed," von Lohmann says. "Sony led the fight for home taping because it had a business in selling VCRs. Today it's harder to think of Sony as an advocate for the public interest because their business is now so deeply intertwined with content. Microsoft traditionally has served as a proxy for the public because they empowered people to use computers in new and creative ways. But Microsoft now has a second agenda, which is to gain market share by wooing Hollywood with the most restrictive digital rights management technologies they can devise. So when these three industries get together in cross-industry groups, the deals they cut sometimes don't reflect the public interest. I don't think we'll see them trade away things like the consumer's ability to time-shift television. But they're perfectly happy to trade away future innovations that would benefit the consumer, so long as they can be assured that everyone must give up those same innovations. That's where legislation, regulations, licensing rules, and tech mandates all come in."

Licensing standards set within the clubby confines of these private industry groups rarely get much attention, but the rulemakers effectively dictate consumer electronics policy for the public, which rarely has a seat at the table during negotiations. Take the DVD. In 1996, Hollywood was all set to launch the new DVD format for playback on DVD players but not on computers. It was only the tech industry's proposal to include copy protection, and a decision by Warner Home Video and Toshiba to fend off a rival format by Sony and Philips called the Multimedia CD, that led the studios to agree to make Hollywood DVDs compatible with the computer's DVD drive. Several studio executives have suggested that if they had to do it all over again, they never would have agreed to allow DVDs to play on computers, given how trivial it was for the encryption to be broken. "Frankly, we made some mistakes last time," says Adrian Alperovich, executive vice president of Sony's Columbia TriStar Home Entertainment. "I think the standards should have been tougher."

Today, Hollywood, consumer electronics makers, and tech companies are back at the bargaining table, hammering out how the next generation of high-definition DVDs will behave. The new discs, under development for years, will hold four to five times more video and audio data than standard DVDs. This time around, studios want an airtight protection scheme, a digital vault that even the best minds at the National Security Agency cannot penetrate.

Stephen Balogh, an Intel business development manager who sits on the standards body hashing out the new rules, says the tech companies must be accommodating to the entertainment industries because Hollywood could decide to simply withhold its movies. "Our philosophy has been, create a legal, protected environment where content owners feel safe. At the same time, content owners' needs must be balanced by the needs and expectations of customers."[8]

It's a fair-minded approach, except the scales have tipped precariously against the customer. Consider the new breed of technologies that may alter the balance of power between Hollywood and viewers even further—effectively eroding the public's digital rights. What once was a battle over piracy and file-sharing networks has moved into other areas, such as personal video recorders and digital television broadcasts.

Hollywood is adding such little-known weapons to its arsenal as "certification" and "renewability"—new forms of copy control that are about to enter the living room by stealth.[9]

When a transaction takes place between a customer and movie studio over the Internet, certification tells the merchant who you are and whether you have the authority to place the order.[10] It can monitor what kinds of movies or programs you've been watching. The technology can be used in other ways as well. Because copy protection on DVDs has been broken and DVD burners are proliferating, the studios are pushing for ways of signaling to a DVD player or receiver that a disc or a recording is authorized. The video would shut down if it doesn't have the proper clearances. Entertainment analyst Tim Onosko predicts: "Next-generation DVD players on the drawing boards will most likely dial a mothership to check the legitimacy of your content. If it's a disc that somehow violates the rules, or is a bootleg or an illegal clone copy, the player will balk."

Renewability means if someone has bypassed the copy protection on a home electronics product, the system can be updated with new copy protection. Also called upgradeable DRM, renewability puts devices on a digital leash, giving the entertainment companies the power to cut the cord to any technology or media player it believes has been compromised—and effectively turning Hollywood into the warden of our entertainment experiences.[11] Nurse Ratchet, meet your match. Because it is impractical to introduce a major new format more than once or twice a decade, the studios' answer lies in retaining a format like DVD but changing its copy protection. Hollywood appears excited by the prospect of forcing all media players to abide by its rules of control. Mitch Singer, executive vice president of digital policy for Sony Pictures Entertainment, said at the 2004 Digital Hollywood summit, "We want to make sure any future devices will be updatable, especially as we move into high-def." Tech representatives have signaled their willingness to add such renewability features in future media players.

You say you want to use fifteen seconds from that new Eddie Murphy film as part of your school project? Today millions of people are able to assert their fair use rights by downloading software from the Darknet to circumvent the DVD's copy protection. Tomorrow, when Hollywood introduces a new copy protection scheme, as soon as a hacker cracks and distributes the encryption key, the studios will be able to send a firmware update to your next-gen DVD player so that the crack no longer works—and you won't be able to snag those fifteen seconds after all. Or, say you transfer movies or TV shows to your Archos portable media player. (The French devicemaker Archos subverts copy protection by letting users plug the device into a DVD player and transfer a movie to it.) If Hollywood has detected that 0.01 percent of Archos's customers are illegally uploading movies to the Internet with the help of Archos players, it could update the software inside DVD players or set-top boxes to prevent the transfer of films and TV shows to *all* Archos players. Hollywood would maintain a "whitelist" of approved devices and a blacklist of naughty devices that aren't sufficiently locked down. Von Lohmann says your DVD player would not need to be online: when you drop a commercial DVD into the player, a hidden track on the disc will update your player's firmware without your knowing it.

Of course, if that happens, some users will be tempted to simply point a camcorder at a TV or computer screen or theater screen to capture the scene they want. The media companies can't stop *that*, can they? But Hollywood may trump you there, too. Cinea of Herndon, Virginia, has devised a Cam Jam technology to modify the image projected on theater screens and some small screens so that you can watch it without noticing anything amiss, but a videotape taken of the same image comes out marred. Engineers at the Dolby Laboratories-owned start-up—mostly the same crew who came up with the Circuit City DivX pay-per-play scheme that consumers so thunderously rejected—came up with the copy protection solution after studying differences between the way humans process moving images and the way cameras record them. No doubt the Cam Jam technology—without an accompanying warning label—will soon be coming to a camcorder near you.

Score one for "information with a ball and chain," as Steven Levy put it in a *Newsweek* column discussing the coming era of digital rights management—technologies that govern how you may use digital media:

> We're entering the age of digital ankle bracelets. . . .
>
> Like it or not, rights management is increasingly going to be a fact of your life. Not only will music, books and movies be steeped in it, but soon such mundane artifacts as documents, spreadsheet files and e-mail will be joining the domain of restricted information. In fact, the next version of Microsoft Office will enable creators of certain documents to issue restrictions that dictate who, if anyone, can read them, copy them or forward them. In addition, you can specify that the files and mail you send may "sunset" after a specified period of time, evaporating like the little tapes dead-dropped to Peter Graves in *Mission: Impossible*.[12]

Von Lohmann sees some of the biggest battles ahead over the public's use of video. "The natural thing for people to do is appropriate, mix up, edit, and play the video that's all around them. That's what we've seen in music with mash-ups and sampling, that's what we've seen in art with collage and pastiche-based expression."

The restrictions on new technologies can only serve to dampen innovation, he says. Von Lohmann tells of a phone call he received from a real-estate developer who builds homes in new subdivisions. The developer told him, "I'm putting in all these houses that can be wired together, and people will want to put personal video recorders in their houses. Once I have a cluster of these houses in a subdivision, I could effectively digitize all television signals, using the different PVRs to record different films and channels. And if they were all connected together, there could be a service for this suburb where you could get just about any TV show you wanted through this distributed network."

Von Lohmann says he responded, " 'Yes, that's a great idea. And you will get sued within a week if you build it.' That chilled him on it. The studios and networks would sue him because this is their nightmare scenario, where the future of television is taken out of their hands and put in the hands of someone like the user or the subdivision developer."

In the end, this may be the greatest potential loss to society: the service that never rolls out, the device that never gets invented, the cultural advancement that never takes place—all for fear of a Hollywood lawsuit.

As participatory culture takes shape, its practitioners face considerable challenges. The same digital technologies that give us new ways to create and interact with personal media also give entertainment companies unprecedented power to limit how we use media.

Consider some examples:

In late 2002, I appeared onstage at an O'Reilly emerging technology conference with Victor Nemechek, marketing chief of El Gato Software, which makes a product that lets you watch, record, edit, and archive television on a Macintosh computer. "Before we started out, we had a team meeting to discuss whether we should take the risk of investing time and money into such an effort if a deep-pocketed movie studio could just come along and shut down our business," Nemechek told the audience. "But we felt strongly that we had to do this."

At first, Apple wasn't interested in supporting the start-up's technology, given Steve Jobs's dislike for television and belief that it takes people away from creative experiences at the computer. But when El Gato's small team unveiled EyeTV at a Macworld conference in 2002, attendees swamped their booth, and Apple changed its tune. Sales have been stronger than expected. It's not a huge market, but more and more people are recording TV on laptops and watching the shows while traveling. Others are using the software in unexpected ways, such as to record video game matches so the participants could watch their battles again in slow motion. Users can cut and paste, edit, e-mail the video, and transfer it over a home network, but piracy has been minimal, Nemechek said, with most people simply wanting to time-shift television to watch it at a more convenient time.[13]

Both El Gato and SnapStream Media, a Texas company that lets you record TV onto a PC, use an analog signal to record television. But their future prospects are clouded under federal regulations governing digital television. If they want the software to record digital television onto your PC, they have to follow new FCC rules. That means grabbing the signal, doing the secret Boy Scout handshake, and encrypting the show so you can watch a lower-grade version of it on your computer or within a home network. But you won't be able to e-mail it, share it with friends, upload it to the Internet, or borrow clips for use in a home movie or homemade political ad, as you can now.

In the digital era, even a matter so simple as recording a television show is no longer something you can take for granted. In September 2002, Cablevision inadvertently invoked copy restrictions on all unscrambled digital TV programming delivered to its 3 million subscribers in the New York metro area. Under the rules of the 5C networking group, media companies can instruct downstream digital devices to copy always, copy once, or copy never. Cablevision turned on the copy never option by accident.

"This is what the future looks like if Hollywood has its way," Kraus tells me on the morning it hit the news. "You press the record button, it doesn't work, and you don't know why. The content providers are getting greater and greater control over how you use content in the privacy of your own home and with your family members and close circle of friends."

Entertainment analyst Onosko observed on his weblog: "Even pay-per-view television allows buyers to make a tape copy for themselves and to share with others, an absent (and soon illegal) luxury under the FCC's new digital cable initiative. And VCRs (as well as hard disk video recorders and DVD recorders) that will record and play back any program, anytime, will also soon vanish under the rules."

For example, consider Microsoft's Media Center PC, which now recognizes a signal from the copyright owner that prevents cable viewers from recording any episodes of *The Sopranos* to DVD. (After all, they sell their own DVD packages.) In late 2004, as von Lohmann predicted a year earlier, Macrovision announced it had developed a feature that will allow the Hollywood studios to place restrictions on how long a digital video recorder can save programming; movies could disappear after a week. Also in late 2004, AllYourTV.com reported that an executive at Time Warner had approached several cable companies to push for a plan that would erase recordings of popular cable series such as *Six Feet Under* from customer' digital video recorders if they are stored for longer than two to four weeks.

Or consider DVDs and devices that stream home media. When Carson Kressley, one of the Fab Five members of *Queer Eye for the Straight Guy*, attended the Consumer Electronics Show in Las Vegas in early 2004, he was asked to give a writer's cluttered apartment a clean, modern look. He gave the writer better access to his music, snapshots, and television shows by eliminating physical media like CDs, photo albums, and videotapes; in their place he digitized and stored all those media inside a digital box connected to a flat-screen TV. But there was one thing Kressley could not do: eliminate stacks of DVDs by digitizing the movies and storing them on a hard drive.

And yet, the technology has existed for years. I spotted one of these DVD jukeboxes in the offices of Intervideo, a small company in Fremont, California, whose flagship DVD software product has 75 million customers. Two of the company's executives cued up the Denzel Washington thriller *Virtuosity* to show off their "time stretching" software, which lets you slow a DVD to help learn the language or, conversely, speed it up, so you can watch a two-hour movie in ninety minutes with the dialogue at normal pitch—handy for short airplane flights, even if the studios might disapprove. But the InterVideo execs were reluctant to show off their DVD jukebox and demo software, which lets you watch a DVD on any networked home TV.

It's illegal to copy an encrypted DVD to a jukebox, or storage device, and then play it back from that device, explains Intervideo's chief technical officer, Honda Shing. "Those are the rules that we have to play by" under Hollywood's Content Scramble System, he says. "We cannot sell this device because of the DVD regulations. Personally, I think this prohibition is kind of backward, but we don't want to get into any lawsuits."

Patrick Lo, chief executive of Netgear, a leading maker of home networking equipment, told the *New York Times* during the 2003 Consumer Electronics Show that media company concerns about copyrights were substantially slowing development of home entertainment systems. "The studios will not let us copy movies onto servers [media hubs], and so we can't distribute them around the house."[14]

A few days after returning from the 2004 Consumer Electronics Show in Las Vegas—the twenty-fifth time he has attended the event—a leading expert on the CE industry, Richard F. Doherty, tells me, "Jack Valenti is still managing to rattle a saber, threaten that there might be a lawsuit in the offing, and get results even if it's contrary to what the marketplace and consumers want. I can tell you that lots of manufacturers we spoke with at the conference are getting a little tired of it."[15]

Doherty, head of the consulting firm Envisioneering Group in Seaford, New York, points to lawsuits against Sonicblue's ReplayTV and DVD software maker 321 Studios and suggests that Hollywood's "extreme paranoia" over digital piracy is stalling innovation in the marketplace.[16]

Michael Petricone, vice president of the Consumer Electronics

Association, says, "It's a very litigious climate right now, and it's being driven by the widespread misapplication of the DMCA. We're currently in a climate where, if you bring out any product that allows consumers to use media in new and flexible ways, you can be fairly confident you're going to face a Hollywood lawsuit. That has profound implications for the consumer electronics industry and for consumers. I've heard from manufacturers, and from venture capitalists who are reviewing proposals from companies that use media in new ways and are wary of the lawsuit risk."

The movie industry lives in fear that once a movie escapes its DVD shell, it will wind up on a piracy channel in the Darknet. For that reason, Hollywood sued 321 Studios, a small company near St. Louis, which sold software that enabled customers to back up copies of their DVDs. (Valenti tells me that DVDs are virtually indestructible—what, he doesn't have grandkids?—but if they are damaged, you can always go out and buy another copy.) In August 2004, 321 Studios declared bankruptcy in the wake of Hollywood's lawsuits. The studios' short-term victory will likely bring long-term costs. 321 Studios had shown its willingness to become a reliable partner in the battle against movie piracy. I bought their product and was impressed with the safeguards built in to allay Hollywood's worries: you could make no more than one backup copy, you could not make copies of copies, and a digital watermark was added so it could be traced back to the source in the unlikely event it wound up in the Darknet or on the black market.

Instead, Hollywood has shut down this avenue, claiming that fair use does not apply to its movies. This despite a GarnerG2 survey in 2002 that found 73 percent of consumers believed they could legally back up videotapes and DVDs. Millions of them will likely venture into the Darknet in the coming years to look for the easy-to-find ripper tools that will defeat Hollywood's DVD protection scheme. Stephan Steiner, a twenty-four-year-old European who operates Doom9, tells me he gets roughly 1 million unique visitors a month looking for tools to back up their DVD movies.

So far, no legal threats have been made against another tech start-up that is dodging Hollywood's sledgehammer. A small company in Grass Valley, California, called Sixteen Nine Time, is doing a booming business in giving people what they want: digital connections.[17]

"There are a lot of high-end videophiles who spend 5 or 10 grand on a plasma-display TV and become annoyed by the fact that they can't get digital video outputs on anything and thus can't record high-definition programming," von Lohmann says.

For a handsome sum, the folks at 169time.com will take your set-top receiver, crack it open, and add digital outputs so you can record over-the-air high-definition television to a digital tape machine or computer. After all, in the coming age of HDTV, we'll still want to time-shift so we can watch shows on our own schedules. Richard Adams, a consultant for Sixteen Nine Time, says the company believes it is acting legally under the fair use provisions of the Copyright Act. If the equipment manufacturers offered digital outputs, it would cost them less than $20 rather than the hundreds of dollars that Sixteen Nine Time charges, but Hollywood has balked at letting its satellite partners provide boxes with digital outputs.

In the months and years ahead, as set-top boxes with no digital outputs are replaced in the market by boxes with encrypted, copy-protected digital outputs, Sixteen Nine Time may find itself on increasingly shaky legal ground because installing unprotected digital outputs could be seen as bypassing the digital TV protection system. "At that point, they will probably be violating the DMCA and the studios will probably sue," tech attorney Burger says.

Von Lohmann adds, "The message is simple: if you want maximum flexibility from your satellite set-top box, send it to 169time today. You'll get a more flexible, interoperable digital output than you'll ever get from your satellite provider. On the other hand, if you want the alternative, and don't care that it won't work with your computer, just wait a little while for the new set-top boxes with digital outputs, locked down with DRM." [18]

Consultant Doherty's[19] own frustration with the prevalence of digital locks is growing. "I shot a high school graduation tape of my daughter. I'm close friends with Steve Wozniak, and our kids are the same age. I made a copy and sent it to Steve, and a mutual friend of ours tried to make a copy and it said, can't do it. Now, imagine the outrage. It's my own copy. My camcorder allows me to make one copy, but two friends of mine can't make a copy from that copy. Who the hell set up this rule? This was going from a Sony product to a Sony product to a Sony product.[20] Sony decided to put this feature into a camcorder because their lawyers are overly deferential to Hollywood's lawyers. But who are we protecting people from?"

Sony Corp. of America declined to comment.

John Gilmore, a millionaire high-tech entrepreneur and peripatetic cofounder of EFF, has a similar story. In a widely circulated essay titled "What's Wrong with Copy Protection,"[21] he fumes at copy protection schemes that prevent users from using digital media in legal ways. He writes, "My recording of my brother's wedding is uncopyable, because my [Sony] MiniDisc deck acts as if I and my brother don't own the copyright on it." Gilmore tells me his two Sony MiniDisc recorders and Pioneer MiniDisc recorder all refuse to record copies of copies, and they let him transfer original recordings only with great effort.[22]

Gilmore's targets are plentiful: computer manufacturers that don't allow you to mix and match video tracks from various artists, the way your CD burner lets you. Companies too cowed by Hollywood to release software that lets you record streaming Internet video, even though the Supreme Court has sanctioned personal home recording as lawful. Intel's High Definition Content Protection, high-speed hardware encryption that lets you watch high-definition programming on a monitor or projector but won't let you record it. Standards bodies that are devising rules to rearchitect disk drives, Zip disks, computer flash memory, and other storage media so copyrighted music and other media would have strings attached—embedded restrictions about how the media could be used.[23]

Sony is among the worst offenders. Its portable MiniDisc audio recorders come with digital input jacks but never digital outputs, instead converting sound to lower-quality analog. Its line of Net MD Walkman MiniDisc player-recorders employs copy protection so you may download audio from your PC to your Walkman MiniDisc, but you cannot upload audio you've recorded from your Walkman to your PC, making the whole point of a digital recorder somewhat elusive.[24] In 2002, a fan site called Minidisc.org sent a petition[25] with two thousand signatures to Sony management protesting the restrictions. Sony responded that it had "no immediate plans" to change its policy.[26] In May 2004, Sony released its first portable digital music player with a hard drive, touted as an "alternative" to Apple's iPod, but absurdly, the Vaio Pocket VGF-AP1 doesn't play MP3s—only Sony's proprietary digital music formats, loaded down with copy protection. Sony made a small bow to reality in late 2004 when it announced that its new Sony players would play MP3s, though its online music store continues selling songs encoded in the closed ATRAC format.

The bottom line, Gilmore says, is this: "Consumer products should serve the interests of the consumers. Products should serve the interests of the people who are paying for them. And they should clearly disclose what they can't or won't do."

To be sure, the free market can take care of some of these concerns. Customers will generally resist such controls, and the marketplace will adjust. But what happens when cartel behavior stamps out customer choice? Too often, the digital restrictions are found in products across the board, locked in by industry consortiums and only rarely disclosed.

Additional private and cross-industry initiatives on copy protection seem to be springing up all the time.[27] Seth Greenstein, spokesman for the 5C—five technology companies that set the rules for copy protection over networked digital devices—says digital rights management often enables more consumer choice, letting users choose from among several licensing terms for a product, for example. And the plain fact is that without copy controls, the entertainment industry would refuse to make movies and high-def TV available in a digital environment.[28]

Greenstein also makes the point that the overwhelming majority of technology enthusiasts are not pirates. "Generally speaking, the people who do the most recording of home audio or video and archive them into personal collections are the ones who buy the most CDs or DVDs."

But pirate coves may be the only refuge for technology buffs who feel unduly constrained by the digital handcuffs being placed on the devices and products they legally buy. As the barbed wire goes up, more people will turn to the Darknet to obtain illegal software to crack copy protection. As the locks tighten and the strictures of law and commerce lose their moral authority, more people will enter the shadow world to trade digital media.

The Microsoft researchers who authored the "Darknet" paper offer a similar warning. Media companies are relying too heavily on technology like copy protection to prevent piracy. "If you are competing with the darknet," the researchers wrote, "you must compete on the darknet's own terms: that is convenience and low cost rather than additional security." In other words, the best thing media companies can do to fight piracy is to offer customers high quality, ease of use, affordable choices, and reasonable rules.

Von Lohmann says the entertainment companies should heed that advice. "All it takes is for one person to break copy protection and post a file on a darknet network, and then the content multiplies," he says. "Yes, posting music or downloading a movie is illegal. But the bottom line is, if artists and content owners aren't being compensated in a world where there will always be a Darknet, let's change the system and create some mechanism so that new markets and new business models are unleashed and creators get paid. Let's change the law to square it with our new reality."

7 A Nation of Digital Felons

R EV. JOHN LOOKS A BIT HARRIED AS HE SCURRIES about in the sanctuary of his stone church in a pastoral suburb of Boston. Technical issues, you see. He fiddles with his DVD-equipped Dell laptop, trying to line it up so the "worship slides," containing hymn lyrics, project clearly onto the big vertical screen set up behind the altar.

Minutes later, fifty congregants file down the speckled ruby-red carpet and settle into stiff birch pews. Two singers' lilting voices, accompanied by a pianist, soar toward the musty, vaulted wooden rafters. *"Come, now is the time to worship. Come, now is the time to give your heart."* In the front row, a grandmother, hair knotted in a gray bun, raises her hands high above her head, closes her eyes, and sways to the lyrics.

Then Rev. John, who is pastor of this evangelical Christian church, begins his multimedia sermon. The worshipers take it in stride, for they have seen him do this before, updating ancient gospel messages for modern times through a familiar emissary: Hollywood. For on this particular Sunday, Rev. John projects a scene from the 1990 movie *Joe versus the Volcano* onto the screen. In the movie, Tom Hanks asks Meg Ryan whether she believes in God. She tells him, "I believe in myself." The pastor pauses the clip just after Meg Ryan says that her father believes most people are asleep and the few who are awake live in a state of constant amazement.

Rev. John uses that exchange as the jumping-off point for a sermon about finding your purpose in life. A thoroughly modern minister, he paces down the aisle wearing black Sketcher shoes, tan chinos, and a forest green sweater that softens his solid, two-hundred-pound physique. An imposing man with broad shoulders and a dark tuft of short-cropped hair atop his six-foot-two frame, the pastor might pass for an outside linebacker, but he also has a geeky streak that makes him far more savvy about computers than most men of the cloth. That can be traced to his previous vocation, as a network administrator for a *Fortune* 500 company. Before that, he was a police officer.

"So how will you discover your purpose in life?" he asks, dialing down the feedback on his wireless microphone. During his half-hour talk, he somehow manages to weave together biblical parables, Muslim precepts, and scattered references to G.K. Chesterton, *The Simpsons*, and mass murderer Ted Bundy's chances for redemption. All in all, a typical eclectic performance from the plugged-in pastor.

Service over, the congregants file out, and he powers down his laptop. "When we use a clip from a popular film, people tend to remember it better than if we just used an anecdote or story," he tells me. "We live in a visual age."

I ask whether his followers would be surprised to learn that his multimedia sermon amounted to a federal crime. "I think they would be, yes," he says quietly. "Technically, I broke the law. I could be prosecuted as a felon."

To capture the short scene in *Joe versus the Volcano*, Rev. John used an illegal software program. Yesterday he ripped the scene from his DVD onto his hard drive with DVD Decrypt, a program that violates the Digital Millennium Copyright Act (DMCA). "The Hollywood studios don't give you a legal way to do this," he says by way of explanation. Although displaying the clip amounts to fair use, making the clip by copying the scene from a DVD violates the DMCA—and fair use is no defense under the draconian DMCA.[1]

This would not be the first or last time the pastor ran afoul of federal copyright law. On a cold fall night he spoke to a group of fifteen students on a local college campus about personal decision-making and choosing a life path. To underscore the theme of his talk, he used a video clip from *Good Will Hunting*—the scene where Matt Damon ends up storming out of the counseling session after Robin Williams tells him to leave. Rev. John used a decryption program to rip the scene from a DVD he owns, encoded it for high-quality playback on his laptop, and pumped it out to a projection screen. During editing, he muted the f-word several times for his young audience.

"I basically challenged the students to figure out what they were trying to accomplish in life," he says. But in pulling together his presentation, the pastor again acknowledges that he violated the DMCA, subjecting him to civil damages. "It's just wrong that this should be illegal," he says.

A few weeks earlier, a pair of friends, Chris and Katie Cutter, stopped by the pastor's home. "Check it out," the pastor told them. As his wife tended to his two children, he popped into his DVD player a video CD of *The Simpsons* that he had burned earlier that day. Sure enough, a new episode of *The Simpsons* filled the TV screen—hours before it was scheduled to debut nationally. Some enterprising stranger had intercepted the satellite feed from the Fox mother ship to a local affiliate, encoded it on a hard drive, and posted it to an Internet newsgroup. Rev. John simply downloaded it to his computer, edited out the commercials, and burned a copy onto a CD. Voilà—a private, world-premiere showing of *The Simpsons*.

"He was totally messing with my wife," Chris Cutter said. "A few hours later we saw the same show on live TV. She was like, 'How did he do that?'"

Confessed the pastor, "I wanted to show off a little. It felt cool that you had the episode before anyone else did."

Rev. John realizes that his actions run afoul of copyright laws. But is he really hurting anyone? Clearly, he doesn't believe so. And to fully appreciate how Internet downloading has become ingrained into his DNA, we should bear in mind that he has been a member of the digital generation far longer than he has been a minister.

During college in the 1980s, John longed to watch television programs that weren't carried in the Boston area, particularly foreign shows such as British comedies and Japanese anime. He got his first taste of downloading on bulletin board services in the late '80s, swapping home computer games over three-hundred-baud modems. Over the years, he became immersed in Usenet, a grand Internet stockpile of more than thirty-six thousand discussion groups. When the open Web exploded in popularity, he went the other way, becoming deeply immersed in trolling the remote recesses of Usenet. As connections became dizzyingly fast, he began downloading and trading anime and obscure foreign television shows.

To quench his anime fixation, he began using fansubs. When anime fans find a Japanese cartoon that hasn't been subtitled into English, volunteers take matters into their own hands and add the translations themselves. In many cases, anime distribution groups called fansubs release the fantasy adventures years before a show is picked up for commercial release in the West. The practice is typically illegal, but Japanese animation firms turn a blind eye because fansubs generate a loyal following. Once a show is licensed for commercial sale, legitimate fansubs cease their production and distribution of the material.

Rev. John takes me upstairs to a cluttered bedroom that serves as his home office. There in the corner, beyond spindles of CD-R trays and assorted bric-a-brac, lies his prize possession, a homebuilt Athlon XP computer. He boots it up, launches a news reader program called Agent, and shows me the scrolling lists of hundreds of TV shows available for quick download. "I probably have two hundred CDs' worth of anime, and I've watched only a quarter of it," he says. "It's surprising how much you accumulate once you have a cable modem. The barriers are no longer about technology, they're about lack of time."

In addition to his anime CDs, he has another hundred video CDs in his collection from downloaded TV shows, including every episode of *The Sopranos* and *Six Feet Under*. He subscribes to HBO, so no penance required, he figures. He also has downloaded a wide assortment of British comedies and dramas such as *Spooks*, an espionage series, and *Red Dwarf*, a sci-fi show. Today he chiefly uses file trading as a sort of poor man's TiVo—video on demand for those who can't afford a pricey personal video recorder. For instance, he missed entire seasons of *24*, *Scrubs*, and *Monk*, so he pulled down copies of all the episodes from the Internet in the high-quality Supervideo CD format and watched the episodes during summer reruns—on his family's schedule, not the networks'.

Every February or March, John's wife throws a little Academy Awards house party for close friends, and sometimes John will download a nominated movie—not yet available on DVD—for the group to watch in the weeks leading up to the Oscars telecast. At other times Rev. John will create a more child-friendly movie from DVDs they own. His wife tells me, "We have a nine-inch TV with a built-in DVD player between the two seats in the middle of our minivan. It's a major pain to have to sit through the FBI warning and the previews and then have to unbuckle my seat belt and do contortions to press 'play' for the kids to see the movie." So John copies the DVD to disc, without the required copy protection, and burns a new disc, without the FBI warning, preview, or play button. (Yes, this, too, is a crime.) "Now we can just pop in the DVD and drive and not worry about it," she says.

Rev. John also turned to the Internet to solve a small family dilemma: one room in his house contained a VCR, where his young son watched movies on videotape. But the high-strung youngster often spent time in the family room, which sported only a DVD player. How to transfer all the movie titles the family owned on videotape to DVD? The pastor turned to the Internet. He went online, downloaded all the movies, and burned them onto disc using utilities he obtained for free from a site called Doom9. The family now uses the movies as spares in the DVD player.

"I know it's a violation," he says. But the minister doesn't figure it will set him back any come Judgment Day. "I don't think it's wrong. We already own the movies, just in a different format."

All of this inevitably raises the questions: doesn't piracy amount to stealing, as Jack Valenti insists? Isn't this a sin? We exchange lighthearted jabs about eternal hellfire and then get down to a serious discussion about how digital media intersect with ethics and morality.

If it sounds as if Rev. John is entirely dismissive of copyright laws, it's not so. His church pays a licensing fee to Christian Copyright Licensing International for the music used in Sunday services. His sermons, released on CD and cassette tape, do not include excerpts from copyrighted movies or music. At home, John and his wife buy more DVDs than most of their friends, even though he could download the movies for free. He downloads computer games from the Net and, if they remain on his computer for more than a month, he'll buy an authorized version. He doesn't download music for free and has never earned a cent from his downloading forays. Neither does he share files with strangers, although, in a bout of charity, he downloaded an episode of *South Park* and burned it onto a CD for a friend who had missed the show.

"I've wrestled with the ethical question, and on a moral level I try to guard against being a freeloader," he says. "Basically, I try to be honest. I want to make sure I'm not taking money out of any artist's pocket. Those of us who dabble in digital media have to keep asking ourselves: am I living up to that standard?"

We walk back to his small office in the rear of the church, and I ask a question no one has put to him before: what might Jesus say about file sharing? He puzzles for a while and finally says, "I don't know. When the teachers of the law came to Jesus and asked, 'What is the most important commandment?,' he said, 'Love the Lord your God with all your heart's almighty strength. But there's an equally important commandment. Love your neighbor as yourself.' And I think that's the question to ask: are you taking money out of your neighbor's pocket? If your heart tells you what you're doing may not be fair or right, stay away from it."

Rev. John knows that his vocation sets him apart from most file traders. At the same time, his computer prowess sets him apart from most Christian ministers. "I'm genuinely concerned about the digital divide in society, where people without access to technology are getting left behind," he says. "But it seems Congress is less interested in remedying that than in criminalizing legitimate behavior through the DMCA and through perpetual copyright extensions." Why, he asks, is there no legitimate way for him to pay a fee to access television shows over the Internet? Why does ripping movies for a church sermon constitute a felony?

Toward the end of my visit, our talk turns to darknets. The pastor has considered this subject, too. "If they come up with a truly anonymous file-sharing network, one that can't be tracked or shut down, a lot of people would find that threatening. But the net benefit to society would be positive. People would have freedom of speech. Whistle-blowers would be free to come forward. That kind of democratization of information really would be a powerful blow against oppression in any form." His two-year-old toddles in, and John tousles his son's hair. "In that sense, I see a direct application to God's work. Once something is out there, how are you going to stop it?"

Driving to Intel's new research lab at the University of Washington at daybreak on April 3, 2002, Donald S. Whiteside drank in the spectacular Seattle morning. The sun glinted off Elliot Bay, the Cascades gleamed in the distance.

Newly minted the year before as vice president in charge of Intel's broadband and content program, Whiteside was one of the executive team's stars. Whether facing hostile congressmen on Capitol Hill or meeting with

Hollywood executives in swank corporate high-rises, he cut a dashing figure. Tall, ruddy-skinned, and imposing, with silvery hair and sculpted features, Whiteside had quickly become one of the leading figures in the digital rights wars because of Intel's vast influence in the technology world. Computers made with Intel's chips are changing modern life more than any other product. The Microsoft-Intel alliance, dubbed Wintel, powers more than nine of every ten personal computers. With $27 billion in annual sales and sixty thousand employees, Intel was the only company with representatives on both the 4C and 5C industry groups, which hammer out the technology rules for recording and networking media throughout a house or a business.

On this particular morning, a congressional fact-finding delegation was convening at the Intel lab, followed by trips to Amazon and Microsoft. For the twenty or so senior and midlevel staffers from the House Judiciary Committee, Senate Commerce Committee, and other key panels, the trip was more than a junket to the nation's java capital. It was an opportunity to press the message that Washington was unhappy with the pace of progress by the high-tech sector in protecting movies and music from Internet piracy. The aides, whose philosophical outlook cut a wide ideological swatch across both political parties, were not of a single mind on the torturously complex subject of copyright law. But many held the view that high tech's potentates possessed a technological silver bullet that could solve the problem of Internet piracy once and for all. At the very least, the technowizards could certainly come up with a solution if forced. Perhaps they needed a nudge from Washington. Many of the assembled staffers on that spring morning seemed to believe that Washington probably would have to intervene in some way to sort out this mess.

If hubris flowed like wine, the Seattle region's vintners would have faced serious competition from this strutting little delegation.[2]

Whiteside parked his rental sedan and greeted his guests in the lab's largest conference room. No reporters were present, so the give and take could be frank and forthright. Whiteside fired up his laptop as a lab employee connected it to a projection screen for a presentation of Power-Point slides. Whiteside, who flew in from Phoenix, apologized for his less-than-dapper appearance: the airline had lost his luggage, and he could rustle up only an ill-fitting shirt this early in the morning.

Whiteside quickly launched into a slide show for the aides and a few interns lurking in the wings. He was an articulate evangelist for Intel's vision of the networked home. While industry titans like Bill Gates and Steve Jobs sometimes seemed a bit out there, preaching about smart homes and the Web lifestyle and pervasive computing that would reach into every crevice of our lives, Whiteside tended to bring the discussion down to earth, talking about the technological forces and business imperatives that were driving the digital revolution. The trend lines were unmistakable: the networked home was very real and quickly becoming an integral part of middle-class America.

The aides, serious men and women in their twenties to forties, seemed caught up by Whiteside's click-and-tell. He briefly recounted the evolution of personal computing. The era of stand-alone boxes was ending, he told his audience. We're now at the dawn of a new phase of the computer revolution. Whiteside called this "the era of the extended wireless PC." That was one way to frame the discussion, although the PC was only one component of this new era of connectivity. (Bill Gates calls this "seamless computing." I'd argue that a better term would be "personal media networks.") By whatever name, these are the connections that are making all our high-tech stuff talk to each other.

This trend will touch all of us in profound ways. Forget the nonsense you may have heard about the digital home. It's not about walking into a room and having the network flick on the lights, turn on the stereo, and mix you a martini. It's not about your smart refrigerator ordering milk when you're a quart low. It's about new ways to share and exploit personal media—bringing digital music, photos, television, movies, voice, and audio together in an intelligent way so that content and communication can flow instantly from one device to another in the universal language of 0's and 1's. Home networks will let you capture a movie or show from the Web or your cable system and zip it wirelessly to let you watch it on the TV in your living room, in your car, or on your boat. Stream music from your PC to the high-fidelity speakers in the family room. Show your latest family photos in a slide show on your TV set. We will bank, learn to cook, and consult with doctors over the network. We'll look in on loved ones when we're at work.

And we will do countless other things no one has thought of yet.

The rudimentary plumbing for this network has already begun to appear in the homes of early adopters. Hundreds of thousands of people have networked their televisions to stream recorded programming from the digital box in one room to another room. Tens of millions have bought TV tuner cards, letting viewers watch television on their computers. Others are taking the MP3 music files on their computers and playing them on their home entertainment systems. Further out, engineers at Intel were working on an ultrasmall "silicon radio" that would be embedded in the corner of every one of the billions of chips it makes as part of this wireless hive. It was all about connections.

The tech industry, mired in the worst downturn in its history, had risen up as one to embrace the idea that its salvation lay in the converged, connected, networked home. Plans were formulated, industry standards were set, and now came the job of making the vision a reality—rolling it out in a way simple enough for customers to use without getting a graduate degree from MIT. (The Yankee Group reports that 30 percent of all home networking products sold are returned because the buyer can't get them to work. It's hard to make this stuff simple, but techies need to get serious about making this their top priority.)

It turns out, however, that the most maddeningly difficult part of this new wireless bazaar was not about how to get everyone connected. The hardest part was figuring out how to allow some connections but *prevent* others. Two reasons for this: you and I don't want our private information—about health, money, shopping habits, political beliefs—to seep out into the digital ether. Tech gurus were tackling the problem, figuring out how a conversation could take place through the air between your PC and your television set fifty feet away, but sealing it off from your neighbor or a stranger on the street. The second reason for restricting certain connections: the efforts by media and entertainment companies to protect and control their digital goods. Here, the issues were even more tangled. When a consumer bought digital content, did he own it, or was he just "licensing" the bits? What rights did he have to watch, use, share, or transfer digital media both inside and outside his house? And who should decide?

Whiteside ended his PowerPoint show with a discussion of digital piracy. Piracy runs the gamut from the casual copier and hobbyist to the hacker, small-scale pirate, and professional pirate. Technology, he said, might be effective against the casual copier, but it almost never thwarts determined pirates. He fired up a video clip. The motion picture *Titanic* flashed onscreen in remarkable clarity and audio fidelity. "I captured this video clip by pointing my camcorder at the television in my living room," he told the aides. The only additional piece of hardware needed was an inexpensive time base corrector to synchronize the television and camcorder refresh rates, available at any Radio Shack and used for a wide range of legitimate purposes. Legislate all the technological safeguards you want, he told them, and piracy still would be this easy to accomplish.

Then it was the congressional staffers' turn. They jousted with Whiteside on the subjects of technology mandates, copy protection, and digital piracy. The government mandated unleaded gasoline, one aide suggested, so why shouldn't it mandate technological measures in consumer devices to protect the content industry? Another suggested requiring companies to place watermark technology in all camcorders to thwart pirated recordings of movies. Some of the aides admitted to downloading songs using Napster, while others fulminated against what they considered to be rampant online piracy being enabled by technology companies. Several staffers spoke up in agreement with an aide who called television's V-chip a great success story. Whiteside alternately sparred, coaxed, cajoled, and educated his guests. A senior aide to a Democratic senator would tell me later, "The session at Intel was by far the most stimulating of the trip."

Toward the end of the meeting, Whiteside fingered the jewel case of a homemade DVD he had created months earlier. He cued up the video in his laptop and froze the opening frame on the projection screen. Time to get personal.

Whiteside explained how the homemade DVD came to be. His nine-year-old son, Timmy, played on a Pop Warner team called the Typhoons, and Whiteside spent the better part of a football season capturing images of the action with his digital camcorder. At long last Whiteside culled together the highlights, imported them into his PC, and began creating his digital masterpiece. "I used a program to copy a few seconds from the DVD of the movie *Rudy*," he said. "It's the scene showing the final game of the Notre Dame season with Rudy's family in the stands cheering wildly when he got to play. I then spliced in some snippets of pro players doing a touchdown dance from NFL Films, and I overlaid it with audio from 'Who Let the Dogs Out?' I stitched this all together with video of my son, and it turned out to be the piece of home video that gets watched the most in our house. When relatives or members of the football team come over, we pop it in and we just laugh. The added scenes and music really bring it all to life."

There was just one problem. "It turns out to do this, I violated the DMCA. I used the DeCSS program to circumvent the encryption and access the movie clips on the DVD that I own," Whiteside told the aides. "The end product is a DVD that I don't sell or distribute but is considered a derivative work under copyright law."

To their credit, none of the congressional aides flipped open their cell phones to call the attorney general. (When I described Whiteside's home movie to Jack Valenti, he said, "He's committing a violation of federal law.")

DeCSS, software devised largely by fifteen-year-old Norwegian Jon Lech Johansen in 1999 to circumvent the digital locks on a DVD, has been widely popular since it first appeared on the Net.[3] (He wrote the code so he could play a DVD movie on his Linux computer. Johansen tells me his original DeCSS code may have been downloaded a million times over the years, and related ripper programs millions more.) Authorities have brandished the Digital Millennium Copyright Act as a club, threatening to use it against anyone who uses, distributes, or even links to a program like DeCSS. First-time offenders are subject to civil fines of up to $2,500, with penalties of up to five years in prison and a $500,000 fine if the violation was willful and for profit. Whiteside said he didn't know he was violating the law at the time and hasn't done it since.

The point of his demonstration, Whiteside said, was not a mea culpa, but a real-world example of how Washington's penchant for legislative solutions can hobble a new, flowering marketplace of innovation. "This is precisely the kind of exciting consumer creativity that should be enabled," he said. "I don't claim to have all the answers. Should I have to go clear rights to use ten seconds from *Rudy* in my son's video, or does it fall under fair use? Should I have to pay pennies for every second of a snippet? I don't know. But I do know that we have to figure out a way for consumers to do something creative without breaking the law.

"To me, this episode was a great way to frame the question: Should copyright law permit this or not? Should the DMCA criminalize this sort of thing? Or should the creative community, high-tech community, and lawmakers get together to try to stimulate this kind of innovative behavior?"

Copyright law was crafted with consumers in mind. But what happens when audiences create media as well as consume it? As we sample, quote, reinvent, and share media in the new participatory culture, the law and our digital lives are diverging at an accelerating clip.

One of the most popular videos on the Internet last year was a political animation called *This Land* that poked fun at candidates George W. Bush and John Kerry. More than 10 million people downloaded the Flash movie, which turned up on several network and cable television shows. But the creators, brothers Gregg and Evan Spiridellis, used the melody of Woodie Guthrie's 1949 classic "This Land Is Your Land" for the sound track. The

Richmond Organization, a music publisher that owns the copyright to the song, threatened to file suit unless the movie was withdrawn from public display. (Guthrie would likely have been appalled at such an assault on free speech.) The threat was withdrawn after the EFF's legal beagles discovered the song may have fallen into the public domain.

"In the old days, Dan Rather had to worry about copyright law, but the average Joe didn't," says Jonathan Zittrain, cofounder of Harvard's Berkman Center for Internet & Society. "What has changed is that the Internet has given us all the power of publishing. And now the culture of the copyright regime is clashing with the culture of democratic media."[4]

Congress thought it had brought copyright into the modern era with a major rewrite of the Copyright Act in 1976. The new law spelled out fair use, which allows the public to use copyrighted material without permission for commentary, criticism, or parody. But only a few years later, special interests were knocking at the door again, looking for new laws to govern DAT recorders, chip designs, satellite broadcasts, personal computers, and computer networks. The digital age had arrived. In 1985, Congress asked its Office of Technology Assessment to study the issue. After more than a year of hearings, testimony, historical analysis, and independent research, the bipartisan office issued a three-hundred-page report titled "Intellectual Property Rights in an Age of Electronics and Information."

"The more we dug into it, the more we came to the conclusion that copyright is conceptually incoherent when it comes to works in digital media. It doesn't even work," Rob Kost, one of the report's authors, tells me.[5] "Copyright was intended to protect authorship in any medium of expression, and yet here were all these officials from the recording, software, and movie industries coming into our hearing room wanting to outlaw or strictly control these new forms of digital expression."

The Office of Technology Assessment staffers conducted a thought experiment, Kost recalls. "Remember, this was 1986, when the Internet was still Arpanet. We said, let's suppose there is a network where I shared a copy of a Mozart symphony with two of my friends, and each of them shared the same symphony with two of their friends every fifteen minutes. If you do the math, in just over eight hours everybody in the world has a copy of the symphony.[6] How do you enforce against that? Little did we see Napster coming."

The OTA's report concluded that from the standpoint of enforceability and legal coherence, it may no longer be possible to prop up traditional copyright in an age of digital media. The report received a lackluster reception on the floor of Congress and was publicly attacked by the recording industry and computer giants like IBM.

Kost, who later became legal counsel of Prodigy and is now a businessman in New York, sounds a bit jaded after watching Congress pass a spate of laws in the 1990s that contravened the report's evenhanded set of policy recommendations. "The fact is the laws are bought and paid for by contributors to congressional candidates. There's no semblance of honest, public-interest-oriented kinds of inquiries here. It's all about, 'which lobbyists can help me?' "

By the mid-1990s, it was easy to understand why the entertainment companies were nervous. The music industry, Hollywood studios, and publishing companies saw the Internet as a major threat to their distribution models. Unlimited digital reproductions, plus worldwide distribution at zero cost, meant that millions of people could potentially rip off music, movies, and books and drain revenue streams. So a legion of lobbyists descended on Capitol Hill. After months of intense negotiations and brutal arm-twisting by all stakeholders except the public, in 1998 Congress enacted the most far-reaching update of copyright law in a generation.[7]

The DMCA—the chief federal law governing the use of content online—went much further than earlier measures. It effectively turns software code into law by outlawing any attempt to route around copy protection on electronic media. If you do, you could go to jail or be sued by the rights holder.

Under this new brand of digital protectionism, copyright law now prevents not only *copying* but also full *access* to purchased products such as a DVD, CD, e-book, or computer software.[8] Content owners now wield exclusive power to control their material through code—with the backing of federal law.

With the new law, Hollywood got the storybook ending it wanted: an airtight legal seal around its goods.

When President Clinton signed the DMCA in 1998,[9] lawmakers thought they had fashioned a grand compromise that would put to rest the simmering feuds between all parties in the copyright wars while preserving traditional rights of the public such as fair use. "When you talk to a lot of folks in Congress, no one anticipated that the anticircumvention provisions would be used to prevent fair use," says Joe Kraus of DigitalConsumer.org.[10] "And yet the courts have said too bad, the DMCA trumps fair use, and if you crack the copy protection on a piece of digital media, you're automatically a criminal."

The DMCA did not simply dust off copyright and update it for the new digital era. Instead, it radically transformed the centuries-old copyright bargain in which creators and the public maintain a balance of rights. As one observer put it, "Copyright's crucial limitations and exceptions are facing a stealth attack, embedded in the structure of the media themselves."[11]

What's new and unsettling is how the law has deputized technology to become a partner of the state. Where once we might have tinkered with a product we paid for and brought home, that was no longer an option. Where once educators, journalists, researchers, and critics could fall back on fair use for accessing cultural works, that's no longer true.[12]

The *Christian Science Monitor* described the new reality of lockdown culture this way: "In a few years, Americans may not be able to copy a song off a CD, watch a recorded DVD at a friend's house, or store a copy of a television show for more than a day."[13]

Already, viewers are not permitted to fast-forward through previews on certain DVDs, forcing us to endure five minutes of advertising. We can't transfer certain copy-protected CDs to an MP3 player. The public is being pushed to accept "trusted systems" that eliminate all unauthorized uses of media and foster a pay-per-use universe. Under the new regime, the freedoms we have long enjoyed—lending an article to a friend, backing up a file, clipping an item for later retrieval—become illegal if done online without the permission of the copyright owner. It's as if you needed to sign in and obtain permission every time you wanted to read a book on your own bookshelf.

"This debate is about whether the content industries will be able to use technology, backed by the force of law, to control what you can do with content that you own," says Gigi Sohn, president of the public interest group Public Knowledge. "If you buy a DVD or e-book, the content owner can determine how you can use it. [One of the earliest e-books was a textbook that expired and became unreadable at the semester's end so that students would not be able to resell it.[14]] Never before has there been postpurchase control by the content industry. They'd like to make you think it's all about piracy over peer-to-peer networks, but piracy is almost beside the point."

So far, the DMCA has been used sparingly by federal prosecutors. Few criminal cases have been brought under the act. But that's beside the point. The *chill* is the point.

I cannot tell you Rev. John's last name because he could be subjected to ruinous fines and jail time. Whiteside no longer makes creative mixes of home footage and Hollywood snippets. Millions of people use ripper programs to unlock DVDs—to back up a copy, to play a movie on a Linux computer—but every such use is deemed a felony, and so almost no one will discuss his or her use of these tools openly.

The entertainment industry sends out thousands of cease-and-desist orders each year to students, universities, corporations, and Internet service providers, threatening to impose massive fines under the DMCA unless copyrighted works are removed from public view. It's a strong-arm tactic that Tony Soprano himself might admire.

For example, in the fall of 2003, internal memos from Diebold Election Systems, the nation's largest maker of electronic voting machines, appeared on the Web. Someone had leaked fifteen thousand e-mail messages and memos that revealed internal discussions about software and security flaws in thirty-three thousand electronic voting machines the company had manufactured. Diebold officials knew its system was vulnerable to hackers but did little to fix it. Students at Harvard, MIT, Swarthmore, and more than two dozen other colleges decided this information was important enough to post publicly, especially in light of Diebold management's aggressive fundraising activities on behalf of President George W. Bush in the 2004 election.

Days after the memos became public, Diebold attorneys sent out scores of "takedown" letters to universities and individuals, threatening prosecution under the DMCA. The tactic worked. In almost all cases, the memos were immediately removed from the Web.[15] The DMCA had become, in effect, an Official Secrets Act—a tool of censorship. As the New York Times reported: "The question of whether the students were within their rights to post the memos was essentially moot: thanks to the Digital Millennium Copyright Act, their speech could be silenced without the benefit of actual lawsuits, public hearings, judges or other niceties of due process."[16] After the students persisted and the company endured a wave of negative publicity, Diebold relented and allowed the memos to return to the Web. But to supporters of free speech online, the episode was a stark reminder of the DMCA's reach.

The EFF's von Lohmann says the DMCA and copyright infringement laws have criminalized activities undertaken by vast numbers of people. "I worry about laws that make tens of millions of Americans into lawbreakers who can be sued whenever the studios and recording labels feel like it. I worry about any country where a large number of people can be brought up on charges at will based on whatever reason the accusing party wants to cite. That's where we're heading with copyright law."

Von Lohmann's colleague at EFF, Cory Doctorow, warns that a combination of the DMCA and next-generation copy protection technologies will almost certainly thwart acts of conscience by whistle-blowers such as those undertaken by Daniel Ellsberg, who leaked the Pentagon Papers, or the three women who blew the whistle at WorldCom, Enron, and the FBI and were named Persons of the Year in 2002 by *Time* magazine.[17] Similar actions may become difficult or impossible in the era of lockdown media. New copy protection technologies will allow companies and individuals to decide whether e-mails, memos, and other digital documents can be forwarded, saved, printed out, or photocopied—all this on top of the threat of sanctions under the DMCA.

Certainly, the DMCA has its good points. Companies large and small supported its passage because it established rules of the road for media in the digital age. But the DMCA's takedown and anticircumvention provisions continue to have unintended, far-reaching effects far beyond the scope of what Congress intended.[18]

In 2001, Princeton's Felten accepted a public challenge by the recording industry to break its new security system for protecting music. But when he announced that he and his team of students had cracked the system and would reveal their findings at an academic conference, the Recording Industry Association of America said some of its members might bring charges against them under the DMCA if they did so. The RIAA reversed course after public outcry. In 2002, Hewlett-Packard invoked the DMCA and threatened to sue a team of researchers who publicized a vulnerability in HP's Tru64 Unix operating system. HP later relented after some bad press. In 2003, Princeton student John Alex Laderman announced on his Web site that he'd discovered how to disable copy protection on a music CD—by holding down the shift key. (Doh!) Software maker SunnComm first said it planned to sue him under the DMCA, then retreated.[19] In the private sector, companies from garage door makers to ink cartridge manufacturers have used the DMCA to stifle marketplace competition.

In the mid-1990s, Peter Jaszi, a law professor at American University, formed the Digital Future Coalition, an umbrella group of academics, librarians, consumer groups, and commercial trade associations formed to participate in the drafting of the DMCA—except the group was largely shut out of the process. Jaszi says: "Instead of being used to prevent piracy, the DMCA has become increasingly a tool of anticompetitive practice on the part of the wealthiest, most powerful entities in the content industry. It's also being used to provide a legal infrastructure for a ubiquitous, pay-per-use content distribution model. It may take a long time, but I'm confident the DMCA will be modified because this crazy law can't remain indefinitely in place."

The first criminal case brought under the DMCA began on July 17, 2001, when the FBI, acting on a tip from Adobe Systems, arrested Dmitry Skylarov as he stepped off a plane to attend a computer conference in Las Vegas.[20] Skylarov, a programmer and assistant professor at a Moscow university, helped write a program for his Russian employer, ElcomSoft, that permitted owners of Adobe's eBook Reader to access e-books through Adobe's standard, less restrictive PDF format. (The software worked only on legitimately purchased e-books.) A reader might have many legitimate reasons for wanting to skirt Adobe's restrictions. A blind reader used ElcomSoft's unscrambler to feed e-books into speech synthesizers. Other people wanted to move an e-book they purchased from a desktop machine to a laptop, or to read an e-book on a Linux computer. Some users chafed at rules preventing them from using an e-book to copy or print out passages from works in the public domain, like Lewis Carroll's 1865 novel *Alice in Wonderland*, George Eliot's 1873 novel *Middlemarch*, or Aristotle's *Politics*. Still, none of that mattered under the DMCA.

After authorities brought charges against Skylarov, newspaper accounts pointed out the incongruity of prosecuting someone for creating software that was perfectly legal in Russia, where it was made. (Indeed, *encrypted* e-books are illegal in Russia and Germany.) Skylarov, the father of a 2½-year-old son and 3-month-old daughter, spent several weeks in jail before demonstrations by tech activists against the feds' heavy-handed use of the DMCA spurred Adobe to seek dismissal of the charges. Skylarov was freed in exchange for his testimony at his company's trial, which ended in acquittal.[21]

Adobe is hardly alone in overlooking fair use and the public domain in the realm of e-books. In 2004 you could purchase an electronic version of the U.S. Constitution on a Microsoft Reader—armored with copy protection that prevented you from printing it.[22] Circumventing such restrictions is illegal.

So far, the courts have uniformly upheld the harshest provisions of the DMCA. In the ElcomSoft case, a federal court acknowledged that copy protection in Adobe's eBook Reader did restrict freedoms once enjoyed by the public, such as fair use and first sale (the idea that once you buy a book you may lend, resell, or dispose of it as you wish), but the court said Congress had the power to "sacrifice" these rights. In a DMCA case brought by eight Hollywood studios against *2600* magazine, another court held that copy protection that stripped away fair use rights was permissible because anyone who wanted to copy portions of a work for criticism, scholarship, or other lawful purposes could still do so by retyping by hand. If you wanted to copy and paste a visual image, however, you were out of luck.

Fair use is a murky doctrine. Programmers point out that code is black and white—a series of 0's and 1's that leaves no room for the muddy grays of fair use. Computers don't understand gray. Ambiguity cannot be programmed into a device. And yet, as tech author David Weinberger has pointed out, fair use is all about wiggle room. This is the fatal flaw of copy protection. It doesn't know if you're going to take a five-second snippet from *Rudy* to add to a home movie, or copy the entire movie and upload it to the Net. Where leeway is the default and rules are the exception in our real lives, when we venture into the digital world, the default becomes: prevent everything.

Not only do copy control systems fail to map fair use and lawful use, they also can't possibly anticipate new social behaviors. As von Lohmann notes, fair use is a dynamic, evolving concept. When Universal sued Sony in the *Betamax* case in 1976, most copyright scholars believed home taping did not constitute fair use. If Hollywood and the tech world had imposed an inflexible copy protection system back then, such things as time-shifting, personal video recorders, ripping software, CD burners, and MP3 players would never have come about.

The public seems to believe it has an expansive set of rights to use materials as it sees fit. Many of us think of "fair use" in a colloquial sense to encompass any use of a work that is fair and reasonable. But in its strict legal sense under the Copyright Act, fair use is a notoriously weak vessel.[23]

What we need is a new term to refer to fair, reasonable, commonsense, noncommercial uses of digital media. I propose *digital rights*. Like fair use, digital rights will sometimes be hard to quantify precisely from case to case. Ultimately the public will determine its contours and reach. Most of us will know it when we see it. Backing up a children's movie on DVD to avoid your kid's sticky fingers probably qualifies as a reasonable digital right. Copying a rented Blockbuster DVD to avoid buying the movie does not.

While fair use and digital rights continue to erode, the DMCA's most chilling effects may be on innovation and scientific research. Scientists have raised concerns about the DMCA's criminalization of security research and legitimate academic inquiry. A number of technical conferences have begun to relocate overseas, and scores of computer scientists from abroad now refuse to travel to this country because of liability concerns under the DMCA.[24]

This is not a matter of concern only to academics and intellectuals. In the summer and fall of 2002, President Bush's top cyberspace security adviser, Richard A. Clarke, called for Congress to reform the DMCA, citing the law's use to chill legitimate computer security research. "A lot of people didn't realize that it would have this potential chilling effect on vulnerability research," he told the *Boston Globe*.[25] (Clarke's critique came well before he wrote a book about the Bush White House and became a lightning rod in the 2004 presidential campaign.)

Techies have lined up against the DMCA for another reason: it effectively outlaws forms of open source software. For example, under the DMCA, an open source DVD player could be considered a "circumvention device" and thus would be illegal.

"In the past, you were supposed to understand how machines did their jobs," Peter Wayner, author of a book about the free software movement, wrote in the *New York Times*. "Today, that kind of curiosity makes you a hacker. The big movie and music conglomerates want to portray the meddling kids who fiddle with DVD players as pirates who are just one click away from breaking into the Pentagon and launching nuclear missiles."[26]

Journalists, too, have raised concerns about the reach of the DMCA. Technology journalist Declan McCullagh wrote an article for tech news site News.com[27] in which he related that a confidential source had given him the secret password to access documents on the Transportation Security Administration Web site. The documents, covering airport security procedures, were encrypted, and a password was required to open and read them. A note on the site warned that this "information is restricted to airport management and local law enforcement." If the reporter typed the password given to him, he could be liable for fines of $500,000 and up to five years in prison under the DMCA, which prohibits anyone from circumventing "a technological measure" that controls access to protected information. McCullagh concludes: "intellectual property rights have gone too far, and arguably interfere with the newsgathering process." It is uncertain whether using someone else's password is a violation of the DMCA.[28]

| | |

The DMCA and other recent changes in the law have tipped the scales toward content owners and away from the public. What can be done to rebalance the scales? Education. Legal reform. Innovative new licensing systems. And the Darknet.

Jed Horovitz shot a documentary to educate the public. The fifty-three-year-old New Jersey entrepreneur, with sharply chiseled features and gleaming bald head, had been running a small video operation called Video Pipeline that took Hollywood films, created two-minute trailers to help promote them, and distributed them to online retailers such as Netflix, BestBuy, and Barnes & Noble, as well as public libraries. In 2000, the Walt Disney Co. filed suit, charging that Horovitz's company was violating Disney's copyright by featuring portions of their movies online. Horovitz lost at trial and was forced to lay off his six employees and dissolve the company in 2004.

During the trial, Horovitz decided to return to his filmmaking roots. Earlier in his career, he had worked at Roger Corman's low-budget movie factory, helping turn out such classics as *Slumber Party Massacre 2* and *Rock 'n' Roll High School Forever*. Originally he planned to call his new first-person film *Mickey and Me*. But as he heard of other similar incidents, he realized the story had a larger context. He and a videographer then spent several months and $15,000 canvassing the nation to create *Willful Infringement*, a call to arms about the clash between free expression and the ownership of ideas.

"My mother was a children's librarian, and she imbued me with a worldview that culture is a conversation, that you don't own stories, you share them," he tells me. "What has happened over the past few decades is that culture has become privatized to the point where we're now facing a crisis. We need to remember we can still quote and sample, we still have fair use. As a free culture, we're still allowed to do things without permission."[29]

Artists, writers, musicians, scientists, and others parade across his lens. Many of them have been threatened, sued, fined, and put out of work in the name of copyright. Horovitz captures it all in a documentary style popularized by Michael Moore in *Roger & Me* and *Bowling for Columbine*. At various points, the iconoclastic Horovitz appears on camera, appearing dumbfounded at the tales of an overreaching Hollywood legal machinery. A preschool director says the MPAA sent letters warning that the school could not show cartoon videos to the children without a license, nor could the school hang likenesses of famous cartoon characters on the walls without permission. Members of a Rolling Stones tribute band tell of performing under a legal cloud. Husband-and-wife party clowns in Anaheim, California, relate how they were warned not to create balloon animals for kids that looked too much like Tigger, Barney, or the Aladdin genie. A young amateur filmmaker named Mazen Mawlawi explains how he and his friends thought it would be cool to make their own twist on the *Star Wars* legend and so spent two years to make a thirty-five-minute film short, set between episodes three and four, that staged new scenes, including laser sword fights and Jedi knights blasting into space. The tribute film was forced off the Internet by Lucasfilm attorneys.

Horovitz distributed copies of his movie to university law schools and other venues, but its central message has not yet bubbled up into the mainstream media. *Willful Infringement* was featured as part of the "Illegal Art" exhibit in 2003.

Critics of tightening copyright control also have begun trying to reform the law. Intel's Whiteside says, "Copyright law has evolved to the point where it is out of balance with the founders' original intentions of balancing creators' rights and consumers' rights. At some point, the law needs to be pulled back to reflect prevailing attitudes in society."

Although the free culture movement has so far struck out in pushing for legislative reforms, it has been more successful with an initiative that works within the confines of current copyright law.

In May 2002, a group of law and technology scholars launched Creative Commons as a way to empower people to customize their own copyrights. With Creative Commons, musicians, writers, filmmakers, photographers, artists, and other creative people define the scope of how others may use or reinterpret their works. Based in San Francisco, the nonprofit rights clearinghouse dispenses with copyright's intimidating legalese by giving individuals a choice of several easy-to-use licenses through its Web site.

The goal is to enable and empower that "sensible center" where Lessig believes most of us reside. Creative Commons helps rekindle the dynamism of artistic creation, reminding us that Shakespeare, Picasso, Miles Davis, and other giants created their works through imitation, adaptation, reinterpretation of cultural themes, and ultimately inspired reinvention.

Executive director Glenn Otis Brown calls Creative Commons a "cheap, no-hassle way to fine-tune your rights or donate your rights to the public." A Creative Commons mark does not mean that copyright is waived but that certain freedoms are granted. A teacher could search the site for drawings she would be allowed to use freely in an online lesson plan. Writers and photographers could allow their creations to be shared without legal hassles. Musicians could make their music available to rappers and DJs to download, sample, and remix as they like. Collaboration across space and time is now a breeze. Using a Creative Commons "attribution/share-alike" license, Colin Mutchler posted a guitar track called "My Life" to a music site, a seventeen-year-old violinist named Cora Beth added a violin track, and the result is a new piece of music called "My Life Changed."

Rev. John uses Creative Commons to share his sermons. Anyone else is free to borrow, rework, or copy his spiritual talks without giving him credit. A project called "Undead Art" challenges students to remix the cult movie *Night of the Living Dead*, which fell into the public domain by accident, and create something new, like a comedy sketch or zombie dance video. Participants then assign their work a Creative Commons license.

Documentary filmmakers, who sometimes spend more time clearing rights than filming, have become quick fans. Rick Prelinger, whose Prelinger Film Archives covers more than forty-eight thousand titles from 1903 to 1980, was one of the first to sign up. His archive includes material from World War II and the Cold War, such as the "Duck and Cover" film that instructed schoolchildren how to duck under their desks to survive a nuclear attack. Now students, scholars, and "struggling artists" can dip into his archive and use footage in their personal projects. "The more we give away, the more we sell," he says. John Halperin of WD Films got free archive material from Prelinger to make a TV series called *Big Thinkers*. British artist Vicki Bennett used free film footage for a digital media festival and for a cinema project called *People Like Us* after finding she couldn't afford any of the material licensed by stock footage companies. "History should be available for commentary to all people, not just those that can afford to do so," she told *BBC News Online*.[30]

Since December 2002, artists have used Creative Commons to share the rights to 3 million writings and pieces of music, video, and digital art. Some four thousand Web pages carry the public domain designation, saying, in effect, No rights reserved. The vast majority of people using Creative Commons say, Yes, you may use, borrow, and build on my work for noncommercial purposes, but if you plan on profiting from it, you need to get my permission. Call it the share economy.

For example, Allan Vilhan, a musician who lives in a village in Slovakia, put his mix of "trip rock" electronica online with a Creative Commons license. Thousands of people have downloaded the free MP3s, but he also received $450 from an Alabama programmer who paid to use the tracks in a video game, and he got $370 from a San Francisco design firm that is using one of his songs on a client's Web site. Listeners also shelled out $1,500 in donations. Vilhan splits all proceeds with his Internet music distributor.[31]

"A lot of us have been fighting for years in the political arena for these goals, and so far we've failed," Lessig, the organization's chairman, says. "The idea of Creative Commons is, let's use private, voluntary action to get the law out of the way to allow for the extraordinary potential of our creative culture. If Congress won't give it to us, and the courts won't give it to us, then we can give it to ourselves."

While Creative Commons offers a welcome first step toward returning a sense of balance to copyright law, at this early stage it's only a pebble in the lake. If you want to include a ten-second clip from a Disney DVD in your home movie project, your only practical option is to commit a felony, given Disney's blanket-no policy. Hollywood and the law remain unyielding.[32]

More likely, people will ignore the law, or try to duck it, as they engage in creative acts of digital expression. Thousands—soon, perhaps millions—of people will make home-brew videos, documentaries, and digital indy films that incorporate snippets of modern movies without clearing rights. They will continue to create fan fiction that borrows from our shared culture. They will mash up music to reauthor familiar songs and riffs into startling new expressions. (They should also properly credit the creators whose works they have transformed, remixed, or parodied.)

But unless the law changes, much of this will be outlaw culture. Users are becoming aware that the law is curtailing their creative freedoms, so they are turning to technology. People have begun taking to the cyberspace speakeasies and high-tech Cotton Clubs of the Darknet, far from the prying eyes of the authorities, just as an earlier generation skirted Prohibition. (Chapter 12 explores such darknets in greater detail.)[33]

Congress, beholden to special interests that fill lawmakers' campaign coffers, has not yet become attuned to the new thirst in the land for digital rights and remix culture. Instead, as Jaszi's Digital Future Coalition learned, the entreaties of public interest groups, trade associations, and others will go unheeded on Capitol Hill as long as the entertainment companies continue to define the debate on their terms.

The law, many Internet users have decided, is stacked against digital culture. When the law becomes unreasonable, they conclude, the most sensible course of action is to route around it. Technology becomes the only tool available to rebalance the scales and reclaim lost rights. The Napster ethos—once a marketplace rebellion against the music industry's excesses—has spread and transformed into something more: a new credo, a way to bypass unsound laws like the DMCA, a social phenomenon that sees borrowing and sharing as among the most harmless, beneficent, and basic of human desires.

8 Personal Broadcasting

R AVEN DOESN'T LOOK LIKE YOUR TYPICAL NEWSMAN. Flanked by a convoy of beefy motorcycle riders, Raven saunters down the yellow line bisecting Main Street in Daytona Beach, Florida, wearing a flowered Hawaiian shirt, burnt-orange shorts, sandals, and a rumpled gray fedora hat over a straggly mane of shoulder-length black hair. If this were the '60s, Raven would be called the hippie-dippie news guy.

The camera closes in tight. "The other TV stations don't do this for you. My name's Raven, and you're watching Biketoberfest live on Internet TV." For the next several hours, as thousands of Web users catch his report from one of the world's largest gatherings of motorcycle aficionados, the forty-seven-year-old Raven will conduct interviews, offer local travelogue color, and provide anything-goes commentary refreshingly free of the conventions of local broadcasting. Raven, you see, has the two ingredients required of an Internet media star: an engaging personality and an utter lack of inhibition.

"We've got blondes, brunettes, blue eyes, green eyes—some of the most awesome babes in Daytona Beach riding on the back of a chopper," Raven reports as he approaches a Harley owner astride his bike. "If you're into bikes, they've got the most awesome machines on the road down here at Biketoberfest. This one's called a Boss Hog, with a Chevy V8 engine. This bike can smoke the tires. It feels like you've got a V8 stuck between your legs, man. It's just like your best girlfriend, baby." The leather-clad bike owner next to him smiles gamely and finally pipes up into the microphone, "It's basically the fastest motorcycle known to mankind. You can't get a faster bike unless you build it at home."

Moments later, a biker built like a small mountain and sporting an old forest growth of tattoos passes by and asks, "Are you the guy from *Girls Gone Wild?*" Raven shakes his head. "No, you're on Internet TV, live to seventy-five countries!" The Human Tattoo and Vicki, his biker chick, seem disappointed that she won't get to remove her top. Instead, she yells into the camera, "Hi, Internet TV! Woooooooo! Blond hair, blue eyes, *au naturel.*"

It's not the first time Raven has been mistaken for a correspondent from *Girls Gone Wild*, a renegade group of video voyeurs who descend on spring break destinations and shoot footage of college women baring their bosoms. "I'm not into that scene. Everything I shoot is family-oriented," Raven, less frequently known as Harold Kionka, tells me later.[1]

In the late 1990s, Raven began his online career odyssey by starting Route66live.com, Albuquerque's first Internet-only radio station. His gift for gab served him well as a DJ, but Webcasting required royalty payments to the recording industry, so in early 2002 he and his family left New Mexico for the video-friendly pastures of Daytona Beach. For income, Raven spends nights mopping floors and cleaning grease traps as a janitor. By day, he serves as owner, station manager, producer, and on-air personality for *Daytonabeach-live*, which brings live coverage of events in the resort town to an average of twenty thousand viewers a day. The twenty-four-hour Internet TV station airs live programming about ten hours a day; the rest is rebroadcast from earlier tapings. When Raven heads off for his night job, he plops an old-fashioned videotape into the VCR and streams it onto the Web. He pulls it off on a shoestring budget. He runs a small production studio out of his home, using a $200 analog Sony Handycam, a few secondhand computers, and a hosting service that splits his Webcast feed into fifteen hundred simultaneous streams for a grand cost of $17 a month.

"None of this is Hollywood quality, but it's all original programming," he says. "I consider a lot of what I do real reporting with no strings attached. When a major event comes to town, I'm there with my camcorder to record everything that goes down while adding some color commentary. On slower days, I still capture the city's day-to-day life."

Last summer and fall, when four hurricanes ripped through Florida, Raven captured some of the most riveting footage of the storms. More typically, he prowls the streets of Daytona Beach covering public events like the Birthplace of Speed, a three-day antique auto festival. During spring break he wades through the quarter-million people who throng the city's main street and interviews college students from around the nation. "I call it the sidewalk commando cam," he says. He does the same during Bike Week and Black College Reunion week each spring and Biketoberfest each fall. He also attends space shuttle launches, power boat races, fishing and beach activities, rock concerts, and more.

"I'm out there interviewing people just like the local Channel 7 news, only I can bring people more complete coverage, and my signal travels a lot farther," Raven says. "Some days it's almost like being a documentary filmmaker. You're showing things to people who can't be here, and that's a community service."

While Raven offers a 24/7 Internet feed, a number of amateur videographers have begun streaming taped video footage of events on their Web sites or weblogs. Lisa Rein, thirty-four, of San Francisco, has become something of a one-woman news crew. During the demonstrations against the war in Iraq, Rein took to the streets of San Francisco and Oakland, camcorder in hand, and shot footage of the marchers and speakers, including Representative Barbara Lee, singer Harry Belafonte, and antiwar activist Ron Kovic. She posted the video clips on her blog, complete with color commentary, providing much deeper, if more subjective, coverage of the events than a viewer would get by watching the local news.

I also bumped into Rein videotaping speakers at three different law and technology conferences we attended. "There are just so many interesting things happening in our lives that would make great programming," says Rein, an instructor for the University of California Berkeley Extension Online. "The networks aren't interested unless it will attract millions of dollars in advertising revenues. Meanwhile, there are people and events all around us that are meaningful and that people would love to watch. I'm trying to show other people how easy it is to create programming and set up your own TV station on the Web—without help from anyone in big media."[2]

Raven, Rein, and others are at the bleeding edge of a new kind of media experience, a meld of entertainment and journalism that might best be called personal broadcasting. Using equipment that has become relatively inexpensive and simple to use, these video pioneers are claiming a stake in territory that used to be the exclusive province of big media. Personal broadcasting is yet another example of the Internet's tendency to smash and fragment the traditional media universe by promulgating new forms of thin media: niche channels catering to small but highly loyal audiences. A few years from now, it's likely that thousands of people will pick up camcorders, connect to an Internet feed, and roll their own personal broadcasting networks.

But for Internet television to truly become mainstream, something epic needs to happen: we need to start receiving Internet feeds over our television sets rather than our computers. I don't mean MSN TV (the former WebTV), Microsoft's television-Web hybrid that never gained mass popularity. And no, not the complex home network setups that allow early adopters to stream Web pages to a television set.

Internet TV heralds something else: a revolutionary shift away from the television programming chokehold exercised by the major media companies and their cable brethren. A move that would permanently open the media floodgates to allow personal broadcasting—material from the personal media revolution. As Rein says, "To get your message out to the masses, it still has to go out over the box and hit them in their living rooms."

Such a sea change would not mean that the 27 million viewers who tune in *CSI* each week would suddenly shift their allegiance to *Daytonabeach-live*. Big brands will still rule. Professional media outlets will still create most of the programming we'll want to watch. But take Raven's twenty thousand viewers, multiply that by hundreds or thousands of channels, and suddenly you've got more than a blip. You're got a further fragmentation of the mass audience that threatens the underpinnings of big media.

More significantly, personal broadcasting and participatory media are likely to have spillover effects that change the contours of big media. David Leeson, a photographer for the *Dallas Morning News* who won a 2004 Pulitzer Prize for his photojournalism from Iraq, created a forty-minute iMovie documentary, *Dust to Dust*, about his experience as an embedded journalist during the invasion. A powerful work, it aired once on a Dallas television station before it disappeared into the ether. Leeson hopes it will gain new life in an online video repository.

"This form of personal storytelling is very powerful, real, and immediate. Nothing is glossed over," Leeson says. "The style will ultimately affect major media. I think we're heading back to the ancient forms of storytelling."

Raven agrees that something important is happening. "Although my stuff is very primitive compared to Hollywood, we are acquiring an audience, and it is growing. That totally amazes me."

The change is coming. But what shape it takes is up to us.

Warren Lieberfarb, the Hollywood insider-turned-renegade, leans across a polished table in his sun-splashed Brentwood office. The white-haired, professorial former president of Warner Home Video crinkles his eyes, club tie slightly askew, and sizes up the forces now sweeping through the media world.

"I see a very, very, very big transformation that's going to change the balance of power in media," he says, choosing his words with care. "It will step away from the broadcast and cable networks to specialized niche programming that will be accessible through on-demand services. That is the revolution. And nothing is going to stop this."[3]

By the sheer force of his personality, Lieberfarb almost single-handedly led the effort to create a new medium for the distribution of movies, cajoling, bargaining and strong-arming Hollywood moguls and directors who opposed the new format, including powerful forces at Disney, Paramount, and Fox. (No fool, he won't name names.) He more than earned his moniker, the father of the DVD.

Remarkably, Lieberfarb now finds himself in a new field, of sorts, at age sixty. The longtime Hollywood heavy hitter, who once presided over the world's largest film library at Warner, has joined the innovate-or-die, tradition-smashing tech world. As a top consultant to the Microsoft team working on home entertainment technologies, he is putting together program ideas for an Internet that will become an increasing source of secure, full-motion, full-screen video procured from a wide range of new, independent voices.

"All this is going to bypass the broadcast and cable networks," he says. "The whole notion that you sit at a television at a designated time and you tune in to watch what they say you watch—it's over. It's going to take a while, but it's over."

Just as the Internet and the proliferation of low-cost digital tools have reshaped other media, so the new technologies will transform our notion of television. A few years from now, when you say "television," it may no longer be synonymous with the box in your living room because you also will be watching it on your handheld mobile device or tablet PC. "What's on TV" may no longer be synonymous with network and cable programming because you'll be able to access video feeds from a wide range of new content providers. When you do watch television in your living room, you'll still wield a remote control, but you may be watching it on a stand-alone digital box or one that's hooked up to a media-center device or wirelessly connected to a PC, giving you the power to pull niche material from a gushing fire hose of sources.

"People are going to discover that content doesn't have to be produced by the major media companies," Lieberfarb says.

Who will provide this new wealth of programming? In many cases, ordinary individuals. Servers—powerful computers that transmit data—were once confined to big businesses, but now they're reaching the consumer market. Even PCs connected to peer-to-peer networks are now fast enough to process large video files, especially with compression technologies like DivX. This portends a major shift in the media ecosystem. It means individuals are gaining power over media at the expense of the corporations that have traditionally controlled the distribution gateways. And it means we need to rethink our metaphors. Channels, after all, are artificial creations. What we really want are not more channels but more choice. Anyone who runs a file-sharing service out of his house has essentially turned into a broadcast station or movie distributor.

Lieberfarb is not saying the old order of big media programming will be overthrown by a cabal of camcorder-wielding Young Turks. But he is saying that the major media companies will no longer exercise exclusive control over what Americans watch on TV. "There is this attitude in the media industry that we're the ones that make the big-time media that people want. Yet it's always been dark horses that the establishment didn't see that have created the changes in the media landscape. HBO was a dark horse. CNN was a dark horse. ESPN was a dark horse. So were VCRs. And the technophobia in the media industry, the resistance to changing business models, the gut instinct to use their monopoly power to extract financial benefits—all this will not serve the media companies well in the coming era."

Formidable business interests will oppose a mass rollout of easily accessible on-demand media for the public because it threatens their existing business models, Lieberfarb says. In the years ahead, vertically integrated media companies will use their marketplace dominance and their clout in Congress, the regulatory agencies, and the courts in an effort to maintain their role as exclusive intermediaries, as gatekeepers of information and entertainment.

"That's why I think audiovisual media, available online on demand, will take place from the edge"—here he holds his hands wide apart—"and not from the center of the media industry. Change is not going to come from the media conglomerates that have too much at stake in protecting the status quo."

As the proliferation of digital video recorders brings true time shifting to the masses and further fractionalizes linear media, we will increasingly turn toward the edges of the media ecosystem to supplement our visual diets.

What does that mean in practical terms? "The edge can mean pornography," Lieberfarb drolly says, surprising me a little. But history bears him out. After all, adult movies, available largely through a real-time video-on-demand system, generate about four-fifths of entertainment profits in hotel rooms nationwide. "Every new media has started with pornography," he says, and the evidence suggests that adult material will be at the leading edge of the narrow-interest programming that people are willing to pay for.

What will kick-start the niche video revolution? Not alternative politics. Not hippie-dippie news.

Cyberporn.

When I first encounter Gregory L. Clayman, president of VS Media, I begin by asking how digital technologies are enabling new business models. But Clayman wants to show me a buxom blonde gyrating on a bed in front of a Web cam. Who am I to argue?[4]

Half an hour's drive from Lieberfarb's office, VS Media's headquarters are tucked into the corner of a remote office park in Calabasas, California, on the southwestern fringe of the San Fernando Valley. Dubbed San Pornando Valley by some wags, the area is where 95 percent of all domestic adult movies are taped.

VS Media's offices are disappointingly staid: tasteful framed prints of David Hockney and Roy Lichtenstein line the walls, but there's not so much as a Safe Sex poster or bawdy bumper sticker in sight. Tanned and cherubic, Clayman sports a trim beard and open-collar dress shirt. He calls his company the world's largest aggregator and distributor of adult content for the Internet. In the grand tradition of Internet media companies, VS Media produces no original material. Instead, they use independent contractors that operate professional studios in Prague, Buenos Aires, and other cities in North and South America and Europe to produce six hundred hours a day of live adult entertainment for more than a hundred thousand adult Web sites, including Playboy, Penthouse, Vivid, Spice, and adult star Jenna Jameson's personal Web site. "If you go to those sites and click on live girls, you're clicking on us," Clayman says. "We're the Time Warner of adult programming online." Founded in 1996, the forty-employee company brings in more than $20 million a year.

A former insurance adviser who now lives in nearby Malibu, Clayman sits down in front of a computer and surfs over to his company's flagship offering, Flirt 4 Free. The live site lets users communicate with what you might call interactive mistresses. When we arrive, the tease show is just heating up.

"Let's talk to Kristen," Clayman says. "She has no idea who I am." He types out a message on his keyboard: "Blow my friend JD here a kiss, please."

Seconds later, Kristen, clad in a revealing negligee, fetchingly purses her lips, cups a hand, and blows a kiss into the camera. I'm a rookie at this, and Clayman notices my surprise. "She can read your remarks?" I ask.

"Oh, yeah!" he says. "She's talking to a bunch of us right now. She will not get naked or do anything too crazy until you take her into a private room. The girls' job is to get you into a one-on-one, at $5 a minute. Then you get to do whatever you want with her: chat with her, listen to her, command her to take her clothes off and show you her butt."

The streaming video image is small and occasionally fluttery, but the interactivity is unmistakable. Kristen caresses her bra in response to the chat messages sent by twenty or so lonely guys hunkered in front of computer screens somewhere. From the comfort of her queen-size bed in a nondescript room—Clayman doesn't know what country she's in—Kristen controls the Web cam, sees an image of herself performing, and occasionally types a comment in response to chat room suggestions. Now someone named socalkid implores, "Zoom in on that sexy ass pleez." When she does, he types, "Yummy. mmmmmmmmmmm."

At first blush, this may not sound like a great leap forward for mankind. But revolutions are messy affairs. People being people, some will choose to make great art, others will try to elevate the individual in the political process, and still others will revel in the glories of Kristen.

Clayman ends our virtual tour by showing me other VS Media assets: a voyeur site with peep cams (yes, "the girls" know the cameras are there); a huge library of private streaming movies; and an adult auction site, where users place bids on porn queen Jenna Jameson's clothing ("used panties! worn & wet!!!"), novelties, photos, and even a Dodge sports car, Jenna Jameson's RT10 Viper Roadster, with an opening bid of $45,995. "Believe it or not, somebody will buy this," he says.

Copyright comes into play here, too. VS Media is the authorized sales agent for the Pamela Anderson and Tommy Lee sex-tape video. Post it on your site without a license, and chances are you'll be hearing from the company's agent, APIC Worldwide. (Steve Easton of APIC tells me they send out a total of three hundred to five hundred cease-and-desist letters a month to porn site operators, with the large number of infringers centered in Eastern Europe.)

Clayman eventually does get around to discussing business models. "Adult content always leads the technology race. It's less expensive to produce than a Hollywood movie, and people will pay for it even though the quality is not 100 percent perfect. Hollywood's in a bind. They're afraid to transition into this new online medium, so they look at it as the enemy."

The next major milestone, looming tantalizingly close on the horizon, is what Clayman and many others call interactive television, but it's really not much different from the on-demand model that Lieberfarb described. Hollywood looks at interactive media as an opportunity to shop or upsell merchandise, but the studios get nervous about true interactivity because they lose control over the entertainment experience, Clayman says.

"Interactive TV over the Internet is the ultimate killer app. This takes us to a whole new level," he says. "When the day comes in twelve to thirty-six months when you're sitting back on your couch or watching on command in a hotel room and you grab your keyboard and cruise over to Channel 70 and you pick the model you like and the girl is sitting right in your TV saying, 'JD, do you like this?'—I've got to be honest, the next closest thing to that is illegal."

Clayman says he is negotiating with several digital cable providers and media companies like Playboy to make it happen. Under early versions of the plan, the cable or satellite providers would not allow viewers out onto the open Internet, where they could watch a channel like *Daytonabeach-live*. Instead, the vision centers on walled gardens: best bookstores, best auction houses, best adult entertainment, with premium offerings from a handful of partners. "It's just a matter of how fast the convergence of TV and Internet access happens and who gets there first," he says. "If this country ever gets ubiquitous broadband into the home, cyberporn will no doubt help finance it."

As the interview winds down, Clayman suddenly straightens, newly energized, and taps a new Web address into his browser. "There's a girl named Sugar I want you to meet."

It's no coincidence that amateur video and digital creativity are exploding at the same time that big media are facing dislocation and fragmentation. Traditional television is broken. At minimum, a historic churn is under way. Ratings continue to spiral downward as millions of people—especially the young—peel away from the tube to make cool stuff and to engage with other media: video games, weblogs, Flash animations, DVDs, mobile devices. As network executives lose their jobs and prime-time schedules get retooled, it never occurs to the media barons that the fundamental problem may lie not in the programming—the shows on the broadcast networks and cable have rarely been of higher quality—but in the medium.

The problem is television itself.

For decades, television served as the prototypical mass medium, a soothing electronic temple that offered a straightforward Faustian bargain: mass entertainment in return for a consumer culture built on mass consumption. But we are increasingly becoming a world of splintered tribes, a niche society where individual culture has replaced the illusion of mass culture. As we fragment in our tastes, habits, and lifestyles, so, too, does our most popular medium.

How to put television's pieces back together? We need to arrive at a new place of user participation and interaction. The tools are at hand: a converged cable TV and Internet gateway that lets subscribers pay a small monthly fee (80 percent of Americans already pay for cable TV or satellite) in return for a high-speed freeway ramp connecting us to hundreds of niche video channels created by entrepreneurs, amateurs, and independent professionals.

Will the companies controlling the pipes into our houses also control what comes through it? Will they continue to be our visual gatekeepers? "No," Lieberfarb says firmly. "People will be able to access any Web sites delivering movies and video." When cable was created in the early 1970s, he reminds me, the government set up an oversight regime with the objective of creating diversity in programming. "If we believe in freedom of speech, a corollary to that is program diversity," he adds with a flourish. Cable took us part of the way. Digital technology and the Internet will take us the rest.

It's not clear whether Microsoft wants to play gatekeeper of the Internet video flowing into our living rooms. But what if the gatekeepers disappear altogether? Already, a fledgling P2P file-sharing system called konspire2b lets you create Internet broadcasts and subscribe to channels that match your interests, with the files arriving—drip by drip—over several hours. Akimbo, a Silicon Valley start-up, has rolled out a personal video recorder that retrieves TV shows through a high-speed Internet connection. TiVo, which pioneered the personal video recorder category, plans to add Internet delivery this year.

Individuals, too, are becoming distributors. Mark Pesce, an American living in Australia, says he plans to string together a suite of open-source software that automatically takes all the digital television programming he has recorded—*The Sopranos*, *ER*, *24*, and *CSI*, among other shows—and make them available on his Web server "so that anyone can access it, at any time, from anywhere in the world." The media companies, he says, are "not forward-looking enough to figure out for themselves how to get in front of superdistribution."

If we're not yet ready for such a vision, other observers believe that video recording services like TiVo could one day compete directly with cable by becoming content distributors. A movie studio or independent programmer could send a film or video short via the Internet directly to recipients through a digital recorder. TiVo has inked a deal with Standard Film Trust to transmit short films directed by celebrities directly to TiVo recorders. And even Disney has expressed an interest in going directly to viewers without a cable or satellite middleman.

"In the long run," TiVo founder Mike Ramsay tells me, "if you turn on your TiVo, you'll see programming. Whether it comes to you from the Internet or over satellite, cable, or a phone line, we don't care, and you're not going to care where it comes from, either."[5]

That's true, as long as the new technology delivers on its promise of blowing away the gatekeepers of big broadcasting, as long as the corporations providing the connections won't serve as choke holds on what material is allowed to enter our living rooms.

Pesce—founder of the Interactive Media Program at USC's School of Cinema-Television and now a visiting lecturer at the Australian Film Television and Radio School—thinks it has already happened. "I'm not telling you broadcasting is *going* to be obsolete. I'm telling you that it's *already* obsolete. It's a done deal," he wrote in a May 2004 essay in *Mindjack*. "We've seen the lightning strike, and all we're doing now is waiting for the thunderclap. The only thing holding broadcasting together today is inertia, marketing, and copy protection. Once a programming producer figures out that they can distribute their programming via broadband, it's all over. . . . All of this can be summed up in a very neat phrase: *as broadband succeeds, broadcasting will fail.*"[6]

9 Edge TV

"T HAT WAS A VERY NICE PRESENTATION," A HOLLYWOOD
studio chief said to a delegation from TiVo after seeing the
device in action. "Now go set yourselves on fire."[1]

Not everyone is thrilled about digital technologies transforming us from
a push society to a pull society. Even as big media continue to send material
down one-way pipes to a compliant passel of consumers—or, more
precisely, delivering millions of eyeballs to advertisers—we are slowly
beginning to demand much greater control over media. To some degree we
expect to interact with media, to create a sense of intimacy. We want media
to bend to our wishes and to become our personal media. That is a profound shift.

The conventional wisdom holds that television is a lean-back experience, while computer users lean forward. The living room is our escape
from the swirl of modern life, a refuge to take time out and be entertained
by someone else. That remains largely true (less so in Japan, where close to
half the public uses computer screens to watch television), but the overall
trend is toward greater engagement. We are becoming more selective in our

program choices, more vocal about the kinds of entertainment and information coming into our homes, and less willing to lend our eyeballs to a single entity to engage us for an entire evening.

In Great Britain, research from the BBC shows that people want to do more than simply lean back. Instead, they want to "get intimate with their TV," a finding that surprised the researchers. The audience wants to actually shape the programs in some fashion. Some people want to create their own material, either from scratch or by using digital editing tools that a broadcaster might supply. Others hunger for more personalized news—ultralocal newscasts focusing on small swaths of communities and towns.

"I think people have leaned back for fifty years because that's all they've been able to do," Ashley Highfield, the BBC's director of new media and technology, tells me by phone. "I don't think people necessarily want a lazy experience for an evening. The game industry has certainly shown that it's a myth to think people aren't prepared to sit in front of a screen and do something."[2]

If television is to thrive again, we must reinvent it to fit into viewers' lives instead of the other way around. No longer will a handful of media executives in New York and Los Angeles serve as gatekeepers to our entertainment and news programming.

Cable companies never imagined such a future when they began experimenting with interactive, on-demand media beginning in the 1970s, resulting in ham-fisted attempts at creating virtual stores and online communities. More interesting was a joint experiment in time shifting begun in 1991 called Your Choice TV. Eight major cable systems, serving a test market of twenty-five thousand subscribers, mimicked the coming world of digital programming by devoting twenty-four channels to a single show apiece. CBS, ABC, NBC, HBO, ESPN, and other networks signed on and contributed their most popular shows. If you missed a program you wanted to watch—say, *60 Minutes*, *Saturday Night Live*, or an HBO special—Your Choice TV would rebroadcast the show repeatedly for three consecutive days.

"The consumers loved it, because it gave them the ability to access programs nearly on demand," recalls John S. Hendricks, chairman of Discovery Communications and founder of the Discovery Channel. "We were convinced that video on demand for a television product would be huge."[3]

Two things finally overtook the original Your Choice TV concept: the media companies couldn't agree on how to split up the revenue, and digital storage experienced stunning advances. "In the early '90s, we couldn't imagine that you could efficiently store a two-hour movie for easy digital access," Hendricks says. That technological advance is ushering in what Hendricks calls the third wave of television.

The first wave arrived with traditional broadcast television, where viewers watched a limited amount of programming pushed to you by the big three networks. The second wave came in the 1970s and 1980s with cable television, giving viewers additional niche program choices divided by genre. "The third revolution of television is at our doorstep, and it's all about offering people television on demand," Hendricks says. "This is the way everyone felt three decades ago with the advent of cable, and the idea is equally compelling and simple: television on your time schedule."

Four advances in digital technology are spurring a shift toward on-demand television: smarter, beefier boxes, an explosion in programming, better compression, and faster pipes. Personal video recorders of one flavor or another are forecast to be in more than half the nation's 107 million homes with televisions by the end of the decade. (About 72 million homes have cable, and 19 million homes get TV over a satellite dish.) The cost of content creation keeps dropping, giving video makers, documentary filmmakers, and Webcasters like Raven an almost level creative playing field with the big boys. Advances in compression enable chunky media files to be sent over the Net without a loss in image quality. And half of Americans now have high-speed Internet connections.

When the history of television's third wave is written, perhaps we'll mark its starting point at 1975, when Sony launched the Betamax, the first home-use videocassette recorder, and cofounder Akio Morita announced the concept of time shifting. Although VCRs have become staples of most American homes, they continue to be dumb, infernal machines that essentially serve as Blockbuster playback devices, as one wag put it. So let's fast-forward to 1999 and the invention of personal video recorders. PVRs, also called DVRs, deliver the goods on Morita's original vision of time shifting. Tellingly, the disruptive digital technologies of the PVR originated with TiVo and ReplayTV, two Silicon Valley start-ups that also had no ties to the entrenched entertainment industry. (Some observers suggest that Sony would never have introduced the Betamax if it had owned a movie studio in the 1970s; it acquired Columbia Pictures, now Sony Pictures, in 1989.)

Time shifting was not an option when I was a kid. I remember dashing home from Little League baseball just in time to catch *Batman* or *Laugh-In*.

That was appointment television: if you missed an episode, it was a six-month wait for summer reruns. How our family could have used a PVR!

It's hard to describe how liberating a personal video recorder can be until you see one in action. "VCR on steroids" doesn't do it justice. TiVo essentially allows every viewer to create her own private television channel.

With a TiVo or PVR, a viewer can pause live television, watch a show from the beginning while it's still being recorded, watch a previously recorded show while two other programs are being recorded, rewind live television to catch the beginning of a show (if it's on the right channel), jump back seven seconds to replay mumbled dialogue, fast-forward through commercials, retrieve recorded programs instantly, scroll through programming choices two weeks in advance, sample obscure fare you never thought you'd try, automatically record all the Harrison Ford movies that come along, and create season passes that made sure you never missed an episode of your favorite shows. Later models allow you to program your PVR from an Internet connection (in Japan, you can do this with your cell phone), view digital photos and home movies, listen to MP3 music files, and network up to ten machines in your home, so you can watch *Six Feet Under* in your bedroom even if you recorded it in the family room.

Little wonder that actor Mike Meyers told an interviewer, "TiVo is my god," sitting FCC chairman Michael Powell said, "TiVo is God's machine," and *New York Times* tech columnist David Pogue wrote, "Live TV is for suckers." (Gadget-hound disclosure: I don't own a TiVo. I own two.)

Some 5 million households now own a PVR, and that number is expected to reach 30 million by 2009. What most purchasers do not realize, as they place these shiny boxes under their television sets, is that the PVR has the heart of a computer. No videotape, just a hard drive, TV tuner card, modem, and software that records shows and downloads an updated channel guide each day. Almost by stealth, convergence has crept into our homes.

Big Entertainment long ago colonized the living room, but as digital technology intrudes into that sacred space, the balance of power is shifting from the television networks and Hollywood studios to the users. TiVo and other PVRs unshackle us from the fifty-year tyranny of the TV schedule. PVR aficionados suggest it will have wide ripples in society: it saves us time, fits TV into our busy schedules rather than the other way around, lets us uncover buried programming gems, frees us from the *three years* we would otherwise spend watching commercials over the course of a lifetime, and even provides a small measure of satisfaction in zinging the media goliaths.

Researchers who have studied TiVo in the wild say it makes us watch five to six additional hours of television per week. But any TiVo devotee will tell you it's not about watching more television, it's about watching *better* television. With a little practice, a viewer can fast-forward through a major league baseball game in forty minutes without missing a pitch, zip through the interminable time-outs at the end of an NBA game, skim through obnoxious socialite Emily Gilmore on *The Gilmore Girls*, or heartlessly shoot past PBS's fund-raising breaks to get to the good stuff.

As we acquire new viewing habits, PVRs are changing us culturally. According to one study, PVR owners don't know which channel they're watching or which network or brand is delivering the shows. "Network line-ups will have less impact on viewers who no longer identify their favorite shows with the networks broadcasting them," the study by PVR Monitor said. "If this trend continues, the network may cease to be a recognizable consumer brand."[4]

I see other changes in my family and friends. My young son thinks television is about sitting down and picking from a list of shows that have been recorded. Relatives tell me that having a PVR is the only way the family can sit down together for a meal. I have friends with PVRs who can barely sit through commercials or watch force-fed movie theater previews. I, too, have been spoiled by the PVR's siren song. At times I find myself in the car listening to the radio, and my finger impulsively twitches toward a nonexistent replay button. On the Web, TiVo fan sites have taken life. Lukas Karlsson built a Web site that shares with the world what show is playing on his TiVo, the lineup of what he has recorded, and what shows his digital pet intends to record for him. Other TiVo users have used RSS feeds to create virtual "networks" that allow friends and bloggers to discover the person's favorite shows. Hello, Everyman TV.

"There's a surprising amount of religious zeal around this," TiVo founder Ramsay tells me in his trademark Scottish brogue.[5] "We felt from day one that we were revolutionizing television. But it's not until you discover what you can do that you realize how much a slave you were to the old way. When you have five hundred channels and there's nothing on, television is definitely broken. Just as the PC revolution and the Internet have empowered people to be in charge of their own information and their own destiny, TiVo is putting people in charge of their home entertainment. My car has a TiVo license plate, so I get messages under my windshield wipers saying things like, 'TiVo has changed my life.' I think we may have tapped into something primal. It reflects a social change we're seeing all around us. If people want to do or change something, they just go and do it. They don't have to wait in line or ask for permission. The ripples from that as a social trend are far broader than television."

One new door that companies like TiVo has opened up is the concept of "space shifting." Ramsay—quick-witted and easygoing, with a neatly combed crop of salt-and-pepper hair and mustache to match—had not heard the term before, asking me whether I meant the space-time continuum. Well, no. Just as time shifting gave people the ability to watch television on their own schedules, so space shifting lets us experience home entertainment—television, movies, video, photos—in any room or on a mobile device. At TiVo headquarters, a low-slung set of white buildings set in a San Jose office park filled with once high-flying start-ups, they call it multiroom viewing: anything you watch on a late-model TiVo you can watch on your second machine.

"The whole question of where you're allowed to watch something has become a source of controversy because of the rights issues," Ramsay points out. Historically, customers have had the right to buy a CD or DVD, play it in a portable player or laptop, and travel wherever they want. But the rules for fluid digital media have not yet been set. The entertainment industry wants tight controls in place to prevent television shows and movies from being traded online. "In the electronic world, your fair use rights are becoming narrowed over the physical world," he says.

TiVo has staked out a middle approach by letting customers transfer a show within a single domain, such as a house, but preventing people from sending a show to a friend, relative, or neighbor over the Net. Customers can hack their TiVo boxes to increase storage capacity, but "military-grade" encryption prevents them from transferring shows to an unauthorized device such as a personal computer. Under pressure from Hollywood, TiVo introduced additional restrictions in early 2003 that prevent people from watching the same program on more than one machine at a time in the same home.

Even that was not enough. In mid-2004, the MPAA and National Football League petitioned the FCC to stop a modest new feature the company planned to introduce called TiVoToGo. The company wanted to give people the ability to watch video on their other devices, such as a laptop or a vacation home TV—super-secure encryption would prevent it leaking into the Darknet. But Hollywood and the NFL objected that customers might share programming with a friend, perhaps in a football blackout zone. The FCC chuckled a bit and, for once, sided with the public. But as Ramsay told me afterward, "It's scary when you feel that you have to go to the FCC for permission to do something."

The company has gone to great lengths to prove to the entertainment companies that it can be trusted with their material. Howard Look, the vice president in charge of TiVo's interface, settles into a modular, *Jetsons*-style purple chair just off the main lobby a few weeks after returning from another road show with executives at Universal, Disney, Fox, Viacom, NBC, and Discovery Communications. He says, "I've met TV executives who vigorously shake my hand and say, 'I love your product. It's changed the way I watch TV.' Then they put on their company hat and say, 'However, we need to talk with you about several copyright issues.' In general, the industry remains resistant to change, as they've historically been. I think we're still in that period where they're not quite sure what to make of us, and our job is to convince them we're a friend, not foe, and this is an opportunity to create new businesses and generate new revenue streams."[6]

Ramsay is a bit more blunt. "It's not unusual that a lot of the innovation in entertainment has not come out of the entertainment industry. Look at Pixar, which for many years was a technology-oriented company that did 3-D special effects. It's now one of the highest-quality animation companies around. There's a benefit to not being part of an industry that's encumbered by all the baggage that comes along with it. A lot of what you see right now in the traditional media industry is people not wanting to change. And that resistance gives outsiders like us an opportunity to think creatively about the consumer's needs and wants. Will digital technology change everything? I think it will. It won't be just DVR. As the media world moves from analog to digital technology, it's opening up opportunities for change that are fundamental and phenomenal."

Perhaps the most profound change lying just over the horizon is what industry insiders call file-serve television, or distributed TV. I think it deserves a less techie name: Edge TV.

The idea behind Edge TV is disarmingly simple: hit a button on your remote and summon up almost any TV show or film, past or present. Say you wanted to watch *Hill Street Blues* or *I Love Lucy*, but your local cable company doesn't carry it. You could enter the title on your TV screen, and a directory listing would report back on ten places where you could download it for a modest fee.

How does it work? One possibility is that the cable company stores the shows on centralized computers you can access. Another possibility is that your PVR connects with millions of other boxes on the edges of the network so they can not only receive and store programs but also pass them along. It would all be legal as long as your bulked-up box had been deputized by the copyright owner to send the show to any paying customer.

Stewart Alsop, who sits on TiVo's board of directors, wrote about file-serve television in his technology column for *Fortune* magazine. Alsop, Ramsay, and Hendricks have kicked around the idea during "blue sky" sessions in the TiVo boardroom, and they expanded on the concept in separate interviews.

A light form of file-serve television is already in the marketplace: cable's video on demand. With video on demand, subscribers can access hundreds of hours of programming at any time. Shows and movies are streamed, not downloaded, so viewers can pause, rewind, and fast-forward but not skip ahead to certain scenes. Selling points: immediacy and no video to return to the store. But standard video on demand is a mostly ho-hum affair, offering mostly familiar movies and recycled cable shows. The biggest such system operating today offers about 1,500 hours of material, and many experts think that scaling much beyond that will be hard because the companies' regional file servers—basically, racks of giant DVD players—pose a bandwidth bottleneck at some point. The National Football League is working on a video-on-demand service that would let you summon up the Catch, the Tuck, the Ice Bowl. Hendricks, who hinted he may like to roll out a Discovery-on-Demand channel one day, says the amount of programming could climb to 5,000 hours in a few years.[7]

But even 5,000 hours is a drop in the bucket. The television and movie industries in this country alone produce more than 130,000 hours of programming a year. Toss in the archives of shows from past years, global programming, and content from creative new sources, and you're into the many millions of hours. The cable companies' vision of video on demand, then, is an advance over its meager pay-per-view offerings, which serve up a dozen or so months-old movie titles—but it's not much of an advance. "You'd be able to access only a narrow funnel of content, just as content programmers now decide what viewers get to see," Alsop says.[8]

By contrast, Edge TV relies not on their machines but on ours. Instead of a modest number of central storage bins owned by cable companies, you'd have a massively dispersed system of hundreds of thousands or millions of devices in users' homes. Such a widely distributed network offers not just the ability to store more data but also solves the storage limitations and network bandwidth choke point of centralized computers. Thus millions of hours of video could be stored and shared, with some of it arriving instantaneously and some of it drip-loaded over time. In such a decentralized system, high-demand material like just-aired prime-time dramas and new hit movies would move out onto many thousands of hard drives, while low-demand fare like *My Mother the Car* would presumably be found on only a few dozen hard drives. The marketplace would decide. Edge TV would differ from the model being devised by Hollywood and the cable companies in this important way: shows would not be streamed and then vanish. Instead, they would be stored permanently on our home devices.

In a 2001 article in *Inside* magazine, Tom Watson and Jason Chervokas explained how video file-sharing might work through thousands of interconnected personal networks: "Using your broadband access, you build a library on your next-generation personal video recorder, or on remote banks of huge hard drives maintained for you for a small fee. With an evolved version of Aimster, you swap that content with like-minded friends in real time—baseball highlights, Ramones videos, *Honeymooners* episodes, amateur porn."[9]

Like the Internet itself, the greatest appeal of Edge TV is its democratic, freewheeling nature. Anyone, from a homeowner to a Hollywood studio, could store video on a digital disc and deliver it on demand. (This is why I think Edge TV is a better name. The term file-serve television refers only to the mode of distribution, while Edge TV suggests a change in the underlying nature of the programming itself—stuff we can access from the edges of the network.)

One of the biggest beneficiaries of Edge TV may be creative professionals whose works flashed by on television or in theaters and then vanished. Kyra Thompson, an Emmy-winning documentary maker whose credits include *Dying to Tell the Story* (about journalists who risk their lives during hostilities), *Soldiers of Peace* (about a group of children from Colombia who were nominated for the Nobel Peace Prize), and *Spellbound* (about spelling bees), points out that PBS, HBO, and four smaller cable networks are virtually the only broadcast outlets for documentaries today, and considerable pressure is exerted to make the works commercially viable. A film such as the ninety-minute *Dying to Tell the Story* is an imposing undertaking; it took nearly a year to make, cost $600,000, and aired two or three times before it disappeared. "The idea of having your work seen by a new audience sounds wonderful," she says, although she cautions that in such a democratic medium, "the gems are not easy to pull off."[10]

TiVo's Howard Look recognizes the consequences of opening up the video floodgates. "To be able to tap into vast libraries of content—whether it's the good stuff that the TV or movie studios have produced over the past century, or stuff that your neighbor or someone halfway across the world produced—that's pretty exciting to me. I have a fascination with bridge building, with anything having to do with the civil engineering of big things. Once every few months a show will come along on that topic. But I would love to have the ability to say, 'Find me every documentary you can on the building of every bridge, every dam, every canal.' And I'd pay a buck or so for every episode I'd come across."

Consider other possibilities for Edge TV: music fans, like Deadheads of old, could follow their favorite bands virtually. Why not U2-TV? Why not a Puppy Channel (an idea pushed by a Cleveland ad executive, without success, since 1996)? Sports would be a natural fit: Lakers TV, Mets TV. Enthusiasts of cricket or Australian rules football could watch their team's latest match. A couple who watched *Sabrina* with Harrison Ford could immediately compare it to the original version with Humphrey Bogart. Vacationers could tune in to travelogues made by people who actually live in those far-away locales and know the hidden-away gems. A news junkie could see how the foreign press is covering the U.S. president. A forty-year-old woman could see how to perform a breast exam, and homeowners stuck on a self-built brick patio could scout out an instructional video.

Grassroots politics also might come into play. Look recalls, "In 2000 I talked with someone from the Ralph Nader presidential campaign. He told me, 'You should see his stump speeches. People never hear his message on the nightly news. Can I get it out there on TiVo?' No, but he could with file-share television."

Andy Wolfe, who was chief technology officer of Sonicblue[11] when it bought ReplayTV in 2001, says the combined company's grand plan was to build boxes that let users connect to each other or even become broadcasters. "We got calls from church people who wanted to distribute their Sunday morning sermons over the TV. Others wanted to create surveillance systems, letting you check in with a babysitter from a friend's house. There was lots of excitement from people interested in building new things on top of this."[12]

Only time and experimentation will tell where Edge TV may take us.

Certainly some untold number of people will want to watch well-made video from sources we never knew existed. The result won't be video nirvana—much of the material will be junk—but we'll likely be surprised by the depth of sophistication and talent found in the hobbyist world.

Then there is Edge TV's appeal to the nostalgia buff in all of us, for the past is where most of our shared cultural reference points now reside. Within a few years, boomers could be viewing long-vanished shows from their youth: *Soupy Sales*, *Captain Kangeroo*, *Lassie*, *Wonderama* with Sonny Fox, *The Mickey Mouse Club*, *The Many Loves of Dobie Gillis*, the early years of *American Bandstand*. We could dust off curiosities like *Sonny and Cher*, *Father Knows Best*, and *Happy Days*, or revel in the kitsch value of *Get Smart* or *Honey West*. Such a service also would prove to be a bonanza—*Bonanza!*—to students of history or culture. Share with your children the 1969 moon landing, just as you saw it.

Edge TV appeals, then, to our love of niche and kitsch. It extols the surprising, the serendipitous, the offbeat—like Ramsay's love of *Monty Python*, or Look's fondness for bridge building.

Now, what we are really talking about is a celestial jukebox for television—a system that gives users fingertip access to vast libraries of video by relying not on big, centralized computers but on peers at the edges of the network. As you might imagine, a few wrinkles would need to be ironed out along the way. How would anyone make money doing this?

First, the material must be protected in some way. (Piracy leaks are inevitable in any such venture, but a convenient, low-cost, legal video service will always beat the Darknet.) Second, older cable lines, originally designed as a one-way broadcast network, would eventually need an upgrade to handle two-way Internet transmissions. Third, viewers would want an easy way to sort through the flotsam and jetsam of available video. Shows would be embedded with metadata listing title, plot, brand, genre, creator, and other key points. Collaborative filtering systems would allow us to record dozens of shows but watch only those recommended by trusted friends. Some company might act as a sort of super Google for video programming by maintaining local directories of the licensed shows scattered on millions of boxes around the country. That's not too different from TiVo's current business model, which offers wish lists and a directory of shows available for recording. Fourth, the content owners would need to give their permission, with a portion of the profits going to the studio, to the pipeline provider, and to the company that has intelligently connected all those boxes. A revenue model would need to be thrashed out, probably either a pay-as-you-go micropayment system or, more likely, an all-you-can-eat subscription buffet through your existing cable operator. Marketing promotions also would factor in: trade your customer data to an advertiser in return for free access to the shows you want. Finally, rights would need to be cleared. For example, music and theme songs were licensed only for broadcast television, not the Internet. Worse, it appears that no one may own the rights for Internet distribution of old shows. It's a mess, and Congress would likely need to step in and grant a statutory license.

Ramsay says the technology for Edge TV is ready today. "The technology is the easiest piece to solve. The stumbling block is rights management. What happens to the broadcast station or cable network that has that show in syndication and is making money off that? What happens to the DVD aftermarket? They don't want to change. So this will happen very gradually. It may take five or ten years or longer for it to happen, but you'll see it."

Hendricks, the pioneering cable CEO, also believes Edge TV is an unalterable force. "Some of my colleagues in the business wish it would go away. But you can't wish it away. I think this is so powerful that it's going to happen. You'll still have a Discovery and TNT and cable channels driven by basic economics. But there will be this whole other set of businesses driven by the world of on-demand file-serve television."

Alsop agrees. "What you're really up against is a mind-set and mentality. The entire idea of file-serve television terrifies media companies. If I'm a media company and my business is selling copyrighted material, then I must control it from end to end, and I must have an absolute assurance that every time I sell a copy of a program it can't be further copied and the value of my copyright can't be diluted. That leads companies with that way of thinking to a centralized approach. It's not a technical issue, but one of culture and business models. Simply put, movie companies and television companies aren't thrilled to have their valuable stuff sitting on hard disks in your living room, where they might lose control over how they make money from it."

I broached the idea of Edge TV with one of the most forward-thinking TV executives I know, Martin J. Yudkovitz, shortly before he stepped down as president of NBC Digital to become president of TiVo. "You have to remember, there is a lucrative syndication market for TV shows that go off the air. That makes a hell of a lot of money for the copyright owners and for the syndicators, stations, or cable networks that broadcast them. [Syndication of *Seinfeld* has been worth about $3 billion; *The Simpsons*, about $1 billion.] Hollywood will not risk killing the golden goose until it knows exactly what the economic impact on the golden goose will be. Until then, they'll let that market develop excruciatingly slowly."[13]

As Warren Lieberfarb predicted, the first movers will come from the edges.

Suddenly, everything about television is up in the air: On what kinds of devices will we watch TV? Who gets to create visual media? How should programming be paid for? Should the government regulate Internet-based TV? What happens when viewers become their own programmers?

And this: Will the broadcast networks survive?

FCC chairman Michael Powell told the *Chicago Tribune* in 2003, "I think free, over-the-air TV is dying. I don't care how much money they made this year, they're dying. . . . In ten years free TV is going to be gone."[14]

Leave aside the future disruptive effects of Edge TV for the moment. The on-demand technologies already in the marketplace may soon bring about the end of the traditional fall season debut of new shows. The widespread rollout of PVRs would almost certainly mean the end of sweeps (good riddance) and Thursday night appointment TV. It will eventually reduce to irrelevance the logistics of scheduling choices, program lead-ins—the entire elaborate machinery by which the $60 billion television industry creates new hit shows.

Wolfe, the former Sonicblue executive who had extensive dealings with higher-ups in the entertainment industry during negotiations over ReplayTV's technology, says, "The TV people have this buggy whip problem. For fifty years they've been taught that their brilliance is in programming, and programming is the art of deciding what shows get watched when. If you sit down with TV execs, that's what they think their skill is. Not creating quality television. Somebody else does that. Their art is in programming, and that's going away. And they haven't learned how to make the adjustment."

Hendricks argues that the third wave of television doesn't mean network programmers—or the networks themselves—will disappear, just as the advent of cable did not vanquish broadcast television. "When one of these evolutionary steps comes along, it doesn't do away with the past step, it just adds to the consumer's choice," he says. Still, the mass adoption of on-demand technologies will have a far-reaching impact on the industry.

In the new era, the content creator will be king, and the network distributor will be secondary. (Most of the shows that air on the networks or cable are today created by Hollywood studios like Paramount, Warner Bros., Universal, or Columbia TriStar.) But the content producer need not be a large Hollywood studio. Hits will emerge based on quality—through collective word of mouth and online recommendation technologies—rather than through the networks' scheduling theatrics and marketing budgets.[15]

Thirty-second commercials will give way to new forms of advertising and payment schemes. Time-critical programs like news and sports and special events like the Oscars and Emmys will become more valuable to advertisers in a time-shifted, fast-forward world. New kinds of armchair critics and electronic guides will rise up to help us find the really cool stuff. Bots will roam the Net, looking for material to match our interests. (Such collaborative filtering technology needs a little work. One TiVo viewer lamented to the *Wall Street Journal* that, based on a handful of shows he had watched, "My TiVo thinks I'm gay!")

Not surprisingly, Hollywood has a very different vision for your television future. It is a future where PVRs, alternative Internet programming, and other user-empowering tools do not figure prominently. Turner Broadcasting System chief executive Jamie Kellner gave a glimpse of the industry's circle-the-wagons mind-set when he told a reporter, "any time you skip a commercial . . . you're actually stealing the programming." He later proposed that PVR users should pay a penalty fee of $250 a year for ad-free TV. (Never mind that a Yankelovich Partners study in early 2004 found that 69 percent of U.S. consumers were interested in products and services that allow them to block, skip, or opt out of mass marketing.)

Rather than embrace the new technologies, the studios and networks have decided to strike back. They have pursued a multipronged strategy that centers on blunting demand for PVRs before they gain popularity.

Step one was to follow the Sicilian proverb "Keep your friends close, but your enemies closer." Viacom, NBC, the Walt Disney Co., and DirecTV invested in TiVo, hoping to steer the PVR pioneer away from some of the more objectionable innovations pioneered by its more aggressive bad-boy cousin ReplayTV. Time Warner, Disney, and NBC became early investors in ReplayTV, hoping to gain inside knowledge and influence.

Step two: target legislators and regulators. For example, the studios and networks lobbied congressional leaders to lean on the Federal Communications Commission to adopt the broadcast flag. The FCC happily complied.

Step three: reengineer the PVR to make it less threatening. Millions of customers will bring PVR technology into their homes only when it becomes largely invisible—folded into next-generation boxes from satellite and cable companies whose sizable customer base gives them a built-in advantage over start-ups like TiVo. (Indeed, TiVo wants to get out of the business of building boxes and instead license its technology to satellite or cable operators.)

Time Warner's Mystro TV announced plans to begin service later this year with PVR-style features. But look beneath the Trojan horse's seat and you'll see several critical differences. Because the service keeps programming on centralized computers rather than the customer's box, Mystro TV can keep a tight leash on its content—and its customers—by disabling the fast-forward button during ads and restricting which programs can be recorded. Comcast, the nation's largest cable provider, has already rolled out a similar service in hopes of thwarting the on-demand threat from chewing into its control-based business model.[16] If they could get away with it, the entertainment moguls would like to see ad-skipping buttons disappear. This is why upstarts like TiVo matter. Customer-friendly features like zipping through commercials or saving a movie on your digital box for months or years could well disappear if Big Entertainment gets control of the technology.

The fourth and final element in the entertainment companies' battle plan has been to hit hard and relentlessly on the legal front. In 2001, Paramount Pictures and twenty-seven other movie studios and television networks filed four high-profile lawsuits that accused Sonicblue's ReplayTV of abetting copyright infringement. The suits also challenged the very foundation of the PVR, including owners' ability to create personal video libraries that let them watch shows repeatedly. MGM, Fox, Universal Studios, and Orion Pictures also charged that a PVR maker violates copyright law if it allows viewers to record and store shows based on genre, actor, director, or program description.

"If a ReplayTV customer can simply type 'The X-Files' or 'James Bond' and have every episode of 'The X-Files' and every James Bond film recorded in perfect digital form and organized, compiled and stored on the hard drive of his or her ReplayTV 4000 device, it will cause substantial harm to the market for prerecorded DVD, videocassette and other copies of those episodes and films," the lawsuit stated.

In essence, Hollywood was trying to take another whack at the Supreme Court's 1984 *Betamax* ruling, which legalized time shifting and the VCR—to Hollywood's everlasting regret, despite the lucrative financial gains from its legal loss.

The public was not privy to the secret discussions between the entertainment companies and Sonicblue executives, but Wolfe agreed to reveal details of the talks for the first time. Wolfe told me that the broadcasters and studios aimed for nothing less than complete control over the home entertainment experience. Press accounts focused on the entertainment companies' objections to a feature in the Replay 4000 machine that let viewers skip over entire blocks of commercials rather than having to fast-forward, and a second feature that allowed viewers to share a show with up to fifteen friends or relatives who also had ReplayTV units. You could send Grandma a show, though she couldn't forward it to anyone else. In any case, the average ReplayTV customer sent one copy-protected show a month to another person.

But Wolfe says of the controversy over the ad-skipping and show-sharing features: "That was a smoke screen. Those things were all negotiable." Hollywood, he says, had a larger agenda. "They essentially wanted to control what anyone could record on TV. They wanted sole discretion over how long you could keep a show after you recorded it. They wanted to limit how many episodes of the same show you could record. They wanted to ban thirty-second skip buttons and to prevent fast forward from reaching a certain speed. We felt those were nonnegotiable items. Nobody makes a consumer device that lets you record *The Simpsons* only once a week. We just didn't want to get into regulating customer behavior in those ways, and we didn't think there was any law that backed up their demands."

The studios and networks also made the curious legal claim that a PVR maker like ReplayTV could not build a hard disc beyond a certain memory capacity. "They wanted to limit the amount of stuff you could record," Wolfe says. "They came up with a number, but I can't tell you what it is" because of ongoing litigation.

I ask, Have we already surpassed the storage limit the studios sought?

"On my laptop," Wolfe replies with an air of mild exasperation.

Wolfe, who is now trying to raise capital for another start-up, gives this appraisal of the different entertainment industry factions: "The New York people were always interested in new business models, and the L.A. people would tell them to shut up. You always expect New Yorkers to be the arrogant ones, but the people we were dealing with from the relatively younger companies like HBO, Showtime, and MTV always wanted to listen. It was the L.A. people from Disney and MGM—relying on a business model developed more than fifty years ago—who ultimately said, 'You don't understand our business, you're a threat to our business,' and they set about to crush us."

Attorneys for the studios declined comment, citing the confidential nature of settlement negotiations. But in the end, no comment was really necessary. Before the case reached a courtroom, Sonicblue filed for bankruptcy, and its ReplayTV division was sold to a Japanese electronics manufacturer. In June 2003 the new owners began repairing relations with the entertainment industry by dropping ReplayTV's commercial-skipping and "send show" features (although an independent site, Poopli, lets owners of older ReplayTV units share shows with one another). ReplayTV's new boxes are less capable than the old ones.

Even TiVo has not entirely escaped the digital rights wars. Not long before he stepped down as president in early 2003, Morgan Guenther told me the company has the technology for users to create their own custom channel—say, a Catholic Mass channel, an animal channel, or a golf channel—by slicing and dicing pieces of programming from the various broadcasters or the Internet. But media companies have objected to having programs from different networks mixed together to create a new "channel"—even if it's one that resides only in your living room. "You'll get a vehement argument from the industry that it's not legal," he said. "It's a gray area right now."

The disruptions brought about by on-demand technologies and Edge TV's grassroots programming are occurring against the backdrop of the nation's transition to digital television. This is wrapped up in its own set of controversies.

As society adopts digital television, Hollywood has been slow to offer digital content because of fears about Napsterization. In the name of preventing piracy, Hollywood has strong-armed its satellite and cable partners to provide technology that gives content owners the ability to decrease the resolution of high-definition digital video, which would make the less pristine broadcasts less appealing to pirates, in theory. All new satellite receivers contain "down-resolution" capabilities ("image constraint," in Hollywood-speak) that can, for example, degrade the image quality of digital broadcasts on HDTV sets that don't have copy protection Hollywood deems sufficiently strong.

This time, Hollywood didn't need to arm-twist the computer and consumer electronics people. The studios made an end run around those groups by getting the FCC directly involved in governing digital delivery systems.

"The FCC is now regulating the equipment, which is something they've never done before," says tech lobbyist James M. Burger. "What's troubling is that you're ceding control of the devices in people's homes to the movie studios. Why should users have their machines controlled by the Hollywood studios changing your picture resolution?"

Privacy rights may be in danger as well: In parts of Europe, whenever a PVR owner transfers a show to a computer or records it onto a DVD, the machine silently reports that fact back to the content owner. And in this country, Hollywood continues to see the PVR as a dagger poised at its heart.

Lieberfarb, the Hollywood insider who became a convert to grassroots programming, says, "The chairmen of the media conglomerates haven't gotten past the risks of the PVR. They're stuck on the PVR, and that's trivial. That's just how people reschedule the shows they put on. What happens when there's all this new content coming into the home? What then?"

While Hollywood wrings its hands about Internet piracy and the PVR, Dallas Mavericks owner Mark Cuban's HDNet is creating more original programming in high definition than all the networks combined—and broadcasting the shows in the pristine hi-def format with no onerous digital locks and no broadcast flag, which Cuban calls "a waste of taxpayer dollars."

But the most interesting experiments in next-generation television may be taking place overseas. More than a third of Great Britain's homes get interactive digital television from Rupert Murdoch's British Sky Broadcasting, allowing them to pay bills, buy books, play games, order pizza, check local news and weather, send e-mail, select camera angles at sporting events, and choose among narrators for a science documentary. A few small cable companies have begun rolling out similar services in California, Illinois, and elsewhere.[17]

The BBC has been at the forefront of inviting people to participate in creating media, routinely publishing photos and broadcasting video sent in by users at news events and providing Internet tools to encourage civic involvement in local communities. It is now experimenting with local newscasts that let regular folks report the weather from the field.

New media director Highfield has spearheaded the BBC's expansion onto the Web and interactive television. Americans tend to think of interactive TV as something like WebTV: an Internet experience clumsily grafted onto an old medium. Not so. Highfield outlined his vision in a speech to Britain's Royal Television Society[18]: "Future TV will be unrecognizable from today, defined not just by linear TV channels, packaged and scheduled by television executives, but instead will resemble more of a kaleidoscope, thousands of streams of content, some indistinguishable as actual channels. These streams will mix together broadcasters' content and programs and our viewers' contributions. At the simplest level, audiences will want to organize and reorder content the way they want it. They'll add comments to our programs, vote on them, and generally mess about with them. But at another level, audiences will want to create these streams of video themselves from scratch, with or without our help."

New research conducted by the BCC revealed what Highfield termed "four new and significant social trends that show that the way in which we consume TV is changing forever."

First, he said, viewers are taking control of their media, choosing not just what to watch but also how, when, and where to watch it. Second, they have begun participating in the media experience by contributing their own video. Third, viewers—especially young people—are multitasking and consuming more media simultaneously. In 1952, 5 percent of all television viewing was a secondary activity; today, that figure is 50 percent. Finally, viewers have begun sharing all this material with each other. "Downloading and sharing this video is the final piece of the jigsaw and will create a killer combination that I believe could undermine the existing models of pay TV."

The killer combination he outlined consists of digital TV, PVRs, and high-speed broadband, plus the ability to share video over peer-to-peer networks on the Internet. In other words, Edge TV.

In such a world, viewers will watch traditional TV, Internet video, programs stored on a hard disc at home, and shows swapped electronically with friends on peer-to-peer networks. As broadband moves into the living room, he says, "this kind of user-generated telly will explode."

One likely scenario is that personal media will usher in an age of video vérité—video footage of individuals' lives shot on inexpensive next-generation high-definition camcorders and edited on personal computers. Just as text-based bloggers and amateur publishers took up outposts that competed with major media on the Web, so, too, will amateur videomakers become a major force when the Web realizes its multimedia potential.

Perhaps because of his age, thirty-eight, or perhaps because he works for a public institution, the BBC's Highfield does not see the onset of Edge TV as a threat to media companies. He and his bosses are working on ways to let users download and share video footage in the BBC archives. The television industry, he said, should be fostering creative solutions by producing shows that can be readily chopped up, consumed piecemeal, remixed with other material, and freely shared.

"I don't know how long the media players can hold out against the demand for this," he says. "Based on the research we've got of shifting consumer behavior away from watching linear scheduled television, we'd better get there and find a way to offer our entire output on demand. Otherwise we're just going to be marginalized."

So far, Hollywood is moving in the opposite direction. The entertainment companies have imposed rights management schemes that prevent users from sending broadcast video to a friend with a handheld device. They are pushing for further restrictions that would take away computer users' ability to manipulate digital media. And they are using hardball tactics— Sonicblue's legal bills came to more than $1 million a month—to prevent users from taking advantage of the full fruits of the digital revolution.

Consider the issue of personal video libraries. The first TiVos held 14 hours, quickly followed by 30 hours and then 80 hours. By mid-2004, top-of-the-line TiVos held up to 300 hours and ReplayTV units stored 320 hours.

Storage capacities continue to double roughly every fourteen months. By 2012, the boxes in our family room will be big enough to hold ten thousand high-definition movies, one hundred thousand uncompressed CDs, and enough MP3s so that you could listen to new songs continuously for your entire lifetime. Twenty years from now, says Rodney Books, director of MIT's Computer Science and Artificial Intelligence Laboratory, we'll be carrying around portable devices with 20 petabytes of storage—20 million gigabytes, compared with 20 gigabytes today.[19] What will we want to do with all that capacity?

It seems inevitable that as digital recorders grow in capacity, users will begin using the machines not just for time shifting but also for long-term archiving and to build personal video libraries. "The content industry is struggling with that," Ramsay says. "Soon we'll be up to 800 hours, and it will be fascinating to see how the content industry adjusts its business models."

Alsop tells me he thinks we will hit a theoretical storage roof at some point because "there's only so much television you can watch." But that assumes people will only store shows they intend to watch. What if the supercomputer attached to your television became an ally to the studios and networks? What if Edge TV enabled users on the edge of the network to become content *distributors*? It's not hard to imagine that Jermaine, your hobbyist friend down the block, could get a piece of the action every time someone visited his TV Recommendations weblog and paid a small fee to download a pastor's weekly sermon or an amateur film he likened to the next *Blair Witch Project*.

Like Highfield, I believe that a share video movement is at our doorstep. The only question is whether it will be sanctioned by the entertainment companies or forced to retreat to the Darknet. The technology is already largely in place, with peer-to-peer pipelines hooked up to wireless broadband that can pump content to any of our video devices. Now, add to this mix the new breed of portable video players. Soon we'll see pocket television sets selling for less than $200, letting us catch up on the shows we missed the night before as we take the train or bus to work.

Entertainment consultant Tim Onosko writes, "Imagine new channels with short-form programming repurposed from existing channels, scheduled MTV-style, in tiny chunks. Don't like what's on now? Wait two minutes. Now imagine that that little TV has a hard disk in it, so, like a TiVo, it could sit around, monitoring the broadcasters while you weren't watching, and grab little bits to the drive: the *Today Show* news, weather, and sports; Letterman's top ten and Leno's monologue from last night; the trailers for the movies that will open this weekend; book reviews from C-SPAN; the best plays from yesterday's ball games; financial features; soap summaries, and on and on . . . so there's always something fresh to watch, always something new that's tailored to your tastes."

Washington Post technology columnist Leslie Walker writes: "It is only a matter of time before millions of consumers will be doing things like creating custom concert videos of their favorite artists. They'll mix and match video from TV shows and DVD recordings which they (hopefully) will have acquired legally—much as music fans have been creating custom music discs and tapes for years."[20]

She's right. Let's leave it to the people. Who, after all, is in the best position to determine what short snippets the public wants to watch? Users could begin digitizing, remixing, and swapping video clips of the best Adam Sandler skits or U2 performances or the top *Saturday Night Live* routines, just as we see hundreds of thousands of people publishing and trading playlists of their favorite songs. The rights of the copyright holders would still need to be respected, so we would need an entirely new online system for clearing rights online, perhaps tied to a micropayment system. The networks and studios could try to slice and dice the material themselves, but what would be the point? By unleashing a viral marketing tsunami— by using the power of distribution from the edges—the entertainment companies would seed further demand for their brands and reach new audiences.

There is an alternative to grassroots video creation and sanctioned forms of file sharing: the Darknet. To see a glimpse of the shows already circulating in underground circles, head to the TV section of VCDquality.com, a site that serves as a sort of *TV Guide* to hundreds of bootleg programs found on underground trading networks. (Because it doesn't host the infringing material, VCDquality is off the legal hook.) Hollywood's best gambit against movie pirates and TV show bootleggers may be to enlist the creative talent at the grassroots level, to embrace the digital destiny of Edge TV by offering users the tools and financial incentives to promote long-forgotten TV shows and movies, and to consider the possibility that some entrepreneur working in a garage may find a way to add value to a studio's prized show.

How the television landscape ultimately unfolds is anyone's guess. Ramsay, the upbeat Scotsman, sees users being able to access "all the information in the world" through high-speed Internet connected seamlessly to their televisions. "A few years out, your entertainment experience will be radically different, and your choices will be different," he says. "I think nobody will go to Blockbuster to rent movies, and the idea of physical media will all but disappear, because media will be electronic and you'll be able to grab whatever you want and watch it in your home."

The question is, what will be stocked on that virtual shelf? Will it reflect a mere reshuffling of top-down media fare, or will it reflect a genuine unleashing of the digital media revolution?

Jonathan Taplin, a proponent of on-demand media who helped pioneer Internet delivery of video to the home, put it well when he told a Senate committee in 2002: "Our country has a choice of two visions of what our media culture might look like. One might be five hundred channels (owned by six corporations) and nothing on. The other might allow consumers easy on-demand access to a world of unique artistry of such power and grace as would melt the heart."[21]

10 The Sound of Digital Music

TONY ABBOTT DOESN'T RESEMBLE A DIGITAL REVOLU-
tionary. When I meet him at his tract house in Rancho
Cucamonga east of L.A., the sixty-four-year-old counselor
at nearby Chaffey College is wearing a short-sleeve plaid shirt, scuffed
brown work boots, and jeans loosened to accommodate an ample girth. At
once affable and dignified, Abbott strokes a trimmed gray beard and ushers
me into his living room.

A longtime gadget freak, Abbott has lately become something of a digital hobbyist. He and his wife, Judith, love music, and a few years ago Abbott
became exasperated by their 100- and 200-disc CD players, which weren't
up to the task of managing their 600-CD collection. So he ditched the
machines and began converting all his songs into the MP3 format using
Musicmatch Jukebox.

"What I like most is that any song is immediately retrievable," he says. "I
don't have to hunt down the dang thing anymore."[1]

He leads me across a green shag carpet and opens up a hallway closet. There, in the place of an old water heater, rests a blinking eMachines computer that can pump tunes through the speakers in any room—or even to the backyard. As we return to the living room, an Ella Fitzgerald melody gives way to Nat King Cole's "Rosetta." Abbott turns on the TV, and we see details of each song through the home network he has set up. Abbott taps a remote, breezing through the playlists of opera, classical, country-western, and dozens of other musical groupings he has assembled. One fanciful playlist is called "Moon tunes," with dozens of tunes that contain the word "moon" in the title.

Abbott is just getting warmed up. A while back he spent $80 on a low-power FM stereo transmitter and started his own tiny FM station. "I just picked a spot on the dial that doesn't have a local station and set up shop."

His neighbors get a kick out of Tony Radio at 107.1 FM—streamed from the humble computer in the hallway closet—with Abbott holding forth as a sort of digital DJ, minus the chatter and commercials. During the holidays, they tune in to hear Christmas music around the clock. "Sometimes I'll take requests," he says with a chuckle.

The FCC allows low-wattage stations like this, which can reach only a few blocks. Thousands of such stations now operate, serving campus dorms, retirement homes, and other niche populations. If Abbott streamed his Webcast over the Internet, however, he would be required to make payments to the recording industry, even if he attracted the same modest audience he gets with his FM broadcast.

Abbott thinks the recording industry exploits its artists but says he doesn't use music file-sharing services such as Kazaa or iMesh. Of the ten thousand songs he has digitized, only one came that way: Kate Smith's "God Bless America." He explains apologetically, "I searched high and low but couldn't find it in any stores."

People are still intimidated by technology, Abbott says, but his setup was simple to put together, and new wireless technologies are making it easier all the time. What seems like a geek pastime today will be commonplace tomorrow. In a few years, he suggests, on-demand digital music formats will be the rule, and "the audio CD will probably go the way of the eight-track tape, and the four-track, if you're old enough to remember."

Soon it's time to leave. As I drive away, I tune into Tony Radio and listen to an old-timey Duke Ellington medley for a few blocks before the music fades into static.

| | |

Abbott has plenty of company in the ranks of digital music tinkerers. In 2002, Erich Ringewald, a former engineer for Apple and Amazon and cofounder of Be Inc., decided with three pals to pool their music collections.

One of them, Morris Dye (a mutual friend), packed up hundreds of his CDs and loaned them to Ringewald. After ripping the tracks to a computer hard drive, Ringewald then loaded up a surplus computer in Dye's basement with their collective goodies. Finally, Dye ran a wire from his new Turtle Beach AudioTron music player to the server in his basement.

The result? Dye entertains us all night long with a sweet stream of modern and classic jazz, plucked from the 19,339 songs on his computer. "This is such a convenient way to access your music," he says. "I'll never go back to the old way." As a bonus, the music player doubles as a digital radio, which plays more than 100 Internet radio stations. The entire system cost less than $500 per household. It's legal to share legally purchased music with a few friends under the Audio Home Recording Act, despite the recording industry's efforts to mislead the public into thinking that any sharing of music is wrong and unlawful.

"Right now, this is something only hobbyists would do," Ringewald says, "but pretty soon it will go mainstream. We're in a period of transition between these little silver discs called CDs and the future of music, which is all-digital."[2]

As Abbott and Ringewald can attest, digital music is not simply music that comes out of a computer. It's music that has escaped its physical container, like a soul leaving a body. (Not all digital songs have soul, but never mind.) At one time, recorded music was bound to its format: wax, shellac, vinyl, eight-track, cassette, CD. Now, music has been unhinged from its physical moorings and reduced to raw information. Liquidity is the essential ingredient—more so than digital music's other features, such as being free for the plucking on file-sharing services.

Too often, discussions about digital music begin and end with Internet piracy. But by viewing this story through such a narrow prism, we risk overlooking the more important fundamental changes that digitization is bringing to music culture. New digital tools are fostering a rebirth of grassroots musical creativity as ordinary individuals begin to compose, recirculate, and reinvent music in imaginative ways.

How has music changed in the digital age? In almost every way. As writer

Kevin Kelly observed, "With digitization, music went from being a noun, to a verb, once again."[3] People engage with music differently now. They have new ways to create it, new ways to experience it, and new ways to share it.

Collecting and managing digital music are becoming simpler by the day. Personal playlists and mixes are replacing CDs and albums as Abbott, Ringewald, and millions of others turn to digital jukeboxes to manage their music. Now we rearrange albums, mix together different artists and songs on homemade CDs, and store thousands of songs on a 3.6-ounce gizmo. For many people, regular music CDs seem like throwbacks.

Discovering new music is getting easier, too. Collaborative filtering tools introduce listeners to new artists they like. Webcasting and satellite radio are stretching our musical tastes in new directions—and broadening market opportunities for artists and labels—by offering hundreds of niche channels that cater to listeners turned off by the wasteland of commercial radio. Subscribers to the XM or Sirius satellite services can find the kind of intimate musical experience that has all but vanished from the airwaves, with channels devoted to kids, Broadway tunes, comedy recordings, talk shows for gays and African Americans, and more eclectic material. Satellite radio scored its biggest coup in fall 2004 when Sirius signed talk show host Howard Stern, the self-proclaimed King of All Media. Stern and his team will earn $100 million a year for five years beginning in 2006. XM, meanwhile, bagged former NPR newsman Bob Edwards.

Increasingly, new artists are getting discovered online. In 2003, the Los Angeles talent scout Joe Berman typed "New Zealand indie rock bands" into a search engine and found Steriogram, a five-lad outfit from Whangerei, New Zealand. After contacting the group and hearing a demo CD, he signed them to a five-album deal with Capitol, the *Washington Post* reported.[4] The band launched a U.S. tour and landed a video on MTV.

The trend could turn traditional media models upside down. Media theoretician Clay Shirky calls it "the Big Flip."[5] The old notion of *filter, then publish* is giving way to a new sensibility of *publish, then filter*. That formula, which animates blogs and amateur publishing, also can work for music. Tools are now emerging that offer the promise of elevating talented new artists and publicizing good new music.

If managing and discovering music have become easier than ever, so has the biggest prize of all: creating music. The digital democratization of music creation has smashed even the last small barriers to entry. In the old days, even punk rockers had to pick up a guitar and learn a few chords. Now, you don't need to practice, read sheet music, or save up for a pricey instrument. For $49 and an Apple computer, aspiring musicians can turn a computer into a recording studio with a program called GarageBand (Apple even tosses in hundreds of royalty-free, professionally recorded riffs to help get you going). PC users can try their hand at composing hits, too. Similar setups would have set you back $50,000 just fifteen or twenty years ago.

The ideal of joining a rock 'n' roll band is giving way to teens huddled in front of the cool glow of computer screens in bedrooms and garages. You still need talent, patience, and pluck to write a decent tune, and let's be frank, most do-it-yourself music is a swamp of mediocrity. But as people create new music, sample digital snippets, and mash familiar tunes into startling new works—as they use specialty tools to combine tracks, speed up the tempo, edit offensive words from a song, and correct off-key singing (a must-have in my household)—they are breathing new life into a suffocating industry. Just as the Brownie camera changed photography from a professional craft to an everyday pursuit, so, too, is digital technology democratizing music.

Welcome to the age of the amateur.

"Before the broadcast era of twentieth century, music was more something you did for your enjoyment, for your friends," Roger Lynn, a session guitarist who wrote Eric Clapton's 1978 hit "Promises," told NPR.[6] "And today too many people think of it as a career. When you think about it, popular music is just another name for what used to be called folk music. The music of the people."

A few professional musicians have taken that idea to heart, trying to spread and preserve out-of-vogue musical forms by using the Internet. One is Roger McGuinn, former lead singer and songwriter of the Byrds, who helped spur the folk rock tradition in the mid-'60s with hits like "Turn, Turn, Turn," "Mr. Spaceman," and "Three Miles High."

McGuinn, inducted into the Rock 'n' Roll Hall of Fame in 1991, long ago left the Byrds for a solo career. He became hooked on folk music at age fifteen the moment he saw Bob Gibson, an old-time folk singer, perform at his Chicago high school. Folk music is a broad term, encompassing traditional Irish and English ballads, bluegrass, acoustic rock, and contemporary folk. By the early 1990s, the tradition was threatened by the homogenization of broadcast radio—"just rap and bubblegum music," McGuinn calls it—together with the record labels' reluctance to sign folk musicians.[7]

Concerned that the genre was in danger of vanishing, in 1995 he launched McGuinn's Folk Den, a site that offers legitimate file sharing. He named the Folk Den after the Los Angeles club where he and bandmate Gene Clark first met David Crosby. McGuinn began recording and posting traditional chestnuts to the site, and he still adds a new song every month. More than a hundred songs are online, available for free download under a Creative Commons license. McGuinn has reinterpreted "John Riley," "Springfield Mountain," "Old Paint," and "To Morrow"—all of which the late Gibson performed at that long-ago high school assembly.

"In the old days, somebody would sit on the front porch, and somebody else would learn how to pick up the melody," says McGuinn, who sounds youthful at age sixty-two. "When I'm recording solo, I'm one on one with the computer, not in front of a large group of people, so in that sense it fits in with the oral tradition of telling stories and preserving folk songs from one generation to the next. What better way to share these songs than through the Internet?"

As an outgrowth of his preservation project, McGuinn took to the road to record *Treasures from the Folk Den*, an album of traditional folk songs, with Pete Seeger, Joan Baez, Judy Collins, and Odetta. (Seeger, too frail to leave home, sang a duet in his living room with McGuinn.) The album was nominated for a Grammy in 2002.

If he could, McGuinn says he would broaden the commercial media's "scope of appreciation" to also include jazz, reggae, world, and classical music. That's not likely because of financial considerations, but new technologies—satellite radio, online music stores, and CD-burning software (McGuinn uses Musicmatch)—give users greater choices than ever before.

McGuinn occasionally peeks in on Kazaa to see how many of his songs are being traded, but he doesn't take offense. In 2000 he defended Napster in testimony before the Senate Judiciary Committee.[8] "As an artist, I think it's just like being played on the radio," he says. In the end, greater exposure leads to additional sales.

As for McGuinn's preservation hobby, it appears that the folk tradition has been reenergized, thanks to the Net and the release of films such as *O Brother, Where Art Thou?* and *Songcatcher*. "Folk music is pretty healthy now," he says. "It's come a long way in just the last few years."

Four years ago, Disney Channel's cartoon series *The Proud Family* aired an episode that resembled a modern-day version of *Reefer Madness*, the unintentionally hilarious 1936 propaganda film that promoted the idea that smoking marijuana makes people go insane, have wild sex, and dance out of control. This time around, Disney took aim at file sharing, according to a report on AlterNet.org[9]:

Teenager Penny Proud, shown the wonders of a Napster-like program called EZJackster, gets addicted to file sharing and begins downloading all the music she ever wanted. Soon, chaos ensues. Her favorite singer doesn't get his royalty check. Her local record store goes out of business. The police arrive and threaten to haul her to jail. Worst of all, her mom takes away her computer. Penny all but destroys the U.S. economy before realizing, in the end, that file sharing is bad news.

In truth, file sharing often contains more charcoal grays and dark shades than Disney's black-and-white cartoon version would have it.

For instance, meet Mike Sciullo.

Sciullo, a twenty-five-year-old help desk employee who works for a global company based in Pittsburgh, amassed a formidable music catalog after ripping music from his CD collection to his hard drive. But Sciullo didn't stop there. To round out his collection, he dipped into Napster, Kazaa, and Morpheus and downloaded hundreds of additional tunes. He wanted to share his good fortune with friends and coworkers, so he set up a music sharing network on servers he runs both at work and at home. These private darknets are closed to the public, but Sciullo has shared his log-on and password with fifty friends who can dip into his files and download any of the twenty thousand songs on his home computer. Another two hundred friends and coworkers in the corporate offices use the six thousand songs on the company's server as a private jukebox or mini-radio station. He did the same thing at his previous job, where an entire wing of a Pittsburgh medical center listened to music from a server he set up. His friends and coworkers love it.

"It creates a nice atmosphere to be able to listen to music while you work," Sciullo tells me. "Even my boss listens to music off my network."[10]

Sciullo is typical of many in his generation. He does not share Tony Abbott's determination to play by the rules. Instead, he echoes McGuinn's view that file sharing is today's radio. Sciullo sings vocals in a rock band that offers free song downloads on its Web site, and he says both legal band sites and renegade outfits like Kazaa build up fan support for little-known acts. Today he purchases fewer CDs but attends more live concerts and buys more DVDs that feature bands he enjoys.

What are we to make of Sciullo's actions? Do all the rules of the physical world apply once a piece of music is digitized? In an age when the online global village draws us together into real communities in ways our town squares no longer do, where should the lines be drawn when sharing music with others?

When I convey Sciullo's actions to Cary Sherman, president of the Recording Industry Association of America, he says, "These people are stealing, plain and simple."[11]

The RIAA, acting on behalf of the record labels, has sent out thousands of cease-and-desist letters to private corporations and universities that tolerate such practices on their internal networks. The RIAA is pursuing the major file-trading services in court, including the parent company of Kazaa, whose software has been downloaded more than 320 million times, making it the most popular free software application of all time. With illegal song downloads far surpassing Napster's peak, in 2003 the RIAA began filing hundreds of lawsuits against individual file traders who make many thousands of songs available on peer-to-peer networks.

Mike Godwin of the public policy group Public Knowledge says, "Reasonable people may disagree about whether sharing a song between two or ten people is fair use, but I don't know of anyone who believes putting five thousand songs up on the Internet for millions of people to download is legal."

Nonetheless, both Godwin and Public Knowledge president Gigi B. Sohn say most of the blame should not be placed on the four out of ten American adults—more than 60 million people—who have downloaded music from the file-sharing services. They say the record companies have not done enough to offer an attractive legal alternative, and they are missing a chance to use P2P technology to develop new business models and markets.

Music companies knew their world had changed forever in mid-1999 when the original Napster launched, demonstrating an insatiable thirst in the land for an on-demand celestial jukebox. The Napster story is well known—books have been written about the musical earthquake Shawn Fanning set into motion—so I'll hew to my early promise to look ahead, not backward, and concentrate on facets of the digital media revolution beyond file sharing. Still, it's worth recalling that in July 2001, when lawsuits shut it down, 57 million people were using the people-powered song-swapping bazaar, which in many ways represented a pop culture revolution—a mass uprising against the recording industry's predatory pricing and customer-hostile practices.

To the record companies, Napster was always about piracy. To college students and millions more, Napster represented an insanely cool technology that offered free songs, yes, but also easy sampling and instant access to almost any tune. Napster was about flexibility, fluidity, and finding stuff more than it was about free.

Whatever you may think about Napster, it was a cultural powerhouse, opening the floodgates to a new world of free-flowing music. Napster brought millions of people into the digital music space, making us see computers and digital devices as the chief ways to access our music. It sped up by years the transition to the new digital marketplace and paved the way for users to see music as not just a product but also a service. By attracting tens of millions of devoted users, it spurred the music labels to open their vaults to legitimate online music stores. Napster also prompted youth culture to pick up the tools for creating, sampling, and remixing digital music. Music executives who could never get past its piracy underpinnings still get cross-eyed when the name Napster is uttered, but we've barely begun to see the outlines of how its imprint will transform not just the recording industry but television, games, and perhaps movies as well.

The record labels blame the file-sharing networks for their current woes, but many of their wounds have been self-inflicted. When the compact disc was introduced in 1983, its shimmering, high-tech gloss allowed the labels to raise the price of an album from about $9 to $16, even though manufacturing a CD soon cost less than pressing an LP record. The record companies—not the artists—got nearly all the extra money. That unhappy arrangement remains to this day. Of $11 billion in annual CD sales, artists receive less than 5 percent. (By contrast, artists get 12 percent for songs sold in online music stores, on average. And they keep about 35 to 40 percent of concert proceeds.)

Other trends in the music business have sowed additional public discontent. The rise of monolithic radio station chains wiped out independent, locally owned stations that catered to local communities and regional tastes and replaced them with bland, bloodless programming. Nearly every song on the radio is bought and paid for by the record companies. Music execs spend millions to create Britney-size jackpots but neglect to cultivate innovative new bands. (Tina Weymouth told a music industry panel in 2004 that if Talking Heads were starting out today, they would never get signed and never get airplay in the current media environment. Weeks earlier, Don Henley said he doubted that a major label would sign Johnny Cash today.)

Record company execs are often portrayed in an unflattering light—and little wonder. The *New York Times* reported that 99.99 percent of audits show record companies to have underpaid their artists.[12] McGuinn sold half a million copies of 1991's *Back to Rio* and never got a penny in royalties. In a music industry magazine in 2002, Steve Albini, who produced Nirvana's *In Utero*, outlined what a typical record deal looks like: A new band might get a $250,000 advance. Its debut album sells 250,000 copies, earning $710,000 for the label. The band, after repaying such expenses as recording fees, video, catering, wardrobe, and tour bus costs, is left *owing* the label $14,000 in royalties.[13] In an essay in *Salon*, Courtney Love did the math for a band that sells 1 million records, nets $6.6 million for the record company, and its members come away with zero—including its music, which the label owns. (Congress passed a law sanctioning such indentured servitude. Book authors, by contrast, own their books and license them to publishers.) Love relates how Toni Braxton declared bankruptcy in 1998 after selling $188 million worth of CDs after a record contract paid her less than 35 cents per album sold. The entire recording industry, Love concludes, "is based on piracy."[14]

The final twist that turned the public against the record companies was the industry's refusal to create a compelling online marketplace for years after Napster's debut. Internet users hungry for digital music had few or no legitimate recourses but for the file-trading networks.

With the record companies' reputation and credibility in such tatters, is it any wonder that file sharing has been such a guilt-free pastime for so many?

More than 60 percent of Americans see nothing wrong with file downloading or peer-to-peer systems and oppose any attempts to restrict them, according to a 2003 study by the Pew Internet & American Life Project.[15] The research firm NPD Group estimated in 2003 that two-thirds of the music on Americans' computers, or 7.5 billion files, comes from illegal file swapping. A Barna Group study commissioned by the Christian Music Trade Association in 2004 found that 80 percent of teenagers had shared copyrighted music in the previous six months, and being a born-again, active churchgoer made no difference in one's file-trading behavior.[16]

Why do people do it? A couple of years ago, tech lawyer James Burger recalls speaking at the National Youth Leadership Forum, a gathering of some of the nation's brightest high school students in Washington, D.C. When the adults left the room, he closed the door. "How many of you routinely download music and burn CDs?" he asked the fifty teens. "Every hand shot up. I said, 'Don't you think you're stealing? Don't you have a little hesitation?' Here's what they told me: 'Do you know what you're asking us to do? How do we find new music without these file-trading services? We know the record labels are bribing the radio stations to jam the latest boy band or CD Barbie down our throats. But let's suppose I hear a song I like. How do I get it, under your system? I've got to ask my mom or dad to drive me to the mall. I buy a $16 or $18 CD, take it home to listen to it, and I like only one song on the album. And I know almost none of the $16 to $18 is going to the artists. So I don't feel guilty at all. I'm being ripped off by the music industry.'"[17]

A nationwide survey by the legal site FindLaw released in June 2004 found that 56 percent of Americans oppose the recording industry's lawsuits against file traders.[18] Even many musicians take a benign view of file sharing. In a 2004 Pew study, 35 percent of 2,755 musicians and songwriters polled said file-sharing services are not bad for artists because they help promote an artist's work; 23 percent said they're bad for artists because the services allow unrestricted copying of their works; and 35 percent agreed with both statements. In addition, 60 percent said they do not think the RIAA's lawsuits against individual music swappers will benefit musicians and songwriters.

The artists look more favorably toward file-sharing networks when it comes to their own careers. The Pew study reported 35 percent of them said free downloading has helped their careers, only 5 percent said it has hurt their careers, 37 percent said it has made no difference, and 15 percent didn't know.

Major artists are split on the subject. Metallica, Madonna, Eminem, Don Henley, Shakira, and Loudon Wainwright III have come out strongly in favor of the recording industry's hard-line legal approach, and Motown songwriter Lamont Dozier ("Stop! In the Name of Love") has written passionately about the emotional and financial toll file sharing has taken on his family. Conversely, other influential artists like Moby, Smashing Pumpkins, Limp Bizkit, Ben Folds Five, Public Enemy, and They Might Be Giants contend that the RIAA crackdown is wrong. "How can a 14-year-old who has an allowance of $5 a week feel bad about downloading music produced by multimillionaire musicians and greedy record companies?" Moby wrote on his Web site.[19] He advised the labels to launch low-cost services that offer free listening, access to unreleased tracks, ticket discounts, and free merchandise—and to "stop putting out shitty records."

Both sides may be right. File sharing is likely to hurt major pop stars, though "hurt" is a relative term. But many lost Britney CD sales are being offset by increased sales for a new act—or even a forgotten one. Free access to music is often the first step in putting money into a performer's pocket.

Janis Ian, who recorded the hit songs "At Seventeen" and "Jesse" and received nine Grammy nominations (her last hit record came in 1975), won widespread acclaim online in 2002 after defending file-sharing networks and crediting them with sparking renewed interest in her music. Ian, who says every royalty statement she ever received claimed she owned the record company money, observed that the major labels prohibit artists from making their music available for free downloading. Not only that, she wrote, "they own our *voices* for the duration of the contract, so we can't even post a live track for downloading!"

By placing on her Web site free MP3s of music she owns the rights to, Ian saw a 300 percent increase in merchandise sales. "I'm not about to become a zillionaire as a result, but I am making more money," she wrote. "At a time when radio playlists are tighter and any kind of exposure is hard to come by, 365,000 copies of my work now will be heard. Even if only 3 percent of those people come to concerts or buy my CDs, I've gained about 10,000 new fans this year."[20]

As pioneering tech book publisher Tim O'Reilly suggests, obscurity—not piracy—may be the greatest threat to the vast majority of creative artists.

All of this is not to excuse fans who routinely download music illegally for free. That's wrong. But the long-term economic losses and economic dislocation caused by file sharing is still an open question. Music album sales rose 3.8 percent in 2004 over 2003. And a major study in April 2004 by economists at Harvard and the University of North Carolina found that file sharing has no negative effect on CD sales.[21] The study, which tracked 1.75 million downloads over a 17-week period in 2002, found that downloading both helps and hurts the sale of CDs, essentially resulting in a wash. Such findings should give us pause before taking precipitous actions against file-trading culture.[22]

Karen Randall, general counsel of Universal Studios, has a friendly word of advice for her counterparts in the music business who continue to file hundreds of lawsuits against individual file traders. "Be careful with the stick," she said at a Digital Hollywood conference in Beverly Hills. "I don't know how, but somehow the music industry has alienated their customers, and they've alienated their talent. On the movie side, we want to make sure not to do that. The public thinks the music industry is a bunch of suits that are bad and making too much money and it's okay to steal their stuff. The same atmosphere just does not apply to the movie industry. People understand it costs $100 million to make a movie and maybe therefore it shouldn't be stolen." Alienating your customers, she said, is not a winning strategy.[23]

How, then, should the recording industry rethink its approach to the digital age?

If we accept that the future of music is digital, as even record company executives who are struggling to hold back the sea admit, then here's a sobering thought: not one of the major milestones in digital music so far—Napster, Musicmatch, MP3 players, Webcasting, the iPod—was achieved by the record companies.

In 1999, Diamond Multimedia produced the Rio 300, the first portable MP3 player, and weathered the recording industry's legal attempts to stop it. Musicmatch Jukebox changed how we interact with music by giving us tools to rip, mix, and burn our own CDs. Apple's iPod put ten thousand tunes in our pocket in an elegant little machine that looked like it was beamed here from the future. Apple's iTunes Music Store wants to be the answer to digital music delivery, if only the record companies will let it.

We often forget, but the music industry does not begin and end with the major record labels. New bands are giving away their music on P2P networks as a way to gain fame first and fortune later. The largest site for legal MP3s on the Web, GarageBand.com uses listener ratings to rank 300,000 independent musicians and 1.8 million songs. Established artists such as Prince, Todd Rundgren, Ani DiFranco, Aimee Mann, Peter Gabriel, Brian Eno, Ween, and others use the Web to interact with fans and sell their music (some through their labels, some not). Years from now, that will be the rule rather than the exception.

Online music stores, which the record companies once wanted no part of, are now widely seen as the music industry's brightest hope. Apple's foray into music has been so successful that it has restyled itself as a digital media company. In October 2001, after just six months of development, Apple gave the world the iPod, a sleek, handheld device that contains more computing power than an early Macintosh. It has sold more than 10 million units—8.2 million in 2004 alone. *Fortune* columnist and TiVo director Stewart Alsop called it "a perfect template for how digital devices should be designed in the future."[24] Michael Bull, a media lecturer at the University of Sussex, interviewed thousands of iPod owners and found that the ability to make your entire music collection mobile changes not only how we interact with music but also how we interact with each other, making public urban spaces colder as we shut ourselves into warmer personal spaces with our music.[25]

In April 2003, Apple launched the iTunes Music Store and immediately gave legitimate online music services a stamp of credibility. Apple's store sold songs for about a buck apiece, with relatively modest copy protection after CEO Steve Jobs personally jawboned several label chieftains who had previously insisted on irritating digital locks. The iTunes Store is selling at a rate of half a billion songs a year. Although songs sold on CD outnumber songs sold on the Web by a sizable margin, analysts expect that within five years online sales may make up as much as a third of the music market, worth several billion dollars.

Jobs likes to say people want to own music, not rent it. But that's not quite true. People want to *listen* to music—on their terms. There's room for both the buy-any-song digital storefront and the rent-any-song celestial jukebox, as long as both models are faithful to customer expectations. That's where the music companies need to follow Jobs's lead and stop trying to lock down their products with copy protection that attempts to undo the liquidity of digital media.

Phil Schiller, the Apple executive who oversees the iTunes Music Store, told *BusinessWeek Online*: "The solution to music piracy is not a technological one. No one can make the perfect safe to put things in. And it won't be a legislative solution of someone passing a magic law that stops all piracy. In the end, the solution will be a behavioral one. Many people will choose the legal and fair route. That's what we hope we've done here—create something that's in many ways better than the free services."[26]

Apple's success story has been extensively covered in the press, but if the music industry is to thrive in the digital age, other companies and business models will need to prosper as well.

Musicmatch, a 160-employee music software company in San Diego, has been something of a scrappy underdog in the digital music fray. When I visit their second-story offices overlooking a lush Spanish Colonial courtyard filled with orange trees and flowing fountains, world music wafts from an employee cubicle into the reception area. Music is often part of the scene here—after all, ten of the employees are former disc jocks. Minutes later, a woman leads her German shepherd down the hallway past a Rage against the Machine poster. But this is no freewheeling, cash-burning dotcom.

At Musicmatch's birth in 1997, a contingent of company reps convened at one of Silicon Valley's leading venture capital firms and made their pitch, outlining a business plan with charts, usage studies, and conservative revenue projections. A VC exec across the table stopped them short. "Where are the ponytails? You guys look too clean-cut to be in the music business." Another said, "Why do you care about revenue and profits? You guys just don't get it, it's about eyeballs! Why aren't you buying billboards on Highway 101 and getting your name up on Times Square?" Eventually Musicmatch found financial backing at another VC firm, one that was comfortable with profits and slow, steady growth.

In late 1998, Musicmatch released the beta version of the first digital music jukebox, which gave users the ability to burn their own custom CD mixes.[27] Almost immediately, it became a hit. "Giving people control over their music turned out to be a phenomenon that unleashed a torrent of creativity," says senior vice president Bob Ohlweiler. "Creating an ultimate party tape used to take all day. Now you could do it in 10 minutes." Today, Musicmatch Jukebox has more than 50 million registered users, a quarter of whom use the software at least once a month.[28]

"The record industry is a $200 billion industry trapped inside a $40 billion body,"[29] says founder Dennis Mudd, a mirthful Mel Gibson look-alike who dreamed up the idea of Musicmatch while sitting in a class at Wharton. (He got a B on the paper; the professor called the idea intriguing but unfeasible.) "Music is one of the most underconsumed resources around. If people had quicker, easier access, we'd be swimming in music."[30]

The holy grail is the celestial jukebox—a customer-friendly model that places all the music in the world at your fingertips. "The technology is the easy part," Mudd says. "We already have a high percentage of all the marketable music in the world on our servers. The hard part is, with all that music, how does a person find the track she wants to hear at any given time? We help people explore and expand their music universe."

Mudd speaks of the music experience in almost reverential terms. "I remember times when I was driving my car and the perfect song comes on—and that just made my whole day. That's such a rare experience in today's radio environment. We're trying to make it much more common."

Services like Musicmatch do far more than graft radio onto the Internet. They also help listeners create a gotta-have-it, personalized playlist of favorite artists along with new music you never knew you liked.

Before he started Musicmatch, Mudd recalls he was stuck in oldies hell, like so many others of his generation. "I never evolved past the '70s and '80s. I was into the Eagles, Boz Scaggs, the Rolling Stones, Yes, REO Speedwagon. I think a lot of people freeze their musical tastes in high school and college. With Musicmatch's recommendation technology, I quickly became exposed to new musical styles like trip-hop and electronica, and a lot of new artists like Morcheeba, Portishead, Wilco, Lucinda Williams. I had never heard of Nickelback, a small outfit out of Canada. I downloaded a couple of their tracks, listened to them, and said, 'Wow, this is amazing.'"

At launch, Musicmatch's original business model was based on selling digital music tracks. Mudd proposed selling songs for 25 or 50 cents a pop, on the theory that such a price point would dramatically increase sales. The record labels would hear none of it. The labels also insisted on what Mudd called "draconian" copy protection that hobbled the songs people purchased, such as preventing a song acquired on a PC from playing on an MP3 player.

In the early days of the company, Mudd recalls, meetings with the record labels resulted in "flashes of optimism followed by crushing defeat." In 1997 he met with the vice president of new media at Capitol Records, who expressed interest but never responded to Musicmatch's licensing requests. "I call it the pocket veto," he says. "It was almost impossible to get a no from these guys. Nothing would really happen." A year or so later, he and a partner flew to New York for a meeting with the head of new media licensing for BMG Music. The record label executive strode in and announced, "I've only got fifteen minutes, so get to the point." Flustered, the Musicmatch execs asked to reschedule. They never got on his calendar.

"One of the folklores in the music industry is that in every record label president's office there are three framed photos," Ohlweiler relates. "The first photo is of the fired record label executive who let radio happen. The second is of the fired record label executive who let MTV happen. And the third is an empty frame waiting for the guy who let the Internet happen."

By 1999 and 2000, with Napster in full swing, the labels were still not ready to sell songs online, so Musicmatch went the radio route, which did not require the labels' cooperation. Each month more than 1.7 million listeners tune in to free streaming music on Musicmatch Radio.

In 2001, Musicmatch launched the first successful music subscription service, described as a "near music-on-demand service" with CD-quality streaming music. (RealNetworks' Rhapsody, America Online's MusicNet, eMusic, and the born-again Napster also offer digital music subscriptions.) Unlike its more limited radio version, Musicmatch MX lets its two hundred thousand subscribers craft personalized music streams based on favorite artists, a year or an era, or more than a hundred genres like blues or funk. Whereas most radio stations' playlists run from thirty-three to thirty-eight songs, Musicmatch listeners can draw from a well of eight hundred thousand songs.

As it grew to become one of the top radio networks on the Net, Musicmatch bumped up against the realities of the law. Thanks to heavy lobbying by the recording industry, the 1998 Digital Millennium Copyright Act micromanages Internet radio programming. Thus no Internet radio station (whether free or fee-based) may announce the name of an upcoming song. An Internet radio station may not play more than three songs from an album in a three-hour period. It may not play more than two songs in a row from the same album within any three-hour block. It may not play more than three consecutive songs from the same artist, nor more than four songs by the same artist, within a three-hour span.

Take that, all you wannabe Alan Freeds and Wolfman Jacks of the digital era.[31]

The DMCA also prohibits the archiving of streaming Webcasts past a few weeks. The law, in short, imposes on Webcasters not only some of the worst baggage of broadcast radio, but also in many cases a tighter straitjacket.

In 2001, Musicmatch and the Recording Industry Association of America sued each other over aspects of Musicmatch's radio service that the RIAA claimed were not expressly permitted under the DMCA. Among other things, the RIAA objected to a Musicmatch feature that let listeners select the tempo of songs to fit their mood. If you liked Bruce Springsteen, you could select his ballads or his rockers. No more. Musicmatch settled the suit by removing the tool and making other minor modifications.

Musicmatch remains tied to the DMCA's hidebound rules for its Internet radio service, but in late 2002 it launched an artist-on-demand service that lets you summon up more than ten thousand musical acts. Create a channel with all Tommy Dorsey or Barenaked Ladies or Alice in Chains. Because the company licensed the rights, it can stream dozens of tunes in a row from jazz artists, hip-hop groups, pop superstars, and other acts. In return, the labels get a piece of the action. In mid-2004, following Rhapsody and Napster, it launched a song-on-demand service.

While Apple beat it to the punch by launching the first store to sell unfettered online music downloads, Musicmatch followed six months later with its own online store.[32] Others have jumped into online music sales: Amazon, Wal-Mart, BuyMusic.com, eBay, and Napster. And Musicmatch made a major stride in the marketplace when portal giant Yahoo purchased the company in September 2004 for $160 million.

Looking ahead, Mudd says Musicmatch and the record labels have forged a healthy relationship in the past two years. "The new generation of record label executives sees the Internet as the industry's future, because the CD business is eventually going to go away. The CD is going to have a long, slow, horrible death, and it needs to be replaced with a more efficient and profitable model. We're undergoing a vast change in our expectations of how we interact with music. Buying one CD every couple of months isn't very interesting. With the technology available today, you should be able to spend about five bucks a month and have millions of tracks available to you."

He sees the day when music follows you wherever you go, a sort of Audio Everywhere environment you can tap into through any device: portable player, stereo, TV, car radio, wireless device, cell phone. "We'll arrive at the day where you can click a button and listen to whatever kind of music you want to listen to, whether you're in your car, in your living room, or walking down the street with a portable device," he says.

However it shakes out, Mudd and countless others won't soon be returning to a shut-in life of Yes, REO Speedwagon, and Bachman-Turner Overdrive.

11 Channeling Cole Porter

A FRIEND RELATES A STORY TOLD TO HIM BY THE mother of one of Silicon Valley's most influential venture capitalists:

"When she was a little girl, Ann went around the neighborhood and encouraged all the kids to draw, to create these terrific little works of art. She took them and decided to create a little neighborhood art gallery in her parents' garage. And then she decided to start charging a quarter admission. If the little boys and girls who created the pictures wanted to see their own drawings and their friends' drawings, they had to pay her a quarter. So, to recap: Ann created no art herself. She relied exclusively on the work of others. And she made more than the artists did."

Sounds a lot like the music recording industry.

Today, the gatekeepers and middlemen are in danger of being innovated into irrelevance. How will the record companies survive the transition from the analog to the digital age? What will the new business models look like?

It starts with Tarzan economics.

"If you're Tarzan, swinging through the jungle, you've got to cling to the vine and stay off the jungle floor because that's death," Jim Griffin says over dinner at Versailles, a funky Cuban restaurant in Los Angeles. "But you've also got to let go of the vine at precisely the right moment to grab the next one. So there is this moment when you abandon the old thing and grab the new. You can't let go too early, because that would be death. And you can't hold on to the old for too long or it won't work."[1]

Griffin, a forty-six-year-old force of nature with broad shoulders, wire-rim glasses, and neatly combed salt-and-pepper hair, is a leading digital-rights visionary. "That's what this debate is all about: which vine to grab, and when to let go of the old," he says, thunderclap voice rolling across dishes of garlic chicken, pork, and fried bananas.

Moments later, a musician and a new media entrepreneur join our table, acting on an invitation I sent earlier on the Pho digital entertainment discussion list. It's been like this since May 1998, when Griffin, his friend John Parres, and a handful of like-minded individuals began gathering each week at Pho 87, a Vietnamese soup kitchen in L.A.'s Chinatown, to thrash out the convergence of music, art, and the Internet.

The get-togethers quickly blossomed into something larger: a mailing list with a thousand members and a network of Pho hot spots—in New York, London, Detroit, Chicago, Seattle, Helsinki, Washington, Philadelphia, Austin—where dozens of musicians, technologists, hackers, attorneys, record label employees, new media chiefs, and others gather over brunch to discuss new business models, the latest antipiracy techniques, copyright reform, and how to midwife the music industry into the digital era. Most members appear to share the McLuhanesque notion that the medium is the message. In this view, the future is about ubiquitous digital music and services, not physical goods and artificial scarcity that mimic the analog world.[2] All that remains is to hammer out the details.

The Pho group has influence beyond its numbers. Griffin says the heads of all the major record labels—Universal, Warner, Sony, BMG, and EMI—either belong to the list or get summaries of important discussions. Napster founder Shawn Fanning, MP3.com founder Michael Robertson, former RIAA chief Hilary Rosen, and industry-bashing rocker Courtney Love were early members.

Griffin was able to bring together such disparate parties for two reasons. First, he has street cred. Griffin was Geffen Records' director of technology from 1993 to 1998. In June 1994 he led the Geffen team that posted online the first legal full-length commercial song, Aerosmith's "Head First"—to the consternation of Geffen's parent company, Universal Music Group. Universal was later acquired by Vivendi, which put an end to Geffen's heretical ways. Griffin now heads the consulting firm Cherry Lane Digital.

The second thing Griffin brought to the table was an open-source approach. He took not only the name pho (pronounced "fuh") from the soothing Vietnamese beef noodle soup, but also borrowed the spirit of conviviality, openness, and hospitality found at such gatherings—starting with Griffin picking up the tab for several years. Whether online or at one of its frequent gatherings, which can attract as many as a hundred people at a time, the Pho community encourages an open, robust exchange of ideas.

At Pho's inception, the recording industry viewed MP3s with hostility, and woe be the turncoat who advocated accommodation with the new digital technologies. By contrast, anyone could come to a Pho brunch for free. Anyone could join the mailing list and espouse any view. "You had this very regimented music industry that was controlling the dialogue about the digitization of art and music," Griffin says, "and we decided, let's do the opposite of that."

By flinging wide its doors to music fans instead of just industry professionals, Pho also encouraged the notion that a fourteen-year-old could teach the record industry a thing or two. "I thought it would help if the music labels and Hollywood found out what was really going on in dormitories and in kids' bedrooms," Griffin says. Young people still belong to the list, and he says they invariably display a keen instinct for indicating where the business is heading.

Many music executives and company lawyers remain mired in the past, however. An hour earlier, Griffin—dressed in a gray suit, immaculate white shirt, and silk tie—appeared on a panel discussing Internet piracy held by the Beverly Hills Bar Association. "An intellectual property attorney on the panel was nearly ranting about Nokia selling a phone with an embedded MP3 player," he says. Such players were ruled to be legal in 1999, but the record companies still haven't accepted MP3.

"That's how bizarre things are," Griffin says. "You and I would laugh at the notion that MP3s are piracy, but in some countries, they are. In England, unlike the U.S., it's a copyright infringement to change the form of a song. Laws aside, the message from today's customer is clear: we'll choose the medium. It's very much a change from push to pull. When I came into the entertainment business, it was all push. It was unheard of to think that a customer would get to choose the delivery medium for her music."

When you speak to entertainment executives privately, Griffin says, nearly all concede that the digital transformation of their industry is inevitable. "But they also take the view, 'Not on my watch. Just don't let it happen during my contract.'"

That, naturally, creates friction. Griffin digs into a plate of chicken, rice, and beans and says, "You know, David Geffen's companies never owned a truck. He was a music guy, and he made distribution deals with others, but he never had to fill a pipeline that involved factories, warehouses, and trucks carrying plastic discs. So he understood that the value of our music was in many ways determined by the size of the crowd we can draw.

"Teenagers instinctively know this. When they put a song on a P2P network, they believe they're increasing a song's popularity and its ultimate value. So the record labels' model of distribution—where they adjust price to meet demand and control every aspect of the supply chain—is a very different world than the one in which a teenager grows up today."

The other two Phosters nod in agreement with this bit of wisdom from the sage in chief. Over the years, Pho members have read or written thousands of e-mails about the recording industry's outmoded business model. Many would doubtless agree with Lyor Cohen, head of Universal's Island Def Jam, who told the *New Yorker* in 2003 that the record industry would have been better off had the CD not come along in 1983. Without the CD, the old record industry would have died in the early '80s, and a new industry would have risen up in its place. Instead of a decaying industry intent on recycling old staples and maintaining the status quo, we would now be awash in new musical forms and exposed to a new generation of artists who today find it difficult to get onto the airwaves or onto the dwindling shelf space for new artists at the three largest music retailers: BestBuy, Wal-Mart, and Target.

Today, the prospects for the music industry's rebirth are less certain. How things turn out is anyone's guess. "We're in the steepest, most turbulent part of the S curve of change," says Josh Warner, the e-commerce guy on my right. "I can see this far in front of my nose right now."

Three main schools of thought seem to have formed about the industry's prospects. The optimists believe that digital delivery is destiny and customers will eventually flock in great numbers to legitimate online music stores or subscription services that tap into a celestial jukebox. NYU's Clay Shirky, for instance, predicts that ten years from now, "the music industry will be making more money than it does today" if it embraces the fundamental tenets of the digital world by lowering expensive physical barriers and expanding the size of the market.

The pessimists believe that file sharing permanently undercuts the possibility of a legitimate music marketplace and that the music business will return to an 1800s model when live performances and songwriting were the main sources of revenue. David Bowie, for instance, has told interviewers he believes copyright "will no longer exist in ten years," that "music itself is going to become like running water or electricity,"[3] and that "the corporate [music] companies will come to an end."[4]

A third school—let's call it the Ubiquity School—advocates universal access to music. The theory goes that accessing media shouldn't be free but it should "feel free." The Ubiquity School's tenets boil down to this: open wide the music vaults, digitize the unreleased catalogs, legalize the file-sharing networks, and exponentially increase music consumption—and revenues—by imposing a blanket license.

All three groups believe, to some degree, that we are in the midst of a historic upheaval in how people use and consume music. They agree, to varying degrees, that the record companies, wedded to megastars and mass tastes, will undergo major disruptions in their business models, and that the late-twentieth-century phenomenon of pop superstars bringing in tens of millions of dollars was an aberration.

They also agree, more or less, that as the digital revolution has peeled away content (music, movies, text) from its corresponding medium (CDs, videotapes, books)—in other words, as information and storage are decoupled—that spells bad news for distributors and intermediaries that can't adjust to the new digital marketplace. As a result, media companies, especially the record labels, are trying to make fluid digital media behave like physical objects through their copy control schemes. But Griffin says, "The digital river has no reverence for gatekeepers."

If there is one overwhelming consensus among all three camps on Pho, however, it is this: artists should be paid for their work. Even those who believe P2P file sharing and people-powered collaborating filtering should replace the recording industry believe we need to compensate and provide incentives to the creators of culture.

It has ever been so. Lyricist Sammy Cahn, the Songwriters Hall of Fame member who wrote such hits as "All the Way" and "Call Me Irresponsible," was often asked, "Which comes first, the music or the lyrics?" He liked to say, "Neither. It's the phone call." When Cole Porter was asked where he gets his inspiration, he replied, "My sole inspiration is a telephone call from a producer."[5] The dollar still drives a lot of inspiration.

If music and art are to flow like fountains, who will pay the artists? Griffin, a leading proponent of a blanket license for music, says, "We create a pool of money, we find a fair way to split it up, and we give people flat-fee buffets of unbridled choice. A civilized society does not long tolerate creativity or knowledge or art losing its financial footing."

The idea of a blanket license is fairly straightforward, though the devil is in the details.[6] Under such a plan, music fans would pay a tax or fee on their Internet access (regardless of whether the person downloads anything), on MP3 players, or on blank CDs. Music file swapping would become not only legal but also actively encouraged, with free downloads for everyone. The more frequently a song is downloaded, the more an artist would be paid. "Let's give up the control but take in the money," says Griffin, who figures it would tack on another 10 percent to the average cable bill. He compares the plan to the pay-one-price admission at an amusement park.

Proposals for a blanket license take many forms. Some apply just to music, while others encompass all digital media, including movies, TV, and porn. Griffin favors a voluntary system devised through private industry negotiations rather than by government mandate. If a voluntary approach doesn't work, he favors the government stepping in to impose a solution. The EFF and some prominent academics are among those who favor that approach, called a compulsory or statutory license.

Proponents point out that the government has intervened in this way on several occasions. In 1909 Congress set up a licensing system so that anyone can record a cover of a song, without having to ask permission from the songwriter, as long as they pay the composer a standard fee based on each copy they sell. That's why you're perfectly free to be the billionth artist to record a cover of "Louie, Louie." "L.A. and Hollywood were built on licensing, and they die without licensing," Griffin says. Later, the government imposed similar compulsory licenses for radio and cable television. "Can you imagine the alternative, where every radio station has to call every rights holder for permission to play any song?" he asks.

It's an intriguing proposal, one worthy of serious consideration. It would solve the P2P file-sharing problem overnight by making the activity legal. It would get money into the hands of artists. It would eliminate the labels' penchant for pernicious forms of copy protection that prevent people from playing legally purchased music on the devices they want. A small fee assessed on blank CDs, as Canada does to compensate artists, certainly seems reasonable.

But I'm not yet ready to sign on to the compulsory license bandwagon, and not just because of the insuperable difficulties involved, such as divvying up the proceeds, forcing fees on third parties, making it work internationally, or persuading people that they should pay fees to subsidize JLo or Britney.

We're still early in the age of digital media. Our cultural attitudes about sharing music and other media remain half formed. Are we ready to abandon the notion that customers want to buy music and pay for art? Not likely. Americans bought about $12 billion worth of CDs in 2003. Business is booming at the Apple iTunes Store, with major retailers rolling out rival stores. If the success of the Apple store and the budding prospects for music services like Musicmatch and Rhapsody tell us anything, it's that customers want their music in multiple formats. Movies already do this: we have a choice of movie theater, DVD, pay-per-view, cable, satellite, TV. Now music needs to come up with a buffet of options.

As Griffin observes, the era of push has given way to pull. History shows that new technologies bring not just disruptions to old business models but also new market opportunities. Innovate or die—the mantra of the technology world—is a frightening concept for any industry. But it's also a cold truth.

Let a thousand business models bloom.

Does the recording industry have a death wish? You have to wonder.

Time after time, the most interesting developments in music have come from outside the industry: from tech companies, start-ups, music software companies—and from the underground.

Consider the biggest music trend to hit U.S. shores recently: the mash-up. Mash-ups inject a note of playfulness and inventiveness into an increasingly sterile pop music scene. These hybrid tracks jams together two songs—usually the vocals of one track and the melody of another—to get a new sound that is at once familiar and wholly new. Such odd couplings—the Ramones and Abba, Chuck D. and Herb Alpert, Whitney Houston and Kraftwerk, Missy Elliott and George Michael—exploded onto Britain's dance club scene in 2002 and began infiltrating U.S. clubs a year or two ago. Mash-ups are the work of underground DJs and amateur music lovers who find it easy to draw from pop culture to create home-brew remixes on their home computers.

Mash-ups are, in short, the epitome of the remix revolution.

Naturally, an art form this inventive must be illegal. Mash-up music can be found in clubs, in underground record shops, on Kazaa, and in the Darknet. But you won't find it on mainstream radio. The record companies hit several British radio stations with cease-and-desist letters for playing unlicensed mash-ups. Most mash-ups are done to create interesting new sounds and artistic statements, not for commercial gain, so clearances are rarely sought or obtained. Little wonder: it took mash-up duo 2manydjs an entire year to clear rights for a CD that took a week to make. A third of their requests were turned down, and the permissions they did obtain prevent their album from being released in the United States.

A few commercial mash-ups have broken through, beginning with Run DMC's collaboration with Aerosmith on "Walk This Way" in 1986 and DNA's remix of Suzanne Vega's a cappella single "Tom Diner" in 1990. (Two British dance producers couldn't get Vega's label to return their calls, so they released it as a bootleg dance remix. Vega's lawyer wanted to sue. Vega didn't. The sides came to terms on licensing, and the single climbed to No. 1.) In 2002, Nike commissioned a Dutch disc jockey, JXL, to come up with a song for its World Cup ad campaign. JXL stirred a little techno with a thirty-year-old Elvis B-side single, "A Little Less Conversation." Afterward, Nike got permission from Elvis's estate, and the beat-friendly remix hit No. 1 on the British charts. But in its report on the mash-up scene, the *New York Times* sounded a warning for remix culture: "That sort of thing will be simply impossible if digital rights management becomes commonplace."[7]

Lately, mash-ups have gone mainstream. Fans of the pop singer Bjork have posted hundreds of remixes of her music on the Web, some of them superior to the original arrangements. In 2004, David Bowie launched a mash-up contest and challenged fans to mix two of his songs into a single track, with the winner getting an Audi sports coupe. Interactive programs on the Web let you search for two songs and toss them together in a virtual blender and hear the result. Creative Commons offers a mash license that gives users permission to take a creation and sample it but not to take a verbatim copy and distribute it.

The record companies should be big fans of mash-ups, given that they breathe new life into older acts and forgotten recordings. Music writer Peter Rojas suggests, "Rather than threaten bootleggers with legal action, a sounder strategy would be to co-opt the scene by skimming the best ones off the top and rereleasing them as 'official' bootlegs. . . . The record industry could even respond by selling its own do-it-yourself bootleg kits, complete with editing software and authorized samples."[8] But the loss of control involved in home-brew media apparently is too much to bear. Thus, armed with copyright law, the record companies have managed to keep mash-ups relatively hidden as a contraband musical genre.

Until February 2004.

In that month, an odd thing happened. Hundreds of Web sites declared February 24 to be Grey Tuesday in protest of the legal assault on a little-known Los Angeles DJ, who had released an album into the underground. DJ Danger Mouse's the *Grey Album* introduced bootleg culture to the masses. The twenty-six-year-old Danger Mouse, whose real name is Brian Burton, used musical snippets from the Beatles' white album (officially titled *The Beatles*, as every good boomer knows) and overlaid raps from Jay-Z's *Black Album*. The mash-up won acclaim from critics and fans as an inventive melding of genres. While Jay-Z's label was happy to clear rights, the Beatles' label, EMI, was not and moved to stop its distribution. (Michael Jackson, who owns the Beatles' songbook, has not allowed any sampling of their music.) Danger Mouse had shared CDs of his remix with members of the hip-hop underground, but by the time he complied with EMI's demand to destroy all unsold copies of the album, it had soared out of the underground and into the mainstream. Within a month, more than a hundred thousand people had downloaded the illegal twelve-song set from the Internet.

"Mashing is so easy," DJ Danger Mouse said at the Web 2.0 conference in San Francisco in October 2004. "It takes years to learn how to play the guitar and write your own songs. It takes a few weeks of practice with turntable to make people dance and smile. It takes a few hours to crank out something good with some software. So with such a low barrier to entry, everyone jumps in and starts immediately being creative. I don't understand why that is illegal." As for the effect of the new technologies on the music business, Danger Mouse said this: "For some reason we [artists] think we should be millionaires for making people smile. But I don't worry too much, because it will be over soon. There won't be a market for making people smile because kids will just do it for free."

Suzanne Vega told the audience at the 2004 Future of Music summit in Washington, D.C., "I think DJ Danger Mouse, taking something from this era and that era, is using it to play the culture as an instrument. It's artistry."

The cause célèbre over the *Grey Album* was revealing on a number of levels. It proved that P2P networks and the Darknet can trump any cease-and-desist order. It revealed a mainstream interest in an activity that has mostly resided in the shadows. Most important, it showed that, while our first instincts may be to defend the right of artists to control any and all subsequent uses of their works, the new digital reality suggests that absolute control over creative works is no longer possible in an ocean of connectivity and liquid media. Digitization has decimated the tidy contours of control.

Instead of trying to turn back the clock, we ought to be exploring ways for do-it-yourself culture to serve both artists and the public. Lawrence Lessig, among others, favors creating a blanket license for remixes. That is, anyone should be able to sample from others' works without permission—just as anyone can record someone else's song without permission—as long as credit is given. For commercial use of a remix, you would pay the original artist a set share of your proceeds.

A good idea—and one that Congress will never pass, given certain opposition by the entertainment companies.

Mark Hosler of California's experimental-music group Negativland told counterculture magazine *Mondo 2000* that a few hundred years ago, artists could use a paintbrush, piano, or lute to interpret culture. In today's media-saturated environment, modern technologies center on capturing things through photography, video, photocopies, or music sampling. "We're against bootlegging, which is just ripping people off, but we're swimming in all this stuff and can remake it into a kind of self-defense against media coercion," he said.[9] Hosler suggests that today's artists must be given wide latitude to sample, borrow, quote, and comment on the world around us. Negativland created a four-minute movie mash-up, *The Mashin' of the Christ*, in 2004 as a response to the Mel Gibson blockbuster. Its Web site said the DVD decryption technique used to create the video collage violated the DMCA.[10]

For each step forward, it seems the record companies take two steps back.

I know of a musician in Tennessee who fell in love with the sounds of some obscure blues artists who performed in the South in the 1920s. Their music has been out of print for decades, and the musician wanted to produce a limited-run CD compilation to help spread and preserve the music. Sony Music demanded a $40,000 payment for the nonprofit endeavor. The musician decided to violate copyright laws and take the effort underground, chancing he would not be caught because distribution would be limited.

In late 2003, two students at the Massachusetts Institute of Technology developed an "electronic music library"—a hybrid library, radio, and CD jukebox that piggybacked on MIT's cable TV network—with the aim of offering a legal on-demand digital music system. The system gave students and professors on campus instant access to thirty-five hundred streaming albums that spanned the musical spectrum from Dave Matthews to Dvořák. It did not permit downloading or file swapping. The goal, said one of the creators, was to create "a new kind of library" that would draw students away from illegal file trading. The imaginative experiment lasted less than a week. Universal Music forced MIT to pull the plug, saying the proper licenses had not been purchased. Rather than working with the students to devise a legal alternative to file sharing, Universal released a statement saying, "It is unfortunate that MIT launched a service in an attempt to avoid paying recording artists, union musicians, and record labels."

File sharing may become the music labels' undoing—not because of P2P file swapping, but because of their response to it. Rather than accepting a certain level of piracy, as the software industry does, and increasing their bottom lines by converting a percentage of file traders to legitimate services, the record companies seem bent on finding a nonexistent magic bullet to kill music piracy.

The Big Five music labels have all financed the development of counter-piracy programs, including a program that scans a computer's hard drive for pirated music files and attempts to delete them; another program that locks up a computer system for minutes or hours; and a Trojan horse that redirects users to Web sites where they can buy a song they tried to download for free, the *New York Times* reported.[11]

Such measures are certain to inflame music fans already upset by the electronic locks placed on digital music files that prevent songs from playing on a wide range of unauthorized devices. Of the handful of copy-protected CDs released to date in this country, many won't play on a home theater system, DVD player, MP3 player, or Xbox. Songs purchased at Apple's online music store will only play on Apple devices. The current generation of DRM is so upside-down that a user who buys (encrypted) songs legally from an online music store can't stream them from his PC to his stereo, but a user who downloads (encryption-free) songs illegally from eDonkey can. The recording industry is working on a new generation of CDs that will contain DVD-like encryption.

Webcasting, also known as Internet radio, has been another source of acrimony among the recording industry, fans, and fledgling innovators. Many people consider Webcasting to be the future of radio, once wireless Internet connections become pervasive. More than just a newer delivery method for radio, Webcasting offers programming diversity, low barriers to entry, a global reach, and opportunities for new artists and DJs to build fan bases.

Already, virtual DJs turned off by the wasteland of commercial radio are streaming millions of hours of music over the Internet. For instance, the San Francisco music portal Live365 lets you upload music to their servers, manage your playlists, and stream songs to the four corners of the world, all for a modest monthly fee that also covers licensing rights. A few miles from my house, David Hollevoet of Mountain View, California, created a station called '80s Obsession, featuring 1980s New Wave hits, while Phillip Keys of Milpitas runs Challenging Sushi, a station devoted to Japanese underground pop music.[12] Today, Live365 carries more than 15,000 Webcasts—everything from churches streaming sermons and sports teams streaming their games to a day trader doing a play-by-play of the stock exchange. "We're about empowering individuals and companies into becoming global Webcasters," chief operating officer Raghav Gupta says.[13] More than 2 million people from 150 countries spend 12 million hours a month tuning in to the portal's channels.

You would think it would be in the recording industry's interests to see Webcasting thrive as a legal, compelling alternative to file sharing. But the RIAA hasn't seen it that way. Hundreds of small and independent Webcasters went dark in 2001–2003 when the recording industry sought to impose exorbitant royalty fees. Under the DMCA, Congress required Webcasters to pay fees to both songwriters and performers, while radio stations have been exempt from paying royalties to performers and their record labels since the 1970s because such exposure gives artists promotional value. Lobbyists for the Recording Industry Association of America argued that Internet radio offers no promotional value to artists. Congress went along. Today, if KROC radio plays a Beatles song, composers John and Paul get paid, but performers George and Ringo do not. If a U.S. Webcaster plays a Beatles song, John and Paul receive a composition fee plus all four Beatles get a performance royalty.

To its credit, Congress later revisited the issue and lowered the statutory fees for hobbyists, nonprofits, and college stations that stream music. But many Webcasters remain unhappy about the outcome. "Over time, as Internet radio gets bigger and goes head to head with broadcast radio, I have an unfair cost structure relative to broadcast radio," one Webcaster told me.

Ann Gabriel, president of the Webcaster Alliance, agrees. "The laws and subsequent rules have been designed with the express goal of stifling the growth of the Webcasting industry. We believe this was done to kill off smaller Webcasters who reached out to and promoted independent artists not affiliated with RIAA member labels."[14] The RIAA maintains that Webcasters must pay their fair share.

The newest looming battleground in the digital rights wars is digital radio. The nearly century-old business of radio—the last major analog communications medium—has begun to join the digital age. Digitization promises to be the biggest update to the medium since FM's debut in the 1940s. (Few now recall, but FM radio was initially opposed by the record industry because the high-fidelity broadcasts were free.)

Digital radio promises to replace the static, hiss, and uneven reception of analog AM and FM signals with crackle-free sound that won't fade in and out. The technology also will allow listeners to rewind to the beginning of a song, program recordings in advance, track favorite shows, and summon up song titles, artist names, traffic updates, weather forecasts, sports scores, Spanish-language translations, and more on high-definition radio receivers. Digital radio receivers went on sale in the United States only in early 2004, and the nascent industry is just beginning to get off the ground. Several hundred U.S. radio stations have begun digital audio broadcasts or are in the process of converting from analog-only broadcasts.[15] The technology research firm In-Stat/MDR forecasts that 1 million digital receivers will be sold by the end of 2006, and that it will take more than a decade for digital to surpass analog radio broadcasts.

The major record companies view digital radio with alarm because it could allow listeners to capture fleeting music broadcasts as permanent digital files, carving in to purchases of CDs or digital songs from online stores. Already, conflicts are apparent. Reports have surfaced that all-digital radio stations cannot play certain encrypted music CDs because the copy protection won't allow the tracks to be copied to the stations' systems.

In early 2004, the RIAA began seeking government intervention to limit the public's noncommercial home recording rights. It pitched the Federal Communications Commission on the idea of an "audio broadcast flag" that would prevent people from retransmitting digital radio broadcasts over the Internet, among other things. The FCC, which has been quietly transforming into the Federal Computer Commission, agreed to begin the process of considering new rules, which would apply to terrestrial AM and FM stations that broadcast digitally (with the same broadcast range they have now), but not to satellite radio or Internet radio.

Such rules, if adopted, could hamstring legitimate uses by the public. Want to record the digital broadcast of Don Imus, Rush Limbaugh, or Terry Gross on your PC and listen to it in your car? Or tape a cool new digital radio station and play it for friends at a party?

Your device may well tell you: I'm sorry, Dave, I'm afraid I can't do that.

A revealing exchange of letters on the subject took place in spring 2004 between RIAA president Cary Sherman and Consumer Electronics Association CEO Gary Shapiro. Sherman wrote that the RIAA was concerned that new audio recording devices "will enable radio listeners to become owners and world distributors of a personalized collection of sound recordings . . . thereby transforming a passive listening experience into a personal music library."

In a nutshell, the recording industry fears a ReplayTV for radio—devices that let you capture, time-shift, and archive perfect digital broadcasts and share them with friends.

Sherman suggested placing a "buy button" on audio devices, letting consumers "quickly and easily purchase music that they hear on the radio."

Shapiro responded in part: "You state that you do not wish to limit the ability of consumers to record over-the-air radio broadcasts. Instead, you apparently want to force them to buy what they have received for free since Fleming and Marconi first made it possible for consumers to hear news and music over the public airwaves. As you know, we have long been concerned about content owners seeking to change the 'play' button on our devices to a 'pay' button."

Cheryl Leanza, deputy director of Media Access Project, a public interest law firm in Washington, D.C., says the recording industry is afraid of the Napsterization of digital radio. "In the analog world, you could tape songs off the radio, give the recording to your friends, and pretty much do anything you want with it. In the newer world, the technology sets the rules and determines how long you can save a recording, how you can use it, and whether you can share it with a friend.

"The problem is, the technology is so ham-handed that it gives all controls to the content creator and no discretion to listeners, users, or subsequent creators. Fair use goes out the window, and we lose the purpose of copyright, which is to spread ideas and promote discourse. If the technology and the new rules eliminate these kinds of legitimate uses, then you will limit a fair amount of the creativity that we would otherwise get as a society."[16]

| | |

To date, the record companies have shown a mistrust of the technologies that will either sustain them or undercut their reason for existing. The record labels need to realize that their salvation lies not in devising a fool-proof copy protection scheme or legislating file-sharing networks out of existence. Their future lies in winning the hearts, minds, and wallets of thir-teen- to twenty-five-year-old music fans who are immersed in digital cul-ture—who spend their days swapping instant messages, chatting, sending e-mails, and mixing, burning, mashing, and manipulating personal media. Sometimes copyrighted media.

"Media companies need to shift their focus from a circle-the-wagons defense of digital intellectual property to innovative strategies for managing online content as a core revenue source," said KPMG International in a Sep-tember 2002 report that painted a picture of corporations too concerned with copy protection to create new business models.[17]

What will the future of music look like?

We'll likely see a new middle class of musicians emerge, subverting the mass music hit engine and changing the dynamics of the music business. Any new business model must assure that musicians and creative artists are compensated fairly for their work—a task the labels have generally failed at. One casualty of a reinvented music industry may be the collapse of the superstar system. The increasing number of fans with diverse, eclectic tastes suggests that record companies need to jettison their lowest-common-denominator approach to popular music.

Peter Jenner, who managed Pink Floyd and now manages Billy Bragg, told the 2004 Future of Music summit he believes the industry will evolve from a mass market to a mass number of niche markets. Instead of ten artists making $10 million, we'll see a thousand artists making $10,000 to $100,000 each. "We've had a bizarre accident of history where some of the richest performers are musicians," he said. "What we'll have is more musi-cians making a living. Right now, most musicians aren't making a living, but a tiny, tiny, tiny number are making an obscene amount of money."

The struggle between old media (trying to hold on to the receding masses) and new media (catering to niche tastes) will continue for the rest of our lifetimes. Even as the major labels consolidate, they will continue to lose mindshare, as the viral Internet and services like Musicmatch and iTunes step in to become the new artists-and-repertoire scouts. The new players could hardly do much worse, given an industry standard that produces nine failures for every hit band. One of the more notorious blowouts came when Vivendi Universal's MCA Records spent $2.2 million in preparing eighteen-year-old Carly Hennessy for pop stardom. Her 2001 album *Ultimate High* sold 378 copies in its first three months.[18] In the dysfunctional economics of the industry, music executives estimate that major-label releases must sell half a million copies just to break even. Less than 2 percent of new albums do so.

How to snap the industry out of its slump? The record companies should try to deliver on Musicmatch CEO Dennis Mudd's promise of Audio Everywhere, a hum of interconnectivity that lets you tap into any song from almost any device. They should get to work on a true celestial jukebox by emulating some of the most addictive features of Napster. Hundreds of thousands of songs—perhaps millions—remain unavailable for legal purchase, including obscure titles, out-of-print classics, derivative covers, and fun remixes. A number of shortsighted record companies, musicians, and songwriters still won't allow their music to be sold online.

While Apple has built a great music store, it should be seen as version 1, not an end point. The labels should be experimenting with bonus downloads, bundled offerings of familiar and unfamiliar tracks, and tools that elevate customers to producer status, giving people the ability to mix and mash songs together, create compilations—and sell them to other music fans right on the site. Playlists are a great entry point for user participation. A site called Webjay.org lets listeners create playlists of songs on the Web.

Instead of raising prices at the online music stores, the labels should be lowering them. Digital music costs nothing to manufacture, ship, or store, so it should always cost less than its CD cousins. Why not wean kids off file-sharing networks today with 25-cent and 50-cent downloads—as Mudd proposed years ago—and provide services and quality superior to what file traders can get for free?

Traditional radio's days are numbered. Legions of devoted music fans are increasingly turning to P2P networks, Web radio, and satellite radio, with their rich choices and interactive features, as antidotes to the puerile sterility of terrestrial radio. Studies show that the more people listen to Web radio, the more CDs they buy. A few years from now, we'll have broadband radio that lets us listen in our cars to audio on demand. Niche, not mass, will rule the highways.

A new generation of devices allows users to capture, time-shift, and transfer audio recordings. Look for the TiVo effect. Just as viewers watch more and better TV with TiVo, so listeners will discover, collect, archive, and dip into ever-expanding selections of personal radio delivered in personalized, narrowly tailored slices by the new breed of amateur Webcasters. Podcasting will grow in popularity, while traditional radio and CDs will increasingly be seen as an outmoded way of delivering music.

RIAA president Cary Sherman tells me the CD is on its way to "the dustbin of history," though it could take a couple of decades to phase out completely. The industry is pushing new formats such as high-capacity audio discs and CD-DVD hybrids with video and extra features. The new formats *do* sound amazing, with heart-melting fidelity and fuller audio range than regular CDs. Why, then, are people are stepping *down* in quality to MP3s, which compress a music file to a tenth its original size, instead of stepping up to Super Audio Compact Disc and DVD Audio? The lukewarm reception could be because the new devices don't play regular CDs, lack digital outputs, and contain digital watermarks designed to shackle the recordings to the disc. Given a choice, most of us choose participation over permission culture.

In the long term, paint me bullish on a reborn music industry's prospects as companies learn how to take advantage of the opportunities in the new digital marketplace. Griffin, too, agrees that music companies will move beyond their obsession with piracy and come to accept that file trading has become a permanent staple of youth culture. Eventually they will figure out how to "monetize the anarchy."

Griffin, a new father, says, "The kind of media world our kids grow up in will be so different from our own, but to them, it will just be the natural order of things. They'll grow up in a world where entertainment and most art and intellectual property will be fluid and friction-free. The idea that a song could be recorded and moved effortlessly over a network or even wirelessly to a cell phone will seem normal. And the idea that this can be stopped—through legislation or a piece of software code or a shrink-wrap contract or a misleading educational campaign—will be preposterous to them."

12 Architects of Darknet

FTER NAPSTER INTRODUCED PEER-TO-PEER TO THE masses, tens of millions of Americans dove headlong into a file-trading binge of instant gratification and overindulgence that Caligula himself might have admired. But the free-music shindig couldn't last forever, and the copyright cops finally raided the party.

For more than two years, users of Kazaa, BearShare, eDonkey, and home-brew campus sharing programs had figured their file-swapping forays were concealed from view, given that they had taken on nicknames like cosmogrrrl or shredderboy99. That sense of security was a mirage, as they discovered when the Recording Industry Association of America began filing lawsuits against individual file traders in 2003.

Cosmogrrrl, shredderboy99, and millions of other P2P users learned that their pseudonyms offered no protection because their machines, in essence, ratted them out. Whenever personal computers go online, they are assigned a specific Internet address—one that outsiders can track and attach to a name. As the record industry's legal assault kicked into high fear, a new breed of high-tech detective agency sprang up, bearing names like Overpeer, MediaDefender, and BayTSP. Mostly, these outfits have been keeping tabs on file sharers, though in some cases they follow their clients' instructions to dabble in a mild form of sabotage by uploading dummy files called "spoofs" or tying up P2P networks by posing as users who wanted to download large files through slow modems. Their aim is simple: to make life miserable for Internet bootleggers.

For a time after the RIAA announced its plans to file lawsuits, file sharing nosedived. But within nine months, file trading bounced back to its dizzying levels. In September 2004 there were about 6.8 million people logged on to the most popular file-sharing networks at any given time, compared to 4.3 million a year earlier. Today, P2P has gone mainstream. ZPoc is file-sharing software that caters to fans of Christian music. On CyberChef you can trade recipes. There's even a P2P service for fans of singer Alicia Keyes.

The entertainment companies remain unbowed. While Sony BMG Music is working with P2P software maker Grokster on a joint business venture, most of the industry still sees peer-to-peer services as the enemy. The music industry continues to file lawsuits against file traders, and Microsoft and major media companies are gearing up for a public education campaign on the airwaves and in the schools on the subject of piracy. The RIAA says it's pleased by the results of its aggressive tactics, but it may not have counted on a side effect: while millions of people have been scared straight into abandoning file sharing, the lawsuits have driven millions of other file traders deeper underground. In the months after the lawsuits started flying, a new generation of insurgent file-sharing sites reported a surge in traffic. So deeply had file sharing become embedded in the fabric of the digital generation that even threats of heavy fines could not stamp it out. Instead, many traders turned to the Darknet.

With an arms race mounting, some observers wonder whether the recording industry is on a suicide march. "The RIAA is breeding antibiotic-resistant bacteria," warns Clay Shirky, a software developer and thought leader on new media and culture.

Recent history bears him out. Napster was a vulnerable legal target for the record labels because it used a central directory that pointed users to music files residing on millions of personal computers. When the courts shut down Napster, the backlash spawned a new breed of decentralized file-sharing networks. On March 14, 2000, Justin Frankel, the twenty-year-old whiz kid who ran America Online's Nullsoft unit, released Gnutella, a grassroots file-sharing program with no commercial aspirations. AOL removed the program from its Web site nineteen hours later, but not before ten thousand users had downloaded it. Today, LimeWire, BearShare, and Morpheus all run by using Gnutella software. In late 2000, Swedish coder Niklas Zennström—now CEO of Skype, a free Internet phone service—codeveloped a new type of file-trading network called FasTrack. It now powers Kazaa and Grokster. Unlike Napster, these new P2P services contain no central directory, making the networks less vulnerable to legal challenge. Generally speaking, however, the services do not mask the digital finger-prints of users, leaving individuals vulnerable to industry lawsuits.

The hottest new P2P program is called BitTorrent. Bram Cohen, the twenty-eight-year-old Seattle programmer who wrote the code as a way to pull down large files from the Internet, told the *New York Times* that using BitTorrent to trade copyrighted files is "patently stupid because it's not anonymous, and it can't be made anonymous because it's fundamentally antithetical to the architecture."[1] Still, millions of people use it to swap movies, software, and TV shows.

So far, the courts have shielded these kinds of P2P networks from legal liability because of their decentralized design. Even if a court ordered them to shut down tomorrow, the networks would live on, nested in the hard drives of millions of connected users. As one magazine put it: Genie 1, Bottle 0. The music and movie industries succeeded in shuttering Napster, but they can't survive many more such victories.

Today, the digital media wars have entered a new phase. Fueled by what they saw as the arrogance of a litigious entertainment industry, a handful of code jockeys have begun a grassroots insurgency, launching a powerful class of P2P file-sharing networks that contain built-in cloaking devices. With names like Blubster, Waste, BadBlue, Tarzan, and Publius (named for the anonymous authors of the Federalist Papers), the new underground net-works are designed to keep its members' activities and identities secret. "Encrypted networks are . . . the next holy grail for Internet file-swappers," the *New York Times* reported in mid-2003.[2]

The new underground networks are the most visible—that is to say, invisible—example of the Darknet's growth. In these resilient networks, not only are the users' identities protected, but also the traded files are encrypted (or scrambled and hidden from view) in much the same way that data are shuttled during a secure online credit card transaction. Outsiders can't tell what music files, movies, and other works are zipping back and forth. It's the twenty-first-century equivalent of hiding bathtub gin under a fake floorboard, as one writer put it.

"With the RIAA trying to scare users around the world, the developer community is pumping up to create networks which are safer and more anonymous," Pablo Soto, the Spaniard who created Blubster, told the *New York Times*.[3] Within months after launch, Blubster had 250,000 users sharing more than 50 million files.

Travis Kalanick, whose MP3 search engine Scour was shut down by the music industry, told CNN that private darknets are the future of online music swapping. "You essentially will have to socialize your way into a network," he said. "The RIAA may be better off penetrating al Qaeda."[4]

The resulting landscape turns the tradition of the open Internet on its ear. Users have begun walling themselves off from prying eyes during certain activities as never before.

The entertainment companies don't appear to be fazed by the tech rebels' new toys. "The fact that most people have to understand is you are never anonymous on the Internet," Mark Ishikawa, founder of BayTSP, told the *San Francisco Chronicle*.[5] RIAA senior vice president Matt Oppenheim told News.com, "We are not aware of any technology that can provide a user with complete anonymity."[6]

Brave talk, but nonsense, chortle the darknet architects. "It's going to be easy to go dark," one boasted. In encrypted networks, it's virtually impossible to learn where a file originated, where it ended up, or even what the file contained.

The entertainment consultant Bruce Forest offers a sober warning for entertainment companies: "The more that they apply ever-thicker layers of lawyers to this problem, the more lawyerproof will be the new technologies that emerge." If litigation, prosecution, and onerous copy restrictions spur a mass migration to these cloaked darknets, he warns, "it's game over."

Not all darknets were born with the battle cry "Give me free Linkin Park MP3s!" One of the largest darknets, Freenet, was first conceived as a way to route around government censorship.

The story begins at the University of Edinburgh in Scotland, where an undergraduate student named Ian Clarke became fascinated with how emergent systems such as an ant colony or a flock of birds displayed intelligent, complex behaviors while remaining decentralized and highly robust.

He merged that curiosity with a strong political predilection for freedom of speech and wrote a paper fleshing out the idea of a highly secure, encrypted network that would facilitate the free flow of information. In essence, he was describing a darknet. The paper earned him a B.[7]

Clarke wasn't done. After spending long nights in 1999 writing the source code for Freenet, he placed it on the Internet and invited others to help make the idea a reality. Within a short while, volunteers began flocking to what would become the Freenet Project, attracted by Clarke's vision of a censorproof, snoopproof bulwark against government intrusion. Today a small group of software engineers continues to make Freenet a faster, more robust service; all of them are volunteers except for one coder in Britain who works at "subsistence levels" and is paid through small donations. Some 2 million people around the world have downloaded the free program—some out of curiosity, some out of necessity. Another three thousand people download it each day and an untold number of others obtain it through a daisy chain of floppy discs.

Articulate and soft-spoken, the twenty-six-year-old native of Ireland has the kind of soft features, sweep of brown hair, and look of wide-eyed wonder that schoolgirls like to sketch in notebooks. "I'm a very strong believer that freedom of speech is essential to democracy," Clarke says. "If you are forced to disclose your identity every time you express your opinion, you're susceptible to retaliation. Remember that the Federalist Papers, which laid the groundwork for the U.S. Constitution, were authored anonymously. The United States might be a very different country were it not for anonymous speech. So I really take an extremist position on that. I believe if two or more people have a desire to communicate, to transfer information, then they should be free to do so without external interference."

Clarke receives reports of foreigners under repressive regimes who use Freenet to trade news and information more freely. For example, dissidents in mainland China took the source code, modified it, translated it into Mandarin Chinese, and distributed it within China. The software has allowed Net-savvy Chinese to visit forbidden sites like CNN.com and access banned information such as the Tiananmen Papers, a transcript of the 1989 meetings between Chinese leaders and students, without fear of being arrested by government authorities. For this reason, the U.S. State Department and Voice of America have lavished praise on Freenet. To bring Western news and ideas to totalitarian states, the Voice of America occasionally sets up servers that act as relays or stepping-stones to the World Wide Web. But in a place like China, how do you tell the dissidents where to find the Web servers without tipping off the Chinese authorities? And if you're a dissident, how do you publish information about the Falun Gong spiritual sect without fear of reprisal? (Any of the 50 million Internet users in China who type Falun Gong into Google come away empty.)

Freenet is set up so that users don't rely on centralized servers that can be easily subverted. Instead, Freenet plays a shell game with information, so that a cloud of encrypted data moves constantly around the network. By setting aside part of your hard drive for Freenet files, you won't know what information resides on your own machine, and neither would an outsider. Users can access a global information library by passing along an anonymous request from one Freenet machine to the next, so that no one knows where the request originated or where the data were eventually found. A dissident using Freenet can not only consume information anonymously but publish as well.

As evidence that no one controls Freenet, not even its creators, consider the fact that the Freenet China group was secretly active for at least a year before Clarke and the core Freenet developers were even aware of its existence. "I understand that these people are not terribly keen to advertise their presence," he says, "but getting them to talk to us is like getting blood out of a stone."

Lately, attention has turned from Freenet's censorship-smashing abilities inside totalitarian states to its equally disruptive effects in the democratic West. Here, Freenet has been put to use not to route around political repression but to route around overly strict intellectual property laws.

In fall 2003, when internal memos from Diebold Election Systems leaked onto the Internet, Diebold attorneys managed to force their removal from the open Web under threat of DMCA sanctions. But when Freenet users posted the memos, they remained accessible to anyone with a Freenet account. The Diebold lawyers had no way to learn who had posted them or where they resided.

Clarke remains outraged that modern copyright laws are being used to quash speech. "Here's a group of people who are trying to promote democracy by pushing for transparency in the elections process, and copyright law is being used to censor what they're saying. That's an affront to the values of a democratic nation."

I spoke with Clarke a few weeks after he returned to Scotland following a three-year stay in Los Angeles, where he formed two ventures to turn the technology behind Freenet into a business application. He left the United

States, he says, partly for personal reasons, but partly because he worried that Freenet's abilities to create a publication network impervious to censorship could attract the wrath of the Justice Department. "Working in the P2P field as I do, it's useful to live in a country where people don't take an automatically procorporate stance so much as they do in the United States." The current political climate fosters laws like the DMCA and new standards that limit the capabilities of personal computers—trends that are inimical to Freenet's goal of enhancing personal freedom.

Clarke is well aware that many of those flocking to Freenet are more interested in snagging free music than in making soaring political pronouncements. Although he is not eager to see Freenet turned into a music and movie file-trading bazaar, if it happens, so be it. "When people just want to get music without paying for it, that doesn't much interest me. But Freenet cannot protect the rights of political dissidents without also protecting file traders." A copyright chip cannot be built into the network's architecture without compromising its most essential feature: its cloaking ability.

It is an intractable conflict, pitting the right of darknet members to remain anonymous against the right of content owners to have their copyrights respected. To Clarke, it's no contest. Copyright law has become dangerously out of balance, he says, and darknets like Freenet offer citizens the ability to push back a little. "It is the advocates of copyright law who are impinging on people's freedom of communication, not the other way around. In order to enforce copyright law, you need to see what bits people are sending to each other, and if you've got some sort of watchdog watching what kinds of bits flow back and forth, then they cannot communicate freely because someone is looking over their shoulder. Ultimately, what is more important to you: copyright or freedom of communication, which is essential to democracy?"

Clarke argues that copyright laws have expanded dramatically in recent years, to the public's detriment. "Intellectual property is essentially a fiction. In the U.S. Constitution, it had a specific purpose, to promote the sciences and useful arts. Unfortunately, that notion has been twisted so dramatically that we see people suggesting that digital information should be thought of as property no different than a house or piece of land. That's absurd. A piece of land is not infinitely divisible, and yet a piece of information can be replicated as many times as you want. So I would start by challenging their basic premise. Information is not property, and therefore the transmission of information is not theft."

Such views are certain to prove controversial should file swappers migrate to Freenet in large numbers. For it is not just music files and movies that could be traded on Freenet, but also Nazi memorabilia, terrorist how-to manuals, kiddie porn, and other material that cannot stand up to the antiseptic light of public disclosure. Clarke acknowledges this, saying, "If it can be represented in digital form, it can be traded on Freenet. It would be simply impossible to design Freenet any other way while still achieving its goal."

After the RIAA began taking legal action against individual file traders, Freenet experienced "a severalfold increase in page views and downloads," Clarke says. "I think Freenet is widely perceived in the peer-to-peer community as the Alamo—the last resort if the entertainment industry gets really nasty."

But we all know how the Battle of the Alamo turned out, and Clarke tells his peers not to assume that Freenet can route around efforts by government and private industry to reengineer the Internet and the personal computer. In early 2004 the computer giant HP announced its intention to incorporate copy protection—Clarke calls it "user-hostile technology"—in every machine it manufactures. "There is a strong sentiment in most countries that the government and large corporations should stay out of people's bedrooms," he says. "I don't want a digital security guard who's working for Sony to be sitting inside the computer in my bedroom telling me what I can and cannot do with the computer I've bought. I don't want to be tricked or forced to buy something that acts in someone else's best interests.

"If digital rights management becomes pervasive in computers, then I think the battle will have absolutely been lost," he says. "Even though Freenet could allow you to get the bits onto your computer, if your computer doesn't allow you to do anything with them, or reports you for having them, then there's nothing Freenet can do to help."

Freenet may be the largest true darknet around, but it's getting plenty of company. Other programmers have coalesced around the goal of creating private networks that exalt personal freedoms and individual privacy.

Justin Frankel, the code warrior behind Gnutella, repeated his impetuous bad-boy act at America Online in May 2003 when he released Waste— only to see AOL pull the code hours later with a terse notice warning that "any and all" copies of it must be destroyed. (Frankel has since left AOL, but I would love to see his employee evaluation.) Again, the P2P software proliferated quickly online. Designed for clusters of fifty people or less who want to share files or chat with friends while protected by CIA-proof cryptography, the program relies on a buddy system based on trust. Only the invited can join Waste, named for the underground postal system in the Thomas Pynchon novel *The Crying of Lot 49*. Consultant Forest calls Waste "the hottest thing in the underground right now."

Although some darknets are used in ways proscribed by law, others are not. Legitimate business applications, such as Groove Networks' collaboration software, are now being used for clandestine communications. Human rights activists in Sri Lanka used a Groove darknet to trade cloaked electronic messages about the country's civil war.[8]

Groove CEO Ray Ozzie told me at the 2004 Supernova conference about troops on the ground in Iraq who were using laptops and his company's darknet software to communicate securely with others about inventory levels at the coalitions forces' Humanitarian Operations Center. A reporter asked him about the danger that darknets will take up bigger chunks of the Internet. "It's not a danger, it's a requirement," Ozzie replied. "We need virtual boundaries around our workgroups. . . . The only way to accomplish that is with darknets."[9]

In a less noble vein, Earthstation5 made a splash when it declared "war" on the major entertainment companies, saying it was making terabytes of music and Hollywood films, including first-run movies like *Terminator 3* and *Tomb Raider*, freely available on its file trading network. Based in a refugee camp on the West Bank, Earthstation5 debuted in mid-2003 with the boast, "The next revolution in file sharing is upon you. Resistance is futile and we are now in control." The service's president, Ras Kabir, announced that U.S. laws "have absolutely no meaning to us here in Palestine" and taunted the record labels and movie studios: "There aren't too many process servers that are going to be coming into the Jenin refugee camp. We'll welcome them if they do." It's not clear if Earthstation5 is really a darknet. While Earthstation5 claims its architecture provides complete anonymity against the authorities, Clarke is skeptical, noting that ES5 has refused to describe in detail how it guarantees the security of its visitors. My e-mails to Kabir were ignored.

It is too soon to say which, if any, of the fledgling new breed of darknets will eventually achieve mass popularity. Many of the digital speakeasies are still clunky and difficult to use. But those drawbacks will be overcome as the technology matures, and the long-term threat posed to Big Entertainment is very real, despite its professed lack of concern.

Eventually one of these darknets could evolve into a doomsday weapon against the record labels and other entertainment companies.

Andrew Frank, a former executive at two media consultancies who wrote an influential report about file sharing cited by Jack Valenti and other entertainment heavyweights in testimony before Congress, says the lesson of Napster, Gnutella, MP3, and DivX is that small bits of code that emerge from obscure places can spread virally and have widespread effects under the right conditions. The largest threat to the motion picture studios and record labels comes not from Kazaa or other aboveground companies that can be held accountable by Congress or the courts, but by darknets like Freenet, which he said present "a new kind of doomsday weapon."

I ask Clarke whether Freenet could turn into a doomsday weapon, expecting a quick demurral. But he doesn't shirk from the term. If the music and movie industries fail to provide people with digital entertainment unencumbered by ball-and-chain restrictions, he says, then the technology will hit back and darknets will flourish. "Yes, certainly it is a doomsday weapon. But like all doomsday weapons, you hope you never have to use it."

Alex Yalen, an undergraduate majoring in journalism and history at the University of Missouri-Columbia, takes a moment when I ask him to describe the prevalence of file sharing among college students today. "There is definitely a casual attitude on campus toward what is essentially electronic theft," he begins. "File sharing, software piracy, hacking, cracking—whatever you want to call it, it's rampant, it's everywhere, and I'm sure it's driving corporate types nuts."[10]

Yalen prefers not to discuss his own file-sharing proclivities, but says many of his friends and peers have no qualms about pulling down software programs, music, movies, computer games, and other material from easily accessible warez sites. "Intellectual property means basically nothing to most of the people I know," he says. "With high-speed Internet access, new computers, lots of free time, and creative minds, the attitude is pretty opportunistic. The majority opinion is, if it's there, take it."

One of Yalen's friends hosts an FTP server on campus with more than six hundred Hollywood movies. "He doesn't go out to bars and get hammered. When Saturday night rolls around, he sits in his dorm room, downloads new films, and watches them. Sometimes he'll borrow DVDs from the campus library, rip them, and return them. He burns them onto CD, and people come to him to rent movies."

Yalen and his university are hardly unique. The share culture is prevalent on hundreds of college campuses. High prices for software, CDs, and movie tickets—even with student discounts—is a major factor. A second motivation: this is just what college kids do today. "Come on. We're teenagers. There's an element of rebelliousness here," Yalen says. "It's kind of like spitting at the Man in our own little geeky way. A lot of kids feel they're being gouged by big corporations, and this is the way to get even."

Morality is no hindrance. "There is absolutely no stigma when it comes to file sharing or software stealing among college students," he adds. "I have run into a select few who choose for ethical reasons not to pirate, but it's funny—they're the ones who get stigmatized. It's a socially accepted and expected practice." Yalen believes artists should get paid for their work, but he has heard countless stories about the record labels ripping off musicians. Guilt does not come easily to the file traders of Gen Y.

Yalen can't speak for an entire generation, of course. Plenty of college kids forsake file sharing and observe copyright laws. Still, the entertainment companies are petrified of Alex Yalen's generation and the revenge of the file-sharing masses. Their first impulse has been to push for tighter controls, stronger locks, and more punitive laws.

One of the latest efforts centers on digital identity or personal ID certificates. Basically, all Internet users would all assemble in the prison yard for our electronic ankle bracelets. Every online transaction or file transfer would allow a third party to track the details of who paid for a rental or purchase—and who didn't.

Lauren Weinstein, a software and network developer in Los Angeles who cofounded People for Internet Responsibility, is among those who believe such efforts will only stoke the Darknet's appeal. "You have to ask, do the current approaches of the entertainment companies do any good, or will they speed a mass movement to the underground? Yes, the restrictions placed on digital media give content owners more control, and the RIAA lawsuits stop some people from trading, but they also foster a sense of us vs. them. In effect, you're encouraging file traders to consider joining these underground networks, and you've set into motion an evolutionary process of survival of the fittest where the systems get better and better."[11]

This will take years to play out. "You don't go from a visible to an invisible file-sharing world overnight," Weinstein says. But one potential danger to the entertainment industry is that file trading could become impossible to track and the heaviest file traders impossible to spot. "We don't know how much of this is happening already, because to the extent they're successful, by definition it's difficult to get metrics about a phenomenon that's hidden down there and you can't see at all."

Attempts to criminalize encrypted, masked, or distributed networks will fail, Weinstein says, because file-trading darknets are using the same technologies that corporations and scientists use to share and store protected data. Many darknets already emulate the kinds of collaboration tools used at successful businesses, which offer a high degree of privacy, security, and the ability to handle large files. HP and Siemens, for example, use darknets to allow managers to share sensitive data with outside partners. GlaxoSmithKline uses a darknet to allow biologists and chemists to collaborate with university researchers on developing a new obesity drug.[12]

"It is quite possible that in the long run, this is a problem that can't be solved through technology or education," Weinstein says. "It may prove difficult to charge people for material that they can obtain online for free. We are probably heading toward a world where the extent to which people can expect to be paid for their work and their intellectual property is going to depend on the goodwill of the population, rather than by trying to force the issue through technology or law. To the extent that you make enemies of your customers and drive them into darknets, that's self-destructive."

Weinstein underscores his belief that artists should be paid for the fruits of their labors, but that doesn't change the reality of the situation. The more that entertainment companies overreact by imposing burdensome new rules that limit customers' ability to use digital devices in fair ways, "you'll see a backlash from users who will view video piracy as legitimate and defensible rather than an illicit activity."

New media expert Shirky, a professor of telecommunications at New York University, agrees. If Napster was the first wave of file sharing, the second wave arrived with P2P networks that abandoned open, transparent, centralized systems like Napster in favor of less efficient, decentralized systems that can withstand legal attack. Now a third wave is beginning to emerge. The newest incarnation consists of social systems where members are anonymous (like Freenet or Blubster) or you have to schmooze your way into a group's good graces (like Waste).

These are the "small-worlds networks" cited by the "Darknet" paper researchers. In such a world, we won't have a Napster-style celestial jukebox at our fingertips, but we will be able to access a smaller set of material from people we can trust. Our searches for digital media will increasingly depend on our social connections. And our online transactions with others will increasingly be done with encryption running in the background, a trend Shirky calls "profound and irreversible."

As a result, he says, "It's an open question whether darknets will be regarded as a victory or defeat for the recording industry. These exclusive clubs may not have the rich catalog of a Napster or Kazaa, but they will also be much harder for outsiders to penetrate."[13]

BusinessWeek Online warned that the RIAA lawsuits will lead many more users to embrace "encrypted P2P networks [that] will allow not only continued trading of pirated music, but also of pirated software and movies."[14] But the motion picture industry appears determined to follow the RIAA over the cliff.

"We made every effort to engage in an educational campaign to alert consumers that trafficking in infringing movies over P2P services is illegal and subject to civil prosecution, but that practice grew and we felt we had to do something to protect our property," MPAA vice president of government relations Fritz Attaway said. "If someone put their hand into your pocket and grabbed your wallet, you'd probably try to stop them, no?" The movie industry is now pursuing individual file traders.

Hollywood is determined to do whatever it takes to neutralize file sharing and other unauthorized uses of copyrighted material. Two key efforts—the broadcast flag and the trusted computing initiative—involve placing padlocks on some doors of the digital home. Both efforts will frustrate ordinary users but have little effect on hackers or pirates. It's hard to argue with the stated goal of either initiative. The broadcast flag seeks to prevent the indiscriminate redistribution of copyrighted digital TV programs on the Internet. In fall 2003, the FCC issued rules requiring every device capable of processing a digital TV signal to respect the broadcast flag—an invisible marker—in movies and TV shows broadcast on over-the-air television beginning on July 1, 2005.[15] Copyright holders may set the broadcast flag to say that any devices detecting it must refuse to transmit that stream across the Internet in an unprotected fashion. Chris Murray, legislative counsel for Consumers Union, points out that more than 75 million DVD players in viewers' homes today will not be able to play flagged programs recorded with DVD machines sold after mid-2005. A show you record in your living room may not play in the den. In spring 2004, the political group TrueMajority mashed up video of NBC's *The Apprentice* with news footage of President George W. Bush. In the resulting video, Trump fires Bush. Such political speech is protected under fair use, but if the broadcast flag were set, commentators would never get the raw materials to create their parodies.

The American Library Association worries that the broadcast flag will prevent the use of TV clips in the classroom and prevent digitally recorded TV shows from being streamed to students in long-distance learning classes. (Public Knowledge, the ALA, EFF, and other public-interest groups have sued to stop the broadcast flag.)

Internet users also will see their digital rights curtailed. "Right before *Harry Potter* hit the screen, a local reporter interviewed my daughter about the movie," says Seth Greenstein, an attorney with the 5C consortium of tech companies. "I thought it would be very cool to take that broadcast and send it to Grandma in Florida or my brother in Israel. Why not use the flexibility and immediacy of the Internet? In the short run at least, the broadcast flag might prevent that."[16]

Joe Kraus of DigitalConsumer.org cites the example of a high school student compiling a multimedia report on the prevalence of violence on prime-time TV, complete with short examples from network telecasts. Such behavior is permitted under fair use, but she might not be able to e-mail her presentation to her teacher and classmates. In the workplace, countless employees will be frustrated when they try to e-mail a flagged digital TV clip from their home to their office.

While the FCC claims it wants to protect such fair uses, those rights seem likely to disappear. (Even if the technowhizzes devise some sort of secure online cocoon environment, such a barrier places an undue burden on users. If you've ever wrestled with a virtual private network, for instance, it's not the sort of thing you want to inflict on poor Grandma.) Fox technology chief Andrew Setos—who unveiled the broadcast flag proposal in 2002—says media companies hope to solve the current shortcomings of the technology within a few years. In any event, he says, such inconveniences are a small price to pay for keeping high-value material on free, over-the-air broadcasting.

Hollywood got its way with the broadcast flag, but what did it achieve? The flimsy bit of code inserted into broadcasts won't thwart pirates. "The technology on its own terms is hopelessly inadequate at addressing piracy," says von Lohmann, rattling off a list of holes that future hackers and pirates can use to beat the restrictions. For instance, the flag won't stop anyone from converting digital shows to analog, redigitizing them, and blasting them into the Darknet.[17]

But Hollywood got something better than copy protection: a process that gives both the government and the motion picture studios a seat at the table in approving new digital television devices.

Representative Zoe Lofgren, Democrat of California, warned that the FCC order would stop innovative new consumer electronics and computing products from ever coming to market. "Do we want the FCC wielding veto power over a new Apple computer, Palm handheld, or Motorola cell phone? Of course not," she wrote in a commentary for the San Jose Mercury News criticizing the FCC's ruling.[18]

Consumer advocates suspect that the greatest impact of the broadcast flag is yet to come. When the flag "fails"—as such a trivial protection scheme surely will—Hollywood will return to Capitol Hill, demanding stronger safeguards for its material. While some critics fret that the studios will get permission to insert additional restrictions into digital television programming—say, monitoring viewing habits or preventing people from time-shifting, skipping commercials, or archiving shows—a more likely scenario is that Hollywood will press its case to "plug the analog hole."

Plugging the analog hole, Valenti tells me, is now the MPAA's top priority. Video content, even when delivered in a protected digital signal, must be converted to an analog format to be viewed on millions of analog TV sets in viewers' homes. Encryption does not survive digital-to-analog conversion. With copy controls gone, the video can be converted back into digital form and redistributed on the Net.

The MPAA's plan to plug the analog hole consists of two parts: First, the MPAA wants Congress to pass a law requiring watermark detectors in all devices that convert signals from analog to digital. Under this scenario, an invisible mark detected by special equipment would be detected by cop chips inside devices that shut down when a watermark violation is detected. Putting a microphone in front of your speaker to copy a song simply wouldn't work. (Again, this would stop casual copiers, but not hackers or pirates. Again, it would trample on users' rights, such as a mother who is unable to videotape her son's first steps because he is toddling near a TV set showing a copyrighted cartoon.[19]) Second, the studios want to phase out the 300 million TVs, VCRs, and DVD players with "unprotected" analog outputs. New devices would be manufactured without analog inputs and outputs. Failing that, they want to add copyright controls to analog outputs. Valenti admits it would take many years to sunset all analog devices, but eventually Hollywood wants to get to a place where the only outputs on consumer devices are digital—and locked down with copy controls.[20]

"They want to get rid of analog because they can't control it," says Mike Godwin of Public Knowledge.

As convergence brings digital devices into the center of home entertainment, computers—not television—have become the real targets of Hollywood's jihad. Media center hybrid TVs, handheld video players, entertainment servers, and other digital gadgets must all be dumbed down. Any computer offering HDTV must weld the hood shut so that the hard drive, DVD recorder, and other components are sealed with copy protection.

"If they ruin television, I'll be upset," Godwin says. "But if they destroy the computer revolution, I'll be furious."

At a Digital Hollywood conference in Beverly Hills I attended, MPAA technology chief Brad Hunt summed up the challenge facing the entertainment and computing industries this way: "How do you make the PC a trusted entertainment appliance?"

Hollywood's preoccupation with wrapping its movies in "security clothing," as Jack Valenti puts it, has begun to dovetail with the efforts of the high-tech industry to make personal computers more secure and trustworthy.

The question is, more secure and trustworthy for whom?

For the past few years, the Trusted Computing Group—a group of high-tech companies that includes Microsoft, HP, Intel, IBM, and Sony—have collaborated to create a more secure environment for users of PCs, cell phones, and other digital devices. Chip manufacturers like Intel and the major computer companies—including HP, Dell, Gateway, and IBM—are redesigning the hardware of PCs to make them resistant to tampering by intruders.

On the software side, Microsoft has undertaken its own trusted computing efforts. In 2006, Microsoft plans to release Longhorn, the code name for the operating system that will succeed Windows XP. Plans call for Longhorn to include a "next generation secure computing base," Microsoft-speak for turning a part of your hard drive into an uncrackable data vault.

Computer users stand to benefit greatly from the security improvements offered by trusted computing. Such efforts are likely to go a long way in curbing viruses, worms, spam, and malicious hackers. For example, with such technology you can ensure that your personal diary can't be read on any other machine without your permission.

But the technology also carries risks. It gives third parties the power to enforce certain kinds of computer behavior against the user's wishes. For instance, it gives Hollywood, the record industry, and software makers much greater control over the way customers can use movies, music, and computer programs.

"It's a two-edged sword," Brian La Macchia, a software architect in Microsoft's trusted platform technologies group, told the *Chronicle of Higher Education*, acknowledging that commercial publishers have demanded greater protection for their copyrighted works.

In a trusted computing system, the operating system and hardware will work in concert to prevent any tampering by outsiders—or by the computer owner. And therein lies the rub.

Until now, computers were ours. They obeyed our orders (when they weren't crashing) without split loyalties. A surprising percentage of users tinker with their stuff, reworking software or engaging in reverse engineering. Studies conducted at MIT's Sloan School of Management documented the importance of user innovation in certain industries. For instance, a quarter of those using computer-aided design software reported developing innovations for their personal use. The original way a technology vendor invents a piece of software or media is not necessarily the end of the creative process.

Such tinkering may or may not jibe with the brave new world of trusted computing. A key component of Microsoft's new technology will be the nexus, a program that creates a secure environment for conducting private transactions or enforcing copyright policies. Microsoft is quick to point out that it doesn't set the rules; third parties do. That's true. The next generation secure computing base isn't a digital rights management system, but it is a trust system that enforces the content controls set by others.

Based on past behavior, we can expect Hollywood to use these new enforcement tools to control customers' after-purchase behavior. Under the new regime, publishers could set tamperproof controls so that a user cannot capture scenes from a movie, copy songs from a purchased music CD, forward an e-mail, or run certain kinds of software. It's a good guess that this region will be a No Fair Use zone.

In a column on the subject, PBS.org tech writer Robert X. Cringely slammed Microsoft's plans, writing that under such a trusted computing system, "the Internet goes from being ours to being theirs. The very data on your hard drive ceases to be yours because it could self-destruct at any time. We'll end up paying rent to use our own data!" Money quote: "It's a militarized network architecture only Dick Cheney could love."[21]

Security expert Ross Anderson of the University of Cambridge Computer Laboratory agreed. Trusted computing "will transfer the ultimate control of your PC from you to whoever wrote the software it happens to be running."[22]

In a white paper praising trusted computing but criticizing this critical element of the proposed security system, the EFF's Schoen wrote, "the computer's owner is sometimes treated as just another attacker or adversary who must be prevented from breaking in and altering the computer's software." He cited the likelihood of "consumer-unfriendly" behavior by third parties, as when a corporation prevents users from transferring a program or file to another machine, forces software upgrades or downgrades on the user, implants spyware that phones home to describe how the person is using an application, or unilaterally revokes documents stored on computers around the world in a way users can't override.

Pointing out that computer owners and third parties often have divergent interests, Schoen proposed something called owner override. Here's the idea: "Don't accept 'trusted computing' unless it's under the control of the user."[23] Undoubtedly, his suggestion will go unheeded.

Let's underscore one point: the scare stories circulating on the Net about Microsoft's plans are largely untrue. The next generation secure computing base will not prevent anyone from downloading MP3s or running unlicensed software on his or her machine. It won't tap the MPAA on the shoulder when you swap files illegally. You decide what programs to run both inside and outside the nexus. In fact, you don't have to run the nexus at all. (Disclosure: I worked as an editor for Microsoft Sidewalk in 1997–98 in the go-go days when Microsoft thought it might become a media company. I immensely enjoyed my nineteen months there.)

Now, you may be wondering: why would anyone buy a "trusted" machine? Several reasons. First, never underestimate herd behavior. Microsoft's market power ensures that tens of millions of people will buy its new operating system. Longhorn will be the default operating system sold on millions of machines after it debuts next year. No one will be given the choice of buying a system that comes without its security features, so any doubts about the nexus will be offset by the bright new eye candy that Longhorn promises. Second, we're in an insecure era, and trusted computing offers real security benefits. Any system that promises to stop malicious hackers, thieves, pirates, and spammers is bound to appeal. For network administrators, trusted computing can ensure the privacy of student records on a campus network. (Students may not be so thrilled if the same network disables file-sharing software or prevents them from downloading MP3s.)

Finally, some users will be lured by the digital goodies Hollywood offers inside the nexus. I'll wager that the studios and record companies will release movies and albums in formats that can play only on Microsoft's next generation secure computing base—and lock out Macintosh computers unless Apple bows to Hollywood's demand for an ultrasecure viewing environment. As for Linux? The open-source operating system won't be allowed to play in Hollywood's sandbox. Some 20 million Linux users are out of luck.

I cornered John Manferdelli, general manager of Microsoft's trusted platform technologies group, at a technology conference in Berkeley, California, in 2003. Outside the auditorium, Manferdelli was debating a student who insisted that trusted computing would give users less freedom and less power vis-à-vis the entertainment companies.

Manferdelli responded in all the right ways, saying Microsoft didn't want to restrict how people can use their computers, that the trusted computing technology was "policy neutral," that it gave both vendors and customers more marketplace choices with respect to digital media, and that the end user had the final say. "Yes, your computer should be under your control!" he said, exasperated, at one point.

At another tech conference in spring 2003, Bill Gates got touchy when reporters asked about Microsoft's new role as copyright cop. "We're building a security system that people can use or not use as they please," he said. "We are not telling anyone what they have to do or not do with their computers or with their content." Other Microsoft officials said their new technology will simply open up new options for enjoying entertainment on digital devices and will give all parties—publishers and users alike—more control over the information they own.

Which completely misses the point.

It may be true that Gates and the Microsofties sincerely believe that their evenhanded approach is policy-neutral. Their intent may be to play it down the middle. But the end result will be strongly skewed to the control crowd.

Individuals have never wielded power or leverage over Hollywood, with its take-it-or-leave-it cartel behavior. For a time, computers and the Internet tipped the balance of power to *our* side just enough to matter. NYU's Shirky wrote, "The architecture of the internet has effected the largest transfer of power from organizations to individuals the world has ever seen."[24] Unless the tech industry is careful, rearchitecting the PC could well shift the balance of power back to large institutions and big media companies.

Consumers won't care.

Users will.

Day after day, the entertainment brain trust and the Darknet rebels continue their escalating arms race. The motion picture studios lobby Capitol Hill for further restrictions on technology. The music labels hire copyright enforcers to hunt down file traders and to pollute the file-sharing networks with bogus spoof files. The file-trading services rewire their networks to increase user anonymity and to outsmart the spoofs. Through it all, the Darknet burrows farther underground, growing more resilient and resistant to attacks.

There is a way of out this.

We might begin with a cold splash of reality: file trading is here to stay. "The darknet genie will not be put back into the bottle," the Microsoft researchers wrote. They correctly point out that media companies need to factor in the Darknet when offering digital wares to the public. "If you are competing with the darknet, you must compete on the darknet's own terms: that is convenience and low cost rather than additional security."

In short, P2P file trading has become a central defining characteristic of our digital culture, one that young people in particular have embraced.

What can compete in such a world? Compelling business models.

Shirky, for one, is optimistic that the record labels will see the writing on the wall and agree to roll out subscription services that cover entire university campuses, as Penn State did when it signed an agreement with the new Napster in November 2003. Some eighteen thousand students get access to unlimited streams of music, paid for by student fees. Students also can download songs to a PC and burn them to a CD for 99 cents per song. If statewide university systems in California, Texas, and Florida follow suit, it could lead to "an incredibly profound turning point" for the future of digital media, Shirky suggests.

Valenti and other entertainment chieftains lament that no business can compete with free. And yet that is exactly what the Napster–Penn State deal is doing, and what the motion picture industry has been doing for years. My techie friends and I have long had the ability to pull movies down from the Darknet for free. None of us does, because Hollywood makes movies available in a wide range of convenient, mostly affordable formats. Yet, more needs to be done.

"The entire industry needs to rethink its business model," consultant Forest argues. "Instead of spending millions on copy protection and copyright enforcement, they ought to be innovating and building the ultimate system for the delivery of digital entertainment to the home." A lasting peace between the warring sides will occur only when the entertainment companies fully embrace their digital destiny.

Forest says the studios should meet the bootleggers head on. "Price it right, make it convenient, and they will come," he says.

If that happened—if Hollywood succeeded in marginalizing the movie Darknet—what would happen to the rippers, couriers, and encoders of Forest's world? They could serve culture better not by freeing movies from their Hollywood shackles but by creating their own works—digital film shorts, remixes, satirical adaptations. Who will become the Woody Allen of cyberspace? Where are the digital auteurs who will give us the next *What's Up, Tiger Lily?*, complete with a spoof sound track?

This is how to stunt the growth of the Darknet: empower users rather than treat them as one-dimensional consumers. Give people high entertainment value at a fair price. Recognize a new hunger in the land for digital media.

When innovation replaces litigation as the entertainment industry's guiding principle, we will see piracy become a footnote in our transition to the age of digital entertainment media.

If Hollywood and the record labels do not take up the challenge, then the true architects of Darknet may turn out to be the entertainment companies and their tech enablers.

13 Mod Squads

Can Gamers Show Us the Way?

STROLLING THROUGH THE VIRTUAL SHOPPING MALL, I consider buying a new dress for my suddenly slim girlish figure. Instead, I turn to go, deciding to keep my flowing red gown. As I walk to the fifth-story balcony ledge and survey the luminous landscape, I raise my arms—they're a bit weary from being aflame all day—and leap into the abyss, soaring over hills, houses, and beaches. Moments later I smack into the side of a condo. Flying takes some practice. So does having a new body.

It's my first time in a virtual world, and I'm immediately hooked. Cory Ondrejka has loaned me an avatar—a sort of three-dimensional alter ego—as we interact with other cyber-residents via a projection screen in the conference room at Linden Lab, a San Francisco company that is simultaneously blazing new trails in cyberspace and cyberlaw.

The bearded, convivial Ondrejka, Linden Lab's vice president of product development, wears a burgundy rugby shirt, tan shorts, and sandals as he gives me a tour of this trippy new world. The company, founded in 1999, released *Second Life* publicly in June 2003. Unlike action-adventure games where the goal is to kill and conquer, *Second Life* is a virtual world—or "persistent world," in the industry lingo—that is, a space where you hang out, explore, and build personal relationships. These visually rich environments may well be what chat rooms will look like ten years from now.

On the other side of the conference room doors, twenty developers, artists, and marketing employees hunker down at computers under exposed ductwork in the spacious second-story loft, answering customer e-mail and working on new functionalities. The Linden Lab team developed advanced tools that let players generate lifelike characters and build three-dimensional objects. A physics engine simulates the physics of the real world (except, that is, for gravity-defying avatars).

With these tools in hand, users have created over 99 percent of the *Second Life* universe. More than fifteen hundred subscribers wander through the world on a typical day. Many choose to homestead, buying plots of land to add a house or tavern here, a marina or lighthouse there. Unlike an old-fashioned game, where a company sells you a disc or you download static content onto your PC, a virtual world is fluid and ongoing. If you sign off *Second Life* and come back a day later, someone may have built a house or changed the terrain. If *Second Life* existed in the world of atoms rather than bits, it would cover thirty-seven hundred acres, or six square miles. Soon it will be as big as Manhattan.

While other online games like the Sims Online force players to perform tasks in pursuit of a goal, *Second Life* lets people express their personalities and display their creativity. In all, more than thirty thousand users have created a rich, diverse landscape filled with more than half a million objects, interesting characters, whimsical domains, and cool getaways like an island retreat and a forty-ride amusement park. Members are busy creating two hundred events a week, everything from open houses and costume parties to scavenger hunts.

Second Life has become such a sprawling landscape that it's hard to keep up with everything. And so Linden Lab hired a thirty-six-year-old freelance journalist in Oakland, California, to start a weblog, New World News, to cover newsworthy events and interview *Second Life* residents, such as the wounded Marine who had just returned home after fighting the fedayeen.[1] Reporter Wagner James Au built an avatar to resemble himself, right down to the glasses and goatee, and his virtual double dons a white suit in tribute to author Tom Wolfe. Au, in the persona of Hamlet Linden, reports on all the doings in the virtual world, including the occasional bit of tabloid news, such as the real-life stripper who opened a "gentlemen's club" in *Second Life*.

How does Linden Lab make this rich, dynamic, interactive world work? By running a distributed grid of more than two hundred computers in a nearby building. The user, however, sees only a single, seamless world, where the interaction is real and immediate. When you build a motorcycle, you're not building it on your PC and uploading it, you're building it on the *Second Life* site in real time. Someone might come along and say, "No, you should build the front wheel bigger, and I've got a texture you might like."

Textures are big here. They bring a splash of the real world into this artificial space, so that instead of having to settle for cartoonlike pastel colors, you can upload designs, patterns, and images for grafting onto 3-D objects. By using textures and the *Second Life* rendering engine, you turn buildings, clothing, and cars into objects that look almost real. You also can assume multiple looks and personas. Some players upload mug shots of themselves to map onto their 3-D avatars. Others upload photos of their family, build a frame around it, and hang it on the wall of their virtual house.

Now, here is where Linden Lab pulls away from the pack by pioneering new rules for the digital age. Other game companies, like There Inc., Time Warner Interactive, or Worlds Inc. let you create characters or objects.[2] But even if you spend countless hours creating a wonderful new character, it's not really yours. You can never move it off the site or sell it on eBay. Linden Lab is the only game company that lets you *own* your virtual creations.

Ondrejka, employee No. 4, tugs on one of his three ringed gold earrings. "We got thinking about intellectual property rights very early. As soon as you have the ability to upload textures and audio, you're opening the door of, 'What do we want to allow?'" The Linden Lab team decided to let people upload ten-second audio clips but not entire songs because they didn't want to become a music interchange and face the RIAA's wrath. As a result, users upload lots of textures as well as voice samples, sound effects, and short clips of music.

Second Life's original terms of service were similar to those of other online games. Recalls Ondrejka: "We were saying to users, 'Come in, invest perhaps forty hours of your time each week to build a new world, and by the way, we're not going to let you do what you want with your items because you have to license them to us.'" That didn't sit right with the executive team. They decided to fix it.

Founder Philip Rosedale, former technology chief of Seattle Internet media company RealNetworks, and the Linden brain trust revisited the issue with a new mind-set and discovered that *Second Life* was as much a *tool* as a game. Adobe Systems, for example, doesn't demand a piece of the action whenever you create a new image or character using its software. Instead of hiring a content team of twenty to fifty artists like a traditional game company, Linden Lab was putting tools into the hands of its users and asking them to build a world together. The design team created templates showing an empty countryside, sea, and islands, but beyond that, Linden Lab served essentially as a Web hosting company.

"Our lawyers shook their heads," Ondrejka says, "but we decided the future of our company isn't tied up in our owning what our users create. In fact, the opposite is true. The long-term success of Linden Lab is keyed to the quality of content created by our users, and the best way to motivate them to really create good content is to say, it's yours."

The company makes its money from subscription revenues, a small amount of advertising—and taxes. The more property you want, the more you pay. Early on, the cyber-citizens staged a Boston Tea Party, with some of the virtual world's land barons donning colonial outfits to protest the rates. The overlords of *Second Life* consented, so members could continue to merrily build grandiose estates. Inside the game's virtual economy, about a quarter million user-to-user transactions for goods and services take place each month.

Elsewhere in the game community, corporate restrictions have stirred resentment. Anything you say or do while in *Star Wars Galaxies* becomes the property of Sony Online Entertainment. Electronic Arts imposes an equally rigid service agreement for players of *Ultima Online*. For a time, the bartering of *EverQuest* items was a hot commodity on eBay. On a typical day in 2000, you could find more than a thousand people selling items, with bids of $1,375 for a killer wizard, $1,400 for a magic cape, or $1,125 for a cloak of flames. (By contrast, a *Sims* rare-breed cheetah went for a mere $25.) Then Sony stepped in and ordered eBay to ban such sales. The players, after all, had licensed the items but did not really own them.

While some players supported the ban on sales, others did not. As a result, a gray market arose, with Hong Kong–based IGE stepping in to become the world's largest trader of online items, including goods from the unrelenting players of *EverQuest* (nicknamed "EverCrack" for its addictive nature). People who don't play online games may shake their heads in wonder, but the value of such trading has become considerable. Every week, *Ultima* items worth more than $110,000 in real money are traded online. One fellow is trying to scrape out a living for a year doing nothing but selling and trading otherworldly goods.

Now, contrast the traditional game world's restrictive policies with Linden Lab's new approach. "You can build a chair using our geometric modeling engine," Ondrejka says. "You can take that to a real-world company like Ikea and say, 'I want to sell you this chair design.' You can sell Ikea the exclusive license to build and sell your chair in the real world."

Depending on your talent and proclivities, you could design a concept car, motorcycle, or prototype vehicle that nobody has dreamed up yet. You could design a character and license it to a comic book artist or the producers of a new TV series. You could play architect and design a subdivision or create a startling new skyscraper and license the plans to a real-estate developer. The possibilities are endless. By opening up this new creative space of garage game design, *Second Life* and the companies that follow in its footsteps will become thriving digital marketplaces.

On November 14, 2003, Linden Lab announced its revised property rules at the State of Play game conference in New York, where Rosedale told an audience of virtual worlds enthusiasts that subscribers would now retain ownership over the digital material they create, including characters, clothing, scripts, textures, objects, and designs. "Persistent world users are making significant contributions to building these worlds and should be able to both own the content they create and share in the value that is created," he said.

The announcement received an enthusiastic reception. Forty-five minutes later, Linden Lab got an e-mail from a developer who asked if he could create commercial Machinima in *Second Life*. You probably haven't heard of Machinima—pronounced ma-SHEEN-eh-ma, it's short for machine cinema—but you will. It's a small but rapidly growing technique for creating a movie inside a virtual world. Unlike animated features like *Finding Nemo* or *Toy Story*, where studios spend millions generating computer images frame by frame, Machinima developers populate a virtual world with characters and a setting and then use the game engine to generate long sequences of action in real time. Then they capture the sequences digitally, resulting in filmmaking for essentially zero dollars.

Machinima artists have been using the robust engines in id Software's *Quake* or Epic Games' *Unreal*, but they have been stymied by restrictive licenses that prevent them from making a profit off their machine-generated movies. At other times, copyright law gets in the way. The artist behind a four-part Mario Brothers Flash epic mixed together narrative and borrowed music to create a sort of operatic story based on the old video game, but the hosting site removed the episodes because of copyright infringement fears.

In *Second Life*, by contrast, a Machinima filmmaker can go to town. By giving players ownership rights over their creations, Linden Lab has brought copyright law—with all its foibles and quirks—into the virtual world. Real-world filmmakers know that all the world is not free to shoot. An entire genre of law has grown up around whether you need permission to capture trademarked material or copyrighted images on film.[3] For instance, Starbucks forbids photography on its property because its fixtures are proprietary works. A filmmaker must clear rights even for incidental copyrighted material that appears onscreen. The movie *Twelve Monkeys* was pulled from theaters twenty-eight days after release because an artist claimed a chair in the film resembled a furniture sketch he'd designed. A filmmaker making an opera documentary shot a scene of stagehands playing checkers while *The Simpsons* happened to be on the TV in the background; he chose to remove the 4.5 seconds rather than pay Fox $10,000.[4]

As you read this, Linden Lab is consulting with Creative Commons to prevent *Second Life*'s virtual world from becoming ensnared in such copyright tussles. Employees are working on a technology that will allow filmmakers and others to identify on the fly whether any elements in a scene are off-limits—that is, if their creations are restricted or if the owners have agreed to give others full access. "This will allow you to throw a virtual filter over your camera, saying, 'Don't capture anything that I don't have the rights to use in my movie,'" Ondrejka says.

He expects many more such uses of Creative Commons as *Second Life* grows and increasingly engages the real world. "I suspect *Second Life* will someday become a final exam question in law school. I could take a set of blueprints of my house in the real world and upload that into *Second Life*. I could then build a house in the virtual world based on those plans. I upload textures to make my 3-D house look real, and all those textures have rights associated with them. I could insert bits of computer code so that when I walk up to my house, the door opens, and that code could be copyrighted. The door could make a noise as it opens, with audio I own the rights to. Someone who walks past my house could take a screen shot of my house and download it to her computer. Now she has captured in the real world an image of my 3-D object in the virtual world that came from my plans in the real world. She could then take the picture and go build a house in the real world. So at the end of this whole chain, who's infringing whom and where? The Creative Commons people find this whole thing fascinating and terrifying at the same time."

As the real and virtual worlds intersect and borrow from each other, the clean lines between reality and fantasy will blur. "*Second Life* is unique in that we do close the circle often," Ondrejka says. "Things that start in the real world move into the virtual world, get exchanged or change format here, and then move back out to the real world. Let's say I take your picture, upload it to *Second Life*, and build an avatar character that looks like you. Someone comes along and says, 'I want to buy your avatar.' They do, and use a screen shot of their new avatar—based on my picture of you—and put that on their sports site. Has anyone been infringed? Those are the kinds of questions we're now dealing with."

When you upload a creation such as a painting to *Second Life*, you are uploading not just the digital bits but also the rights that accompany it. *Second Life* will soon be using Creative Commons licenses in its code so that users deal directly with such issues as: Do I let others modify my work? Do I let them make copies? Can they borrow it for personal use but not for commercial profit?

Copyright also is the reason why online worlds are largely music-free zones. For instance, *Ultima Online* has a piano, but it can't play. *Second Life*'s jukeboxes don't work. Game companies have negotiated with ASCAP to license songs, but so far the music publishers don't know what to make of virtual worlds, suggesting payment schemes based on a site's total membership rather than how many players might gather in a given virtual bar on a given night. "The licensing rules for music haven't caught up with online worlds yet," Ondrejka says.

Despite not being able to play copyrighted music in *Second Life*, users are making do. Ondrejka says a lot of people underestimate what a bit of talent and a lot of perseverance can accomplish. Players have created balloon races, a resident-abducting alien spaceship, and underwater lairs worthy of Dr. Evil.

"What we see over and over is that, given the right tools, people are incredibly creative," Ondrejka says. "They amaze us every day, devising ways to create the items and features they want, even ones we didn't think were possible."

He sums up the *Second Life* team's most fundamental discovery this way: "The future is the users. Understand that and get out of the way."

| | |

Gamer-created content is not new, but it's certainly the biggest trend in computer games today. The $10 billion game industry has come to rely increasingly on mods, or modifications to games created by hobbyists. The mod movement took off in 1993 when fans of *Doom* started posting new game levels and new tools on Compuserve. Id Software noticed that the piracy was causing a boom in sales and soon offered license agreements that gave users access to source code and developers' tools—handing customers the know-how to manipulate *Doom*.[5]

In the underground world of mods, players become designers and artists, taking game play in directions the original game makers never intended or imagined. These amateur programmers modify the graphics, sounds, or contours of a game in any number of ways. Typically, someone adds an extra level or new character to a game. A cartoon figure might be changed to resemble a reviled teacher, who meets an untimely end. Fan-made files let you play *Doom* as a gun-toting Homer Simpson blasting away at the despised purple dinosaur Barney. In a modded *Star Wars* game, Kiss singer Gene Simmons appears as a Jedi knight.

Two to three years ago, home-brew modifications moved from the geeky fringe to the gaming mainstream. Modders now number in the hundreds of thousands worldwide,[6] a small but influential portion of the more than 87 million people who play online games[7] (a figure that includes online games such as chess, backgammon, and puzzles). Some of the best-selling games— *Half-Life*, *The Sims*, *Quake*—owe their success to tinkering by users.

One of modding's biggest success stories came in 1999, when a twenty-three-year-old Canadian college senior named Minh Le worked with a friend in his parents' basement to turn *Half-Life*, a traditional action game created by Valve Software of Kirkland, Washington, into *Counter-Strike*, a multiplayer game that let players around the globe hook up online to pit soldiers against terrorists. *Half-Life*'s owners were so impressed by Le's mod that they bought the rights, released *Counter-Strike* commercially, and wound up selling 1.5 million copies for $40 million in revenues, making it the most popular multiplayer action game in the world. More than 2.5 million players spend over 6 billion minutes a month playing the game. That's more minutes than viewers spend watching a top ten TV sitcom.

Unlike most modders, Le did not just create new characters, he also reworked *Half-Life* into an entirely new game. As *Business 2.0* magazine reported, "Elsewhere in the entertainment industry, this is the point at which lawyers would come knocking on Le's door. But gamers tend to have a less rigid notion of intellectual property."[8] Valve gave away both the game's source code and the software tools for modifying it. The company is now making sure its new release, *Half-Life 2*, is mod-friendly.

While players have long created mods that breathe new life into old games, it has only been recently that their activities have been encouraged by the industry. Today, most PC game makers produce titles that are open to tinkering by players. Game makers understand that they benefit from free labor and outside-the-box thinking that takes play in new directions. They see that modding fosters sales and increases customer devotion. Many games are now released with the same software tools used by their developers, giving anyone with the skills and desire the ability to create mods. Player modifications aren't a hobby anymore—they're the lifeblood of the industry.

When Microsoft was finishing a new PC game that let players crossbreed animals—say, an elephant with a shark—it gave a group of modders a chance to tweak the final product. By the time *Impossible Creatures* hit shelves in 2003, the tinkerers had developed unofficial variants, released as free downloads, that extended the game in new ways.

Dan Ternes, a seventeen-year-old high school student in Charlotte, North Carolina, created a mod for *Unreal Tournament*, making the game's firearms bigger and badder. In the mod tradition, he has shared his mod—Codename: Gatling—on the Net with other gamers.[9]

In early 2003, Electronic Arts began selling a combat game called *Command and Conquer Generals*. The game giant built in options enabling players to download mods from Web sites and message boards that altered the game in hundreds of different ways. Weeks later, when the Iraq War began, modders retooled the game to allow users to slug it out with Saddam Hussein's troops. Uniforms worn by generic U.S. and Chinese forces combating a make-believe Global Liberation Army were changed to the uniforms worn by the 101st Airborne Division and the Republican Guard.

Other companies have caught mod fever. Sierra Entertainment's *Die Hard: Nakitomi Plaza* and Infogrames' *Tactical Ops: Assault on Terror* began life as free mods. Vivendi Universal Games in Los Angeles extended the life of its *Tribes* series of games for years by making them moddable. Epic Games, Atari, and graphics card maker Nvidia are paying $1 million in cash and prizes to the person or team that devises the most inspired mods of the popular first-person shooter *Unreal Tournament*.[10] Epic includes an editing tool package in its game releases and a DVD with step-by-step instructions on making mods. Epic sponsored a two-day mod-making seminar, while Electronic Arts hosted a week-long "mod university." Epic's lead designer, Cliff Bleszinski, told the *New York Times*, "I think this industry is really kind of grounded a lot closer to its fans, to its roots, than a lot of other businesses."[11]

Why do modders do it? For fun, creativity, love of games, bragging rights, and in some cases as a virtual résumé. Occasionally it works. id Software hired a group of British modders after seeing their mods of *Quake 3*. Another *Quake 3* modder, Bryan Dube, was hired as a programmer at a game design studio in Madison, Wisconsin. Epic Games hired half its early staff from the mod community. The mod movement has become so entrenched that online gaming spot Gamespy.com hosts hundreds of Web sites for modders and gets 18 million visitors a month.

But not all is love and roses in the mod world. While most game makers see benefits in software mods that alter game play, players occasionally resort to creating cheat software that gives them an insider advantage. Some rogue hackers have written codes to give them perfect aim in shooting games, for instance.

Then there is the gray side of the mod movement: hardware mods. This is a nebulous landscape where violators butt up against the antitampering provisions of the DMCA. With a hardware mod, someone takes a game console and rewires the box, adding a mod chip. (You also can buy premodded consoles.) PlayStation mods require soldering equipment to rework hair-thin wires on the motherboard, and disabling the built-in copy protection. Xbox mod chips require screwing in a circuit board and doing a firmware update. An underground economy has sprung up around mod chips. Hundreds of Web sites, many operating in the Darknet, now sell mod chips. Mass-produced mod kits are available off the shelf in many places.

The problem is, mod chips can be used for both legitimate and illegitimate ends. Here are some arguably legitimate reasons: You may be a college student who can't afford a computer. Microsoft's Xbox is the cheapest computer on the market and, with a little tweaking, it can run the Linux operating system. Or perhaps you want to turn your Xbox into a media player to play movies. (More than one Microsoft employee has modded his Xbox for this reason, although add-on kits now let you watch DVDs or DivX movies.) Or perhaps you want to upgrade your aging console without having to shell out for a PlayStation 2. Or perhaps you want to make your legally purchased games run faster by storing them as virtual drives. Or perhaps you want to back up a purchased game onto a CD and play it if your original disc becomes damaged. Or perhaps you want to copy a legally purchased game to the unit's hard drive because you don't want to hunt down the disc every time you wish to play. Or perhaps you live in a country where region coding prevents you from playing a purchased game that hit U.S. store shelves many months before. Region coding, also a hallmark of DVD movies, divides the world into different spheres to maximize entertainment profits. For instance, *Final Fantasy X* for PlayStation 2 was released in Europe six months after the U.S. release and two weeks after the Japanese release of *Final Fantasy XI*.[12]

Proponents of hardware mods say they are simply abiding by the principle that people should be free to modify and experiment with the products they buy. EFF attorney von Lohmann told the *New York Times*, "The principle of tinkering with the stuff that you own was the principle on which the entire personal computer industry was founded. This is basic business and basic science in the technology world and we think that this right to tinker, this freedom to tinker, remains legally protected."[13]

An entire subculture of hackers and technophiles has sprung up to unshackle the Xbox so that its inner PC can be released. But tinkering with mod chips isn't always done strictly for intellectual curiosity. The *San Francisco Bay Guardian* ran a story on a twentysomething man in Silicon Valley who nets $6,000 a month selling and installing mod chips for the Xbox and PlayStation.[14] For $70 he'll mod your system so you can play pirated games or use the device in unauthorized ways. The *New York Times* profiled a thirty-one-year-old Manhattan financial executive who soldered a mod chip and installed Linux on his Xbox, which then let him transfer three thousand MP3 music files and illegal copies of thirty-five hundred old-time arcade games.[15]

It seems beyond argument that most, but not all, uses of mod chips are for playing pirated games. The three major video game console makers—Sony, Nintendo, and Microsoft—have used the courts against sellers of mod chips, relying on the DMCA to go after violators. A twenty-two-year-old Virginia man was sentenced under the DMCA to five months in jail and $28,500 in fines in April 2003 for selling mod chips. The Interactive Digital Software Association calls mod chips "illegal infringing devices."

Two weeks after my interview with two underground movie figures, entertainment consultant Bruce Forest put me in touch with a game pirate who took the name Scarface for our interview. The twenty-two-year-old recent college graduate is a member of several game and movie release groups. The process he described for "freeing" games closely resembled the system used by the movie groups.[16]

First, he said, an employee of a retail store, production company, or manufacturing plant obtains a game and supplies it to the group. Then a ripper copies the game and compresses it onto one or two CDs. Next he uploads the files onto the Internet, where couriers spread the game to private FTP sites and IRC warez channels "in a matter of minutes." Suppliers or donators provide the equipment for the groups to use.

Scarface, a courier, says, "I do it because people shouldn't pay ridiculous prices for games, plus it's the adventure for me." He says he would rather pay $3 for a blank DVD-R disc than $50 to buy a single game. He mods game consoles, though he knows it's illegal, and says the arrest and jailing of a mod dealer in 2003 "had little or no impact in the scene. Mod chips are still being sold all over the world and they're getting cheaper all the time."[17]

It should be noted that a substantial number of gamers who download pirated games actually do buy the game. Many simply want to see whether a certain game works on their system.

Scarface says release groups chiefly target PlayStation 2 games because Sony's device dominates the market (60 million sold vs. about 15 million for Microsoft's Xbox) and thus "more games and better titles" are released. "Release groups always try to target the hyped games—mainly games that cost $40 and up and that have been marketed a few months in advance." For example, months before its release, a fair chunk of *Half-Life 2*, the sequel to the popular PC shooter game, was available in piracy circles.

Scarface, whose personal tastes run to strategic games such as *Rogue Spear*, *Civilization*, and *Halo*, is upfront that his activities are illegal. "Of course it's piracy, there are no other ways to describe it. Game designers produce it, we steal it and release it, but in our world it's considered good because the game designers are overcharging for games." (The full text of the interview is at Darknet.com.)

Analysts predict that within a year or two, game consoles will become more widespread than PCs. *Fortune* magazine reports that Americans now spend more time playing video games—75 hours per year on average—than watching rented videos and DVDs. As we become more entranced by interactive entertainment, we need to thrash out the rules of the digital age.

The issues surrounding hardware modding raise fundamental questions: Do customers have the right to fiddle with the innards of products they buy? How far may individuals go in modifying hardware and software they have legally purchased? What limits should there be? Do the corporations decide, or do individuals enjoy a presumption of certain digital rights when buying products for personal use?

The creativity forged by software modding raises equally profound questions. Game companies have discovered that by unshackling their products and turning users into cocreators of their media experience, it's a win-win where players and businesses benefit equally. Why are such interactive, collaborative experiences limited to the game community? How can traditional entertainment companies take advantage of customer-created content? Is Hollywood looking at the Internet the wrong way, as a piracy vehicle that needs to be locked down rather than as a tool for unleashing users' creative potential?

As the *New York Times* mused in an article about modding, "Imagine buying the latest 'Lord of the Rings' DVD and discovering that the cameras, lights, special effects and editing tools used in its making had been included at no extra charge. Or finding your favorite CDs crammed with virtual recording studios, along with implicit encouragement from the producers to remix the music, record your own material and post it all on the Internet."[18]

That's indeed hard to imagine, given the current Hollywood mind-set where tinkering is seen as a threat to bottom lines[19] and any use of digital media that varies from an entertainment company's directive is met with a lawsuit or a cease-and-desist order. But as these new spaces open up and modders and users begin sampling, transforming, and reinventing other media (often in the Darknet because of unbalanced copyright laws), we need as a society to address these issues head on and come to terms with our digital destiny.

Influential game pioneer Raph Koster, designer of *Ultima Online* and *Star Wars Galaxies*, made the point well in a speech at the Game Developers Conference in San Jose in 2002: "There's an intense amount of learning, craft, and skill that goes there, and I hate to say this to all the film directors, writers, poets, painters, and everyone else out there in the world: Get over yourselves. The rest of the world is coming."

14 Remixing the Digital Future

I LEAN BACK IN MY CHAIR, SHROUDED IN DARKNESS inside a time capsule. Or so it seems. The floor of the small room begins to vibrate. On the wide screen in front, a space shuttle rumbles on the launching pad. The visuals startle: instead of a fuzzy long-range shot, it seems as if we're standing fifty feet from the spacecraft. The NASA video appears astonishingly crisp, the sounds remarkably vivid. Suddenly, with a teeth-rattling roar, the shuttle screams into the sky. "*Endeavor*, throttle up," the flight engineer says.

"Whoa, baby!" I hear myself reply over the din.

To my right, Victor LaCour smiles. The twenty-nine-year-old creative producer of the University of Southern California's Integrated Media Systems Center is wearing a rumpled black blazer and blue jeans to go with shaggy brown hair, frizzy sideburns, and an insatiable curiosity. LaCour, a scientist with a strong creative streak, is one of the wizards working on the immersive Internet, an effort to transform the Net into a rich, interactive, *whoa-baby* experience that stimulates all the senses.

Minutes later, the shuttle footage gives way to an animated Viking sea battle and a Duran Duran concert so lifelike it feels as though you're right there. Again, the high-quality, full-immersion 3-D images and sounds dazzle. LaCour leans over. "Everyone thinks a machine in this room is piping this out." Not so. The video, a step well beyond high-definition TV, is being streamed to L.A. from a server in North Carolina over an ultrafast Internet2 connection. (Internet2 is a consortium of more than two hundred universities working with industry and government to develop next-generation Internet technology.)

What LaCour showed me, inside this squat, red brick building, is more than home theater on steroids or high-definition video on demand. The technology, called Remote Media Immersion, brings information and entertainment experiences to the next level. The center's project engineers are fusing 3-D technology, video compression, spatially placed sound, and wickedly fast pipes to create visually and sonically rich virtual worlds.

"You can get these kinds of experiences only at an amusement park right now," LaCour says. "We're saying, it's coming to your home. The Internet will be television for the people."[1]

LaCour might well have said *of, by,* and *for* the people, for the immersive Internet is as much about independent video as it is about supercharged pipes. The trend lines are unmistakable. Only in the past year or two did it become practical to edit a full-length feature film on a home computer. It's just a matter of time, he says, before anyone will be able to pick up a high-definition camcorder, shoot a movie, store it on a supersize hard drive, and transmit it instantly around the globe (1.5-terabyte hard drives are expected to be commonplace by 2008). Still newer technologies add depth of field, simulating a 3-D experience.

All this holds major implications for Hollywood. "The studios won't disappear, but they will face stiff competition from individuals and small teams of creative people doing very high-quality work," LaCour predicts. "The Internet will serve as the gathering place for high-quality media creation and exchange that rivals and sometimes surpasses what you see in the professional arena. I guarantee you, this will change the entire dynamic of home entertainment."

Now imagine, LaCour says, instead of watching an ancient sea battle from your seat in the theater, you're one of the participants in an interactive, immersive, navigable environment. Picture the kinds of ingenious, creative efforts that can take place with travelogues, do-it-yourself documentaries, online games wedded to realistic city landscapes—the full range of personal media coupled with always-on mega-bandwidth connections.

Already, the center has hosted a live interactive music duet with the performers stationed hundreds of miles apart. Down the road, the researchers plan to host a concert with a virtual audience and a full orchestra whose members are scattered in forty cities. Can you say global jam session?

The immersive Internet opens up other possibilities for art and commerce. Teleconferencing will improve so dramatically it feels as though you and your Tokyo counterpart are negotiating at the same table. Line your wall with a plasma TV screen that perfectly replicates a coral reef or exotic shark exhibit. Or, suggests center director Ulrich Neumann, "Set up a TV at the end of the Thanksgiving table and invite Grandma over. It's not that far-fetched, once that screen is in your home."[2]

The goal, Neumann says, is "an Internet that is not just text and images but art and interactive experiences with multiple participants. It comes down to what creative people invent and what society gravitates toward. A few years ago, no one predicted people would be tapping little text messages to each other on their cell phones. We're in for similar large-scale changes in our living rooms."

Media companies aren't quite ready to cede control of your living room. Their idea of the digital future consists of high-definition TV with limited interactive features running over pipes that go mostly one way. (Today's Internet connections were built for consumers, not users. Uploading is more difficult and about ten times slower than downloading, making it harder for users to share personal media they've created.)

But as Forrester Research predicted in a 2000 report, "Broadband's potential isn't in faster Web pages or interactive afterthoughts overlaid on old TV assets. Instead, a new form will emerge to redefine interactivity, immersing the audience in a collage of content and commerce."

Disney and Microsoft are already on the case, teaming with scientists to make the Internet thousands of times faster, with the goal of launching video-on-demand services so attractive that users will no longer be tempted by illegal sites. Researchers elsewhere are working on ways to turbocharge the Internet so that 100 million U.S. homes can pull programming from the Net at rates more than a hundred times faster than today's top speeds. In California, the Gigabit or Bust Initiative is working toward wireless data access—hundreds of times faster than today's broadband—for every home and business in the state by 2010.

When Americans begin to connect with each other through super-broadband, how open will the information commons be? How will the architectures we're designing today affect the social spaces where we will gather tomorrow? If we're only 2 percent of the way into what the Internet has to offer, as former IBM Internet technology chief John Patrick likes to say, what does the remaining 98 percent hold in store?

In early 2004, IBM Business Consulting Services released a landmark study predicting that major changes in the media and entertainment land-scape over the next five to seven years will force tectonic shifts in the business models of movie and television companies. The report advised companies to convert all content to digital form and create "open media" by giving users the freedom to "compile, program, edit, create and share content."[3]

Above all, the IBM researchers wrote, media companies must include customers in the creative process. "Encourage independent publishing ini-tiatives—comedy blogs, online game characters, short feature films, new music—as a way to develop markets." Companies that make it in this new world will let customers access media on their own terms, "such as intercut-ting an episode of a popular sitcom with personal digital footage."

So far, the media powers have not shown a glimmer of interest. Motion picture studios, television networks, and record companies—long used to dominating their industries—are wary of a future in which they lose their roles as entertainment potentates. Sharing the stage with amateur creators doesn't come naturally to the entertainment giants, which contributed $40 million in the most recent federal election cycle[4] and are pressing their advantage in Congress, the state legislatures, the courts, and in private cross-industry forums to maintain the status quo.

As the digital media revolution seeps into every aspect of our lives, I think it's inevitable that participatory culture will prevail in the long run. But the short run is a different story. I don't share Larry Lessig's famous pes-simism, which earned him the sobriquet "the dean of darkness," but as one looks out over the prospects for digital freedoms in today's public policy arena, it's hard to be optimistic.

In April 2004, the U.S. Department of Justice established an Intellectual Property Task Force to crack down on file traders. Congress is considering bills to allow the Justice Department to file civil piracy lawsuits, to outlaw P2P networks that carry infringing content, and to enact harsher penalties for those who use digital media in ways not approved by the rights holder, regardless of fair use. Regulators are considering giving media companies the power to reach into users' homes and restrict what they can do with works they have paid for. The MPAA has successfully lobbied at least seven state legislatures to pass sweeping new DMCA-like laws that criminalize the use of "unauthorized" home entertainment equipment. You might be breaking the law by hooking up a PVR, VCR, PC, modem, or webcam without obtaining the permission of your cable or satellite operator, ISP, or phone carrier.[5]

Some legislators have gone off the deep end. Senator Orrin Hatch, the Utah Republican who chairs the Senate Judiciary Committee, said during a hearing in 2003 that all future computers should be required to include "kill switches" that could be activated remotely to thwart peer-to-peer piracy. He said he was drafting legislation under which a copyright holder would give an offender two warnings before activating the kill switch to destroy or disable the violator's computer. "Requiring kill switches is an extreme step, but if the private sector can't stop piracy on its own, the government will," he said.

In response, a growing number of public-spirited organizations have begun a broad-based movement on behalf of digital culture. In April 2004, students at Swarthmore College founded Freeculture.org, an international student campaign to preserve digital liberties. Other groups that have joined the digital rights wars include Public Knowledge, the EFF, Consumers Union, the American Library Association, the Center for Democracy and Technology, DigitalConsumer.org, the Alliance for Digital Progress, Protect-fairuse.org, the Home Recording Rights Coalition, Media Access Project, the Digital Speech Project, Anti-DMCA.org, New Yorkers for Fair Use, and Britain's Campaign for Digital Rights, among many others.

In some ways, the grassroots efforts resemble the fledgling protest movements of the early 1960s. James Boyle, a Duke law professor, has likened the issues surrounding digital rights and intellectual property to those of the environmental movement before the first Earth Day.

Just as environmentalists span the political spectrum, so do supporters of digital culture. On his Instapundit weblog, conservative blogger Glenn Reynolds assessed Congress's sidling up to big media interests this way: "These legislative initiatives aren't just about copyright. They're about building a regime that's hostile to content that comes from *anyone* other than Big Media suppliers."[6]

In March 2004, another conservative, pro-business group joined the fray: the Committee for Economic Development, a sixty-year-old policy group that left its mark on such initiatives as the Marshall Plan and the Bretton Woods agreement. Susan Crawford, a professor at Yeshiva University's Cardozo Law School and coauthor of the committee's report, told the *New York Times* that Hollywood was blurring the distinction between digital content and physical property. "Bits are not the same as atoms. We need to reframe the legal discussion to treat the differences of bits and atoms in a more thoughtful way."[7]

Efforts by movie and television studios and record companies to push for tough new legislation to protect copyrighted materials is bad for U.S. business and economic growth, the group concluded. Many of the new restrictions supported by Hollywood, such as limitations on home use of digital television programming, would upset the already precarious balance between the rights of copyright holders and the public. The committee urged a two-year moratorium on new copyright laws or regulations and called for a robust public debate on these issues. "Our first concern should be to 'do no harm,'" the report said.

A spirited public debate on issues of personal media, participatory culture, and intellectual property in the new era is long overdue. With that in mind, I'll offer this ten-point digital culture road map:

1. We are users as well as consumers.

    Once we begin to think of people as creators, producers, designers, and users of media rather than as strictly passive consumers, the entire basis of the conversation changes. As users and stakeholders, citizens should have a seat at the table in efforts to restore the centuries-old balancing act between copyright holders and the public. Users are entitled to have their voices heard in the corridors of power alongside Hollywood's gleaming lobbying machine.

2. Artists must be compensated for their works.

    All sides should recognize that artists, musicians, authors, songwriters, and other creative people should be paid for commercial uses of their works. As *Time* magazine put it, "After all, you can't have an information economy in which all information is free." We should remember that what most users want is not *free* use but *fair* use and the right to participate in our culture.[8]

3. The public's digital rights should be affirmed.

Most people believe they have a "fair use right" to use, borrow, and transform cultural works in their daily lives. The law should be changed to reflect those cultural norms. Congress should specify users' digital rights by mapping out an expansive, affirmative set of rules delineating the scope of the public's right to sample, reuse, build upon, and share the digital works they legally acquire. Such a declaration, with reasonable protections for copyright holders, should include the right to time-shift, space-shift, make personal backup copies, change formats, tinker with stuff you buy, engage in personal editing, and share personal media with others, depending on the circumstances.[9]

4. The DMCA requires a dramatic overhaul.

A suburban Boston pastor incorporates Hollywood images into his sermons. An Intel vice president adds a few seconds of a Hollywood film to a homemade video. Users bypass Hollywood's region code to play an imported movie.[10] Others bypass digital locks to play a DVD on a Linux computer. A scientist discovers a security flaw in a major corporation's encryption system and wants to share his findings with colleagues. The Digital Millennium Copyright Act outlaws all these legitimate activities—none of which has anything to do with file sharing or piracy.

The DMCA chills entrepreneurial innovation, repeals citizens' fair use rights, turns digital devices into black boxes off-limits even to their owners, and relegates Webcasters to second-class status. Those provisions should be repealed.[11]

5. Celebrate participatory culture. Don't outlaw it.

The past few years have seen the most remarkable flourishing of participatory culture in history. We should do everything in our power to foster its growth. In the new era, users sample, remix, mash up, reinvent, and share digital media, drawing from the culture at large in transforming the borrowed material into something new. The law should recognize and legitimize these new forms of digital usage and creativity. Congress should enact new compulsory licenses that permit commercial remixing and sampling of prior works—music, movies, television, games, and art—for a reasonable fixed fee. Personal, noncommercial uses such as home movies, political commentaries, or artistic statements should be permitted for free.

6. The Darknet is the public's great equalizing force.

Some have suggested organizing a mass protest march on Washington to redress the balance of power. I believe a better course is simply to pick up the tools of digital media. When millions more people begin ripping and remixing their culture, the inequities of current law will become plain. In many cases, users will flock to the Darknet to route around copy controls and unbalanced laws. In this way, the Darknet might well serve as the public's great equalizer—a counterbalancing force and bulwark to defend digital liberties. The Darknet will grow in scope, resilience, and effectiveness in direct proportion to digital restrictions the public finds untenable.[12]

7. The Internet is not an entertainment medium.

The Internet is not a delivery system for digital entertainment. It's not a set of pipes or wires. It's a network of networks with a default architecture of participation. On his LawMeme weblog, James Grimmelmann wrote: "Trying to force the Internet to be the perfect delivery system for the RIAA is like draining a Florida swamp to put up an apartment building, only to watch the building slowly sink. The swamp is the natural state of things."

Jaron Lanier, the acclaimed scientist and musician who coined the term "virtual reality," told me this: "If the Internet remains unfettered and entrepreneurs keep coming up with better ways to display compressed video and amateurs create more varied, interesting, and open material, the Net will turn into a superior competitor to Hollywood and traditional television." Any attempts to rewire the Internet or reengineer the personal computer into an entertainment appliance are "profoundly misguided," he says. "The Internet is the future of all communication that's not face to face."

8. To make file sharing and the Darknet irrelevant, innovate.

The way to marginalize file sharing and the Darknet is through innovative, market-based solutions—not through laws, government mandates, lawsuits, digital locks, or misleading educational campaigns. The best defense to piracy is a smart business model.

"We're in this really critical period where the panic and fear of the future can get some real mistakes hard-coded into the system," book publisher Tim O'Reilly warns. "The best way to prevent the piracy that the music and movie industries fear is to provide what people want at an affordable price."

9. Trust the marketplace.

Media companies need to learn to let go. Successful entertainment companies will create new products and pricing schemes, embrace fair use by giving customers flexibility in choosing how they want to view or listen to a work, and give outside innovators the freedom to tinker with and improve existing products. Media companies should embrace their digital destiny, even as their business models suffer short-term dislocation. Record companies, for instance, may need to stop relying on megasales for a few top artists and learn to cultivate a variety of acts. As they always do, industries will adjust, and everyone will win. Says consultant Jim Griffin, "Every time we crave control, we lose. Every time we let go, we profit."

10. Efforts to enrich the public domain should be encouraged.

By continually extending copyright terms, Congress benefits large corporations and the distant heirs of creators, but such actions prevent tens of thousands of cultural works from ever reaching the public. Digital culture advocates have proposed returning to the copyright terms of 1976 (for instance, a fifty-year term for individuals, with a $1 registration fee), plus other measures to enrich the public domain. The public wins if a classic work can be restored or reinterpreted without permission. Those who want to restore balance to copyright laws should support private efforts like Creative Commons that offer fair and flexible alternatives to long, restrictive copyright terms.

These are only a few ideas to get the ball rolling. We may collectively decide that, to protect entertainment interests, our devices need to be locked down while cop chips frisk everyone for unauthorized content. We may decide to welcome "a legal troll squatting at the center of the network, demanding tolls and blocking new experiments," as *Salon* managing editor Scott Rosenberg put it. But that should be an informed choice, not one made behind closed doors by political insiders and corporate interests. We need vigorous public discourse and dustups on these subjects across the land.

As the digital media revolution disintermediates power and gives people an easy outlet to sample and express and share, it can be both threatening and enervating. Over the long term, there is every reason to expect a Hollywood ending to this story. Movie studios will continue to flourish, more recording artists will be able to earn a livable wage, and we'll still be watching television into our golden years. But expect the major entertainment media to look decidedly different. Amateurs and creative individuals at the grass roots will play no small part in that.

To see where we're heading, look where we've been. Today you can hold in your hands a computer a thousand times more powerful than the first PCs at one-fifth the cost, with a high-speed wireless connection to boot. Semiconductor chips—which now power everything from MP3 players and digital cameras to cell phones and kitchen appliances—are 10,000 percent cheaper than they were five years ago.[13] As a result, the average home will soon go from having four computers to having four hundred.[14]

American culture is becoming digital culture.

As the pace of technological progress accelerates, cultural dislocations are inevitable. New technologies will bump up against stolid traditions. In 2003, Japanese bookstores launched a national campaign to stop "digital shoplifting" by customers using the latest camera-equipped mobile phones. Young women who spotted a new hairstyle or outfit in a glossy fashion magazine began using their mobile camera phones to take digital snapshots and e-mail the pictures to friends. Store owners and publishers objected, but it's likely the practice spurred more people to buy the magazine.

Over lunch at Pop!Tech, I sat next to a Maine middle school teacher. She told me school officials imposed a rule that restricted the use of instant messaging in the classroom. Within days, tech-savvy eleven- and twelve-year-olds had broken through the restriction by downloading IM packages from smaller outfits that were off the adults' radar screens.

This is the way we live now. We want to use media on our terms.

"To most young people today, the digital world is close to oxygen," John Seely Brown, former director of Xerox PARC, says. "They don't need to think about it. They breathe it."

Technology has redefined how we use media. It has changed our expectations of how we interpret, interact with, and give back to the world at large. Today's users expect their online activities to be steeped in collaboration, interaction, and expressiveness. Our ethics and social mores adapt to meet technology's steeply sloped curve.

Ten years from now, we will be carrying entire libraries of digital media on our keychains. Alongside our personal collections of favorite Hollywood movies will be visual diaries recorded by friends, photo montages created by college bloggers, and heartfelt personal vignettes shot by seventy-year-old storytellers. As the rules for this new digital world fall into place, it would be tragic if grassroots creativity is crushed or stunted just at the moment when millions of people have been handed the tools to participate in the culture.

For all the technological ferment, some things remain constant. In his Brentwood office, Hollywood visionary Warren Lieberfarb shows me his pride and joy: the turn-of-the-century Victrola he bought years ago in a little shop outside Budapest. The most prominent markings on the device are the patents taken out by the Victor Talking Machine Co. of Camden, New Jersey.[15]

Lieberfarb reverently cranks up the mahogany machine, and the turntable begins to spin. He lowers the needle to the vintage record. A Hungarian waltz wafts from the ancient horn. He leans down and squints at the machine. "You notice all the patents inscribed on the side? We're still fighting about that. I bought it because it's so symbolic of our industry. It shows we haven't really changed all that much."

Acknowledgments

This book was a collaborative effort. The insights and occasional bits of wisdom you may find between these covers owe their origins to others. Any mistakes, omissions, or lapses in reporting are mine alone.

Darknet benefited enormously from an online brain trust of grassroots contributors. Draft chapters were circulated in three places: the Darknet.com blog, where a number of readers—especially Eric Schulman—offered helpful feedback; the Darknet wiki, where Rachel Courtland and user2976 made especially valuable edits; and Howard Rheingold's Brainstorms community, where the manuscript was dissected with care by Bryan Alexander, Michael Corrado, Annette Leung, Gregory D. Esau, Glen Blankenship, Charles Cameron, John Mulligan, and Jesse Walker.

Shel Israel provided generous and wise editing help with many of the chapters. Howard Rheingold offered early guidance and encouragement. I compared notes along the way with Dan Gillmor, another early proponent of participatory media. Ross Mayfield set me up with a Socialtext wiki. Jane Black started me on the right track. Keisha Franklin did some brief reporting for me in chapter 1. Ernest Miller and Ernest Svenson set me straight on several legal matters. I had illuminating conversations with Kevin Werbach and Esther Dyson at Supernova, Bob Metcalf at PopTech, and the organizers of South by Southwest and Digital Hollywood. Thomas Huntington, Jennifer Roberts, Fritz Friedman, and Jenny Miller opened doors to the right people. John Battelle, Jessica Litman, Gary Price, Robert S. Boynton,

Gary Rivlin, Charles C. Mann, Joe Trippi, Hank Barry, Chris Anderson, Shayne Bowman, Chris Willis, Ben and Mena Trott, Rusty Foster, Jim Romenesko, Craig Newmark, Mark Glaser, Carrie McLaren, Håkon Styri, Rick Heller, Stephen Downes, Damien Newman, Bernie Goldbach, Glenn Fleishman, and Buzz Bruggeman also provided valuable contributions.

This book could not have been written without the generous efforts of those profiled in these pages, especially Jack Valenti, Lawrence Lessig, Warren Lieberfarb, Rev. John, Donald S. Whiteside, James M. Burger, Cary Sherman, Andrew Setos, Jaron Lanier, Gigi Sohn, Mike Godwin, Clay Shirky, Tim O'Reilly, Raven, Jim Griffin, Joe Lambert, Siva Vaidhyanathan, Bruce Forest, Jordan Greenhall, David Clayton, Stephen Balogh, Gregory L. Clayman, Mike Ramsay, John S. Hendricks, Martin Yudkovitz, Stewart Alsop, Benjamin S. Feingold, Adrian Alperovich, Jed Horowitz, Paul Kocher, John Perry Barlow, John Gilmore, Fred von Lohmann, Cory Doctorow, Seth Schoen, Wendy Seltzer, Joe Kraus, Chris Murray, Peter Jaszi, Miriam Nisbet, Henry Jenkins, Emery Simon, Gary Shapiro, Glenn Otis Brown, John Manferdelli, Richard Doherty, Dennis Mudd, Bob Ohlweiler, Edward Felten, Tony Abbott, Jonathan Potter, Michael Miron, Seth Greenstein, Jonathan Zittrain, Andy Wolfe, Lauren Weinstein, Ian Clarke, Cory Ondrejka, Honda Shing, Victor LaCour, Beryl Howell, Jack Driscoll, Andrew Frank, Roger McGuinn, and the underground pirates and file sharers who entrusted me with keeping their identities confidential.

Authors David Weinberger and Doc Searls helped build the intellectual framework on which I hung my arguments. Many of the issues surrounding digital rights have been explored in earlier books by gifted academics and writers such as Lessig, Siva Vaidhyanathan, Jessica Litman, David Bollier, Pamela Samuelson, and others. Building upon their works was an honor.

I'm also indebted to the talented journalists who have written with care and uncommon understanding about these issues, including Steven Levy, Kara Swisher, Walt Mossberg, Drew Clark, Jon Healey, James Poniewozik, Declan McCullagh, Amy Harmon, John Markoff, Frank Rich, Leslie Walker, Scott Rosenberg, Brock Meeks, Steve Outing, Dawn C. Chmielewski, Paul Boutin, John Naughton, Heather Green, and the editorial teams at *Salon*, *Slate*, and *BusinessWeek Online*. Fellow bloggers helped inform my understanding of the digital culture wars, especially Dave Winer, Jeff Jarvis, Jay Rosen, Jenny Levine, Marc Canter, Rebecca Blood, Meg Hourihan, Evan Williams, David Sifry, Joi Ito, Jon Lebkowsky, Anil Dash, Mitch Kapor, Seth

Finkelstein, Donna Wentworth, James Grimmelmann, Robert Scoble, Mark Cuban, Halley Suitt, David Rothman, Susan Mernit, Mary Hodder, Kevin Heller, Frank Field, Sheila Lennon, Denise Howell, Steve Rubel, Ben Edelman, Tim Jarrett, Derek Powazek, Christopher Lydon, Leonard Witt, Tim Porter, Morrie Johnston, Lisa Rein, Matt Haughey, John Patrick, Mitch Ratcliffe, Om Malik, Christian Crumlish, Ben Hammersley, Scott Matthews, Dave Farber and his mailing list, and countless others.

I owe a debt to my instructors at the Squaw Valley Community of Writers, especially James Frey, James Houston, and Anne Lamott, who taught me the importance of writing "shitty first drafts."

My family provided a constant source of comfort and support through two years of travels and weekends spent in a tiny office. I love you, Mary.

Finally, a generous thank you to my agent, Deirdre Mullane (as well as to Katya Balter) at the Spieler Agency, who believed in this project from the start, and to Eric Nelson, my editor at John Wiley & Sons, who really gets it.

Notes

To simplify matters for readers, I've changed several long URLs to tinyurls. See Darknet.com for the most up-to-date Web addresses for source material.

1 | The Personal Media Revolution

1. Harry Knowles, "*Raiders of the Lost Ark* Shot-for-Shot Teenage Remake Review!!!," *Ain't It Cool News* (May 31, 2003). Online at www.aintitcool.com/display.cgi?id=15348

2. Jim Windolf, "Raiders of the Lost Backyard," *Vanity Fair* (March 2004).

3. Chris Strompolos, interview with the author (November 17, 2003).

4. Greg Beato, "After Napster," *Soundbitten* (December 7, 2000). Online at www.soundbitten.com/aftnap.html

5. "Amateur" is no pejorative. Jay Rosen reminds us that the root of the word "amateur" is "lover." Whereas media companies create material for profit, amateurs do it out of passion.

6. Marc Canter, interview with the author (February 25, 2004). Canter made similar comments in the "We Media" report discussed in chapter 4. It's important to keep in mind that forms of personal media have been around for centuries. Books, letters, parchments, vintage records on Victrola players, Brownie cameras, 16mm movie cameras, boom boxes—the analog age gave birth to personal media. But the digital age is empowering talented individuals who feel shut out of the mass media machine to express themselves and share their works as never before.

7. Shigeru Miyagawa, "Personal Media and the Human Community," *Technos Quarterly* 11, No. 2 (2002). Online at www.technos.net/tq_11/2miyagawa.htm

8. Bruno Levy, interview with the author (December 11, 2003).

9. Andrew Potter, "Will It Be Free, or Feudal?," *National Post* (May 15, 2004).

10. Sheldon Brown, interview with the author (April 28, 2003).

11. Henry Jenkins, interview with the author (April 29, 2003).

12. Clay Shirky, "RIP the Consumer, 1900–1999," Shirky.com (Spring 2000). Online at www.shirky.com/writings/consumer.html

He also expanded on the theme in another essay, "Weblogs and the Mass Amateurization of Publishing" (July 2003). Online at http://shirky.com/writings/weblogs_publishing.html

2 | Now Playing: Hollywood vs. the Digital Freedom Fighters

1. The Universal representative, Jerry Pierce, said he did not recall such a proposal, saying, "There were some wacky things that came in and came out." Interview with the author (March 25, 2004). Three other participants who were there did recall such a proposal. The incident has not been previously reported.

2. James M. Burger, interviews with the author (October 15, 2002, July 2, 2003, and April 19, 2004).

3. Adrian Alperovich, interview with the author (May 28, 2003). See full interview on Darknet.com. To be fair, the region coding system also protects the revenues of local theaterowners in foreign countries.

4. For the complete transcript of the author's correspondence with >NIL: see Darknet.com.

5. Stephen Balogh, interviews with the author (September 26, 2002, and April 9, 2004).

6. Disclosure: I worked for Microsoft for nineteen months in 1997–1998 as an editor for its Sidewalk city guide.

7. Mary Hodder weblog at napsterization.org/stories/

8. The full text of Carly Fiorina's speech is available at the HP site www.hp.com/hpinfo/execteam/speeches/fiorina/ces04.html

9. Eric Eldred became the plaintiff in *Eldred v. Ashcroft*. The complainants challenged Congress's passage of a twenty-year copyright extension in 1998 because they believe it robs the American public of the rich and diverse public domain guaranteed by the Constitution. The Supreme Court ruled against Eldred 7–2 in January 2003.

10. Donald S. Whiteside, interview with the author (November 13, 2002).

11. Politech mailing list, "News Corp's Peter Chernin: 'The Problem with Stealing'" (November 22, 2002). Online at www.politechbot.com/p-04181.html

12. Figures from the Center for Responsive Politics, www.opensecrets.org

13. The original movie rating system was G, M (for Mature), R, and X. It has been revised several times since it was created in November 1968.

14. The full text of Valenti's speech is online at the MPAA site www.mpaa.org/jack/2003/2003_02_24.htm

15. Jack Valenti, interview with the author (November 14, 2003). For a full transcript, see Darknet.com.

16. Jack Valenti, "Thoughts on the Digital Future of Movies: The Threat of Piracy, the Hope of Redemption," presented to the Permanent Subcommittee on Investigations, U.S. Senate Committee on Governmental Affairs (September 30, 2003).

17. The public domain is often defined as the state that materials fall into once

their copyrights expire, but others say the public domain is much broader than that. The public domain includes not only works that have been placed there but also such things as the right to listen, to share, and to sell or give away used books, records, and other media. In this view, everything starts out being in the public domain, and the only things not in it are materials covered under Section 106 of the Copyright Act, which gives the copyright owner rights for limited times, subject to Sections 107 to 122.

18. Adam D. Thierer and Wayne Crews, *Copy Fights: The Future of Intellectual Property in the Information Age* (Washington, D.C.: Cato Institute, 2002), p. xxvi.

19. As the *Los Angeles Times* reported, "Those who favor expirations for copyright point to what happened with Frances Hodgson Burnett's *The Secret Garden*, the ageless tale of a boy and girl spiritually renewed after discovering a hidden garden on a Yorkshire estate. First published in 1911, the work entered the public domain in 1986. There are now at least 12 print versions of the book as well as two online versions. There has been a TV adaptation, a musical, a big-budget Warner Bros. movie, a cookbook. No one owns *The Secret Garden* anymore, consequently everyone owns it." David Streitfeld, "The Cultural Anarchist vs. the Hollywood Police State," *Los Angeles Times* (September 22, 2002). Online at http://tinyurl.com/2dmnr

20. Lawrence Lessig, interview with the author (February 11, 2003). For a full transcript, see Darknet.com.

21. As the *Economist* magazine said in an editorial after the Eldred ruling, "Copyright was originally the grant of a temporary government-supported monopoly on copying a work. It has never been a property right. Its sole purpose was to encourage the circulation of ideas by giving creators and publishers a short-term incentive to disseminate their work." Editorial, "Copyrights: A Radical Rethink," *Economist* (January 23, 2003).

22. See Steven Levy's profile of Lessig, "Lawrence Lessig's Supreme Showdown," *Wired* (October 2002). Online at www.wired.com/wired/archive/10.10/lessig_pr.html

23. Lessig cited Dan Bricklin's writings for influencing his thinking on this subject. Bricklin's weblog is at danbricklin.com/log/

24. Stewart Brand's full quote is: "Information wants to be free—because it is now so easy to copy and distribute casually—and information wants to be expensive—because in an Information Age, nothing is so valuable as the right information at the right time."

25. Robert S. Boynton, "The Tyranny of Copyright," *New York Times Magazine* (January 25, 2004).

26. Because I'm concentrating on the current activities of the free culture movement, I've left out some history from the main text. The free culture movement owes a nod of recognition to a movement in the software field with similar but not identical ideological tendencies. The open source movement began in 1984 when Richard Stallman, a computer scientist at MIT, quit his job and set up the Free Software Foundation. Concerned that proprietary software makers were locking down code and stunting progress, he became a leading advocate for the free distribution

of software. Recipient of a MacArthur genius grant, Stallman created the "copyleft" license that stipulated a program could be copied and modified as long as the source code to all changes is made accessible to all users. A Finnish student named Linus Torvalds used major contributions from the GNU Project in the early 1990s to create Linux, now installed on more than 20 million computers worldwide. Stallman gives a history of Linux and the GNU Project at www.gnu.org/gnu/linux-and-gnu.html

Over the years, Stallman has taken aim at copyright, software vendors like Dave Winer, and book publishers like Tim O'Reilly. While Stallman, whom I've met in person only briefly, doesn't demand that everything should be free, some of his positions have caused considerable discomfort among potential allies in the free culture movement.

27. Barlow's essay "The Economy of Ideas: Selling Wine without Bottles on the Global Net" is online at EFF: www.eff.org/~barlow/EconomyOfIdeas.html

He adapted the piece for an article in *Wired* magazine in 1994.

Barlow also wrote "A Declaration of the Independence in Cyberspace" in 1996, warning government to back off from regulating this extraordinary new space, although some of his ideas about the separation of the Internet from the purported real world have been roundly criticized. The declaration is online at www.eff.org/~barlow/Declaration-Final.html

28. Drew Clark and Bara Vaida, "Digital Divide," *National Journal's Technology Daily* (September 6, 2002). Here is Valenti's complete quote: "There is this new technology mind-set that there should be no regulation, no rules of the road, and that this is Dodge City without a sheriff," Valenti said. The Internet is no different from cable, satellite, or United Parcel Service, he said. "Every other delivery system operates under ground rules, so why is the Internet to be exempt?"

The article is online at http://notabug.com/2002/nationalJournalDigital Divide.html

29. Barlow reminds us of the second half of Stewart Brand's famous quote; see note 24.

30. See, for example, John Perry Barlow, "The Next Economy of Ideas," *Wired* (October 2000).

31. Doc Searls, "The Choice," *Linux Journal News Notes* (March 6, 2002). Online at www.ssc.com/pipermail/suitwatch/2002q1/000016.html

32. Pollack addressed PopTech on October 19, 2002.

33. Roundtable with John Perry Barlow and others, "Life, Liberty, and . . . the Pursuit of Copyright?," *Atlantic Monthly* (September 17, 1998). Online at www.theatlantic.com/unbound/forum/copyright/barlow2.htm

34. Jordan Pollack, "Should the Right to Own Property Be Preserved?," Edge.org (December 4, 2001). Online at www.edge.org/documents/questions/q2001.3.html

35. Amy Harmon, "Studios Using Digital Armor to Fight Piracy," *New York Times* (January 5, 2003).

36. Some have put the number of recorded songs at 2 million to 3 million, though that's clearly understated. ASCAP, for example, represents 4 million musi-

cal works. It's likely that less than 20 percent of music ever recorded is currently available for purchasing or listening through legal means.

37. Lawrence Lessig, *Free Culture* (New York: Penguin Press, 2004), p. 314.

38. Warren Lieberfarb, interview with the author (November 19 and 21, 2003).

39. Chris Murray, interview with the author (January 20, 2004).

40. Specifically, at the Digital Hollywood conference in Beverly Hills, September 23–25, 2002, Randall said: "Movie companies want to sell our stuff to the public in multiple formats, but to a large extent our hands are tied. Our contracts with Blockbuster, with our pay-TV provider, and with others really limit what we can make available to consumers when they want it, during the theatrical window. Many of these contracts are very long-term."

41. Delivered in November 2002 at the Association for Computing Machinery DRM conference. The "Darknet" paper can be downloaded at http://crypto.stanford.edu/DRM2002/darknet5.doc

42. Microsoft denied my requests to interview any of the researchers, saying the Darknet paper speaks for itself and its authors will not grant interviews to anyone.

3 | Inside the Movie Underground

1. I interviewed Bruce Forest on several occasions by phone and on October 27, 2003, at his house.

2. Forest is the one who came up with this estimate, and even he admits no one knows how many files are being traded in the Darknet. His estimate came on one of the busiest movie weekends in history, in May 2002.

3. For a transcript of the exchange with beneaththecobweb, see Darknet.com.

4. John G. Malcolm, interview with the author.

5. Benjamin S. Feingold and Adrian Alperovich, interviews with the author (November 20, 2003). For a full transcript of Alperovich's comments on the region coding system, see Darknet.com.

6. IDG News Service, "Three Minutes with Rob Glaser" (January 16, 2004). Online at www.pcworld.com/news/article/0,aid,114297,00.asp

4 | When Personal and Mass Media Collide

1. Interviews at the Center for Digital Storytelling took place on September 19, 2002.

2. The father of the digital storytelling movement was Dana Atchley, a whimsical figure who adopted the alter ego Ace Space. Atchley created *Road Show*, a stage production crafted from sixty to seventy short video vignettes he pieced together from people's lives. At the end of the show's run, Atchley and Lambert cofounded the Storycenter. Atchley died in 2000. A tribute is online at www.storycenter.org/dana.html

3. This particular iDay took place on February 8, 2003.

4. Moses Ma in his venture capital newsletter the *Pitch: Insights and Foresight into the Future of Technology* (Spring 2004), p. 4.

5. To its credit, BMG dispatches digital evangelists to meet with any executives, artists, or managers still wary of the Internet. Evelyn Nussenbaum, "Technology and Show Business Kiss and Make Up," *New York Times* (April 26, 2004).

6. Section 1008 of the Copyright Act. Jessica Litman writes in her law review article "War Stories," 20 *Cardozo Arts & Entertainment Law Journal* 337 (2002): "Under the old way of thinking about things, copying your CD and carrying the copy around with you to play in your car, in your Walkman, or in your cassette deck at work is legal. Borrowing a music CD and making a copy on some other medium for your personal use is legal. Recording music from the radio; maxing different recorded tracks for a 'party tape,' and making a copy of one of your CDs for your next-door neighbor are, similarly, all lawful acts. The copyright law says so: section 1008 of the copyright statute provides that consumers may make non-commercial copies of recorded music without liability. Many people seem not to know this any more."

7. Fritz Attaway, interview with the author (November 9, 2004).

8. It should be mentioned that obtaining permission to use copyrighted material from individuals is almost always easier than obtaining it from corporations. Eric Schulman, a Ph.D. astronomer and science writer, tells me he has never had trouble getting permission to use photos that individuals have taken and published on their Web sites (and he always grants such requests as well). But when he writes to corporate entities, he gets no response. For instance, he sent an e-mail to Atari requesting permission to use a screenshot from the game *Civilization* to illustrate the concept of civilization but never received a reply.

9. Philip Gaines, interview with the author (February 11, 2004).

10. Siva Vaidhyanathan, interview with the author (February 10, 2004).

11. Ernest Miller, interview with the author (February 23, 2004).

12. Saffo told the *Washington Post*: "The more people get on the Web, the more the Web becomes the vaster wasteland that is the successor to the vast wasteland of television. I don't care what the majority of people are looking at, because the majority of people are really boring." Joel Achenbach, "Search for Tomorrow," *Washington Post* (February 15, 2004). Online at www.washingtonpost.com/wp-dyn/articles/A42885-2004Feb14_3.html

13. J.D. Lasica, "Citizens as budding reporters and editors," *American Journalism Review* (July–August 1999).

14. The report is available on the Pew site www.pewinternet.org/reports/toc.asp?Report=113

15. The report summary is at www.ced.org/docs/summary/summary_dcc.pdf The full report (101 pages, PDF) is at www.ced.org/docs/report/report_dcc.pdf

16. James Wolcott, "The Laptop Brigade," *Vanity Fair* (April 2004), p. 144.

17. O'Reilly posted the comments on Dan Gillmor's eJournal (January 11, 2004).

18. Moses Ma, op cit.

19. Another site, *FANlib: People Powered Entertainment*, offers a collaborative storytelling environment created by fans. Online at www.fanlib.com/cms/

5 | Code Warriors

1. I visited DivX headquarters on August 23, 2002, and followed up with Jordan Greenhall by phone on January 28, 2004.

2. Paul Boutin wrote perhaps the best roundup of the sneakernet phenomenon in his *Wired* magazine article "Burn, Baby, Burn" (December 2002), online at www.wired.com/wired/archive/10.12/view.html?pg=2

6 | Cool Toys Hollywood Wants to Ban

1. David Clayton, interviews with the author (Spring 2004).

2. David and Diana Miller, interview with the author (November 17, 2002); follow-up (April 2004).

3. For details, see John Redford's "Doomed Engineers" essay (February 1996). Online at www.world.std.com/~jlr/doom/armstrng.htm

4. Hearing before the U.S. House Judiciary Committee, "Home Recordings of Copyrighted Works" (April 12, 1982). Valenti's testimony is online at http://cryptome.org/hrcw-hear.htm

5. Paul Sloan, "The Offer Hollywood Can't Refuse," *Business 2.0* (May 2004), p. 91.

6. Kraus's Senate testimony is online at http://tinyurl.com/2hzwz

His testimony before the House Committee on Energy and Commerce is online at http://tinyurl.com/3dosj

7. The Web site is at http://illegal-art.org/

8. Intel has devised a set of "first principles of content protection" for the digital world, which Stephen Balogh outlined this way:

- Intel understands and depends on intellectual property rights and respects the rights of copyright holders.
- The company is focused on creating a legal, protected digital environment. In so doing, Intel looks at content protection technology chiefly as a deterrent, not as a perfect or complete solution to copyright infringement.
- Content protection solutions need to be flexible and need to enable new flexible media experiences that balance consumer expectations with rights holders' interests. To that end, content protection should enable consumer choice rather than dictate the availability of the digital media experience. Comprehensive disclosure is also needed, chiefly through product labeling, so that consumers know what they can and cannot do when they buy digital media that use copy protected systems.
- Finally, markets—not mandates—are the best way to deliver consumer satisfaction. The market will stimulate technological innovation, bringing about compelling products and business models that meet consumers' demands and expectations.

9. Another feature, called "selectable output control," allows copyright owners to turn off a viewer's set-top box's outputs under certain circumstances, as when a copy protection scheme has been hacked. But consumer groups and electronics companies say honest viewers shouldn't be prevented from, say, playing HDTV

movies or recording high-def television just because someone somewhere else foiled the industry's copy control system.

10. Balogh says, "The first step is forensics, which identifies who you are. Then certification says, are you authorized to use this content in the way you want? Certification is like a watermark in a piece of media that says, 'This piece of media is copy x times and it's being played back, and this content says it's a first-time movie release and it's supposed to be on a DVD-ROM, but I see it's not a DVD-ROM, it's a recordable hard drive,' and so the machine will say, 'You're not certified to play this movie, it's supposed to be a hard piece of plastic that has a burned-in ID, etc.'"

11. Balogh expanded on renewability this way: "Through renewability, the system can be replaced so you don't have to replace the entire machine to get it back up to a secure environment. One of the ways you can do renewability is with revocation. If somebody stole a key, you can revoke that one key and its clones for that one device. Another form of renewability is the wholesale replacement of a downloaded module. So if you're in a cable set-top box, you want to replace the firmware running in that, it's just a download because it upgrades whatever hole was left in the implementation. That's renewability."

12. Steven Levy, "Info with a Ball and Chain," *Newsweek* (June 23, 2003), p. 59.

13. Victor Nemecheck, interview with the author (September 10, 2002).

14. Saul Hansell, "At Big Consumer Electronics Show, the Buzz Is All about Connections," *New York Times* (January 13, 2003).

15. Richard F. Doherty, interview with the author (January 22, 2004).

16. For example, in July 1999 Panasonic launched the world's first high-definition digital VCR. Chiefly intended for showrooms to introduce the public to high-definition TV, the PV-HD1000 was an immediate hit with buyers, who ponied up $1,000 for a device that let them record ultrasharp images on digital tape. But Hollywood was nervous about people recording programs in such a pristine format. "Executives at Panasonic told me they were pressured by Hollywood attorneys to get them all off the market," Doherty says. "Many of the units were recovered and brought to a factory where their 1394 ports [permitting high-speed digital connections] were cut off, leaving them emasculated. That, to me, is extortion." A second person with knowledge of the situation confirmed the account, adding that Panasonic also built a set-top box for DirecTV with a 1394 port, or Firewire output, that connected the box to Panasonic's tape deck so people could record satellite programming in high definition, but Hollywood pressured them to remove the high-speed digital port before the box shipped. Panasonic declined comment.

By 2002, Mitsubishi and JVC started shipping similar digital VHS decks to record high-def TV. But what viewers really wanted was a unit that records high-definition TV onto a hard drive. Those units are just beginning to come onto the market—with airtight copy controls.

17. Von Lohmann tells me:

The lack of digital video outputs creates a number of problems for consumers, both for recording and viewing:

1. For viewing—lower-quality video on "fixed pixel" displays (plasma, DLP,

LCD—anything that is a fixed pixel digital display), because it requires an extra and unnecessary conversion from digital (source) to analog (component outputs) back to digital (in the display). If the technology allowed direct digital outputs to these fixed pixel displays, the whole thing could be made cheaper and higher-quality (because you could eliminate several unnecessary analog to digital conversions).

2. For recording—no ability to record programs in high definition. While it is theoretically possible to record from component analog high-def outputs, there are currently no reasonably priced technologies that do that—it's much easier to simply move the signal as an MPEG digital file rather than rendering it to high-def analog, then redigitizing it in high def. You can pretty easily make lo-def recordings from analog outputs (on a VCR, for example).

18. Von Lohmann, follow-up interview with the author (May 4, 2004).

19. Doherty says companies like Sixteen Nine Time are better able to skirt Hollywood's pressure by not attending cross-industry standards meetings. "These are highly charged meetings, and they are dominated more by lawyers than by the marketers or engineers who are trying to give consumers what they want," says Doherty, who has attended many such meetings. "Design decisions about consumer devices with digital capabilities are made on the basis of emotion rather than hard evidence. Very successful consumer electronics brands with track records of customer loyalty stretching back decades have found themselves incredibly frustrated by this pressure being put on them, sometimes with a legal threat, sometimes with a commercial threat."

20. Specifically, from Doherty's Sony PC-5 to a Sony PC-100 and a Sony DV deck model 1000.

21. John Gilmore, "What's Wrong with Copy Protection" (2001), Spectacle.org. Online at www.spectacle.org/0501/gilmore.html

22. Gilmore e-mails me: "It has been quite an 'interesting' exercise trying to get some of the irreplaceable live recordings off my MiniDiscs. So far I have been able to transfer ten or twenty, with great effort. The replaceable ones I'm ignoring (buying used CDs of them, which is both cheaper and more reliable)." E-mail interview (April 27, 2004).

23. In the same e-mail, Gilmore writes:
In the flash memory market, there's only one viable form factor remaining that doesn't include copy protection: Compact Flash. MMC never gets capacity upgrades; the compatible but copy-protected "SD" (Secure Digital) format does. Sony Memory Sticks all have copy protection. In the hard-disk market, what happened was that the copy-protection standard got sufficient public opposition that it was never made a standard in the public standards committee. But, of course, disk drive makers are free to implement nonstandard "extensions" and disk drive purchasers are free to specify these. For example, the disk drives in every TiVo are password-locked so that they if you remove the drive and plug it into a PC, you can't access it to extract the recorded television signals.

As a second example, computer makers like Dell buy hard drives that are actually larger than advertised, but that are software-locked to pretend to be a smaller size. Then Dell offers their buyers "downloadable" hard-drive upgrades that make the drive "bigger." E.g., you may get a 40GB drive that is really a 120GB drive—but you can only get at the other 80MB with some secret commands negotiated between Dell and the drive maker.

24. See, for example, www.minidisc.org/minidisc_faq.html#_q82

25. The petition is online at www.minidisc.org/netmd_petition_support.html

26. Sony's response is online at www.minidisc.org/netmd_upload_sony_reply. html

27. Here are a few: IBM's extensible Content Protection program would allow media companies to put controls on content distributed over home networks. The Broadcast Protection Discussion Group issued a disputed report that led the FCC to mandate adoption of the broadcast flag. Hollywood formed the Analog Reconversion Discussion Group in early 2003 to address the piracy issue.

28. Seth Greenstein, interview with the author (October 16, 2002).

7 | A Nation of Digital Felons

1. Copyright owners like to say there is no "fair use right" and that fair use is just a defense to infringement. There are others who believe that fair use is a right. The EFF says: "Fair use is the principle that the public is entitled, without having to ask permission, to use copyrighted works so long as these uses do not unduly interfere with the copyright owner's market for a work. Fair uses include personal, noncommercial uses, such as using a VCR to record a television program for later viewing. Fair use also includes activities undertaken for purposes such as criticism, comment, news reporting, teaching, scholarship or research." Making "mix CDs" or copies of CDs for the office or car are other examples of fair use that are potentially impaired by copy-protection technologies.

2. I interviewed Whiteside, members of the delegation, and one other person who was present during the exchange.

3. In an e-mail on March 23, 2004, Johansen tells me: "Neither I or the two other DeCSS authors 'cracked' CSS. Cracking a crypto algorithm means discovering weaknesses. DeCSS does not exploit any CSS weaknesses. Your set-top DVD player and DeCSS decrypt DVDs using the exact same method."

4. Jonathan Zittrain, interview with the author (June 30, 2003).

5. Rob Kost, interview with the author (March 27, 2004).

6. My math genius of a brother-in-law tells me that number would be 8,589,934,590.

7. See the Free Expression Policy Project for the origins of the DMCA, which had its origins in the 1994 "Green Paper" that the Clinton administration produced in response to industry concerns about the potential for widespread copying and sharing of books, articles, movies, music, and virtually any other expression online. The problem of electronic piracy was—and remains—a serious one. The question is how to address it without undermining copyright's free-expression

safety valves. The Green Paper took a radical approach, asserting that every reading or viewing of a work on a computer should be considered a reproduction requiring copyright permission. Cited by Jessica Litman, *Digital Copyright* (Amherst, N.Y.: Prometheus Books, 2001), p. 95. Online at www.fepproject.org/policyreports/copyright2dins.html

8. Drew Clark, "How Copyright Became Controversial," *National Journal's Technology Daily*. Online at www.cfp2002.org/proceedings/proceedings/clark.pdf

9. The DMCA passed the Senate by unanimous consent, passed the House on a voice vote, and was signed into law by President Clinton on October 28, 1998.

10. See Kraus's testimony before the Senate Judiciary Committee during the hearing, "Competition, Innovation, and Public Policy in the Digital Age: Is the Marketplace Working to Protect Digital Creative Works?" (March 14, 2002). Online at http://tinyurl.com/2hzwz

11. Brodi Kemp, "Copyright's Digital Reformulation," *Yale Journal of Law and Technology* (April 2003), p. 8.

12. Princeton computer scientist Edward Felten has become one of the leading critics of overly restrictive digital rights management systems. At a DRM conference at the University of California, Berkeley, in early 2003, he decried the use of DMCA-backed copy protection systems that threaten the free flow of information online and that strip away users' ability to control devices they buy. "DRM strategies tend to take devices, whether they are computers or media players, and turn them into black boxes, black boxes that users are not allowed to analyze or examine or understand," he said. "Technology, God knows, is hard enough to figure out. What we don't need to do is make it harder." Transcripts of the conference are online at www.law.berkeley.edu/institutes/bclt/drm/resources.html

13. Noel C. Paul, "Digital Copying Rules May Change," *Christian Science Monitor* (August 19, 2002).

14. From Digitalconsumer.org FAQs.

15. See Kim Zetter, "E-Vote Protest Gains Momentum," *Wired News* (October 29, 2003). Online at www.wired.com/news/business/0,1367,61002,00.html

16. Robert S. Boynton, "The Tyranny of Copyright?" *New York Times Magazine* (January 25, 2004).

17. *Time*'s article is online at www.time.com/time/personoftheyear/2002/poyintro.html

18. See the EFF's "Unintended Consequences of the DMCA," online at www.eff.org/IP/DMCA/unintended_consequences.pdf

19. Jon C. Dvorak, "Free Speech at Risk," *PC Magazine* (October 13, 2003). Online at http://tinyurl.com/2768x

20. For more, see FreeSkylarov.org/

21. ElcomSoft CEO Alex Katalov said that the DMCA charges took their toll on his company, which spent hundreds of thousands of dollars to defend itself. He also said his experience with U.S. copyright law should send chills through the entire worldwide development community, especially among those who make software designed to test security and crack codes, as such programs also could run afoul of

the DMCA: Alan Wexelblat, "ElcomSoft Is Being Bled Dry by Legal Fees," *Internet Law News* (April 2002).

22. Lawrence Lessig pointed this out on his blog at www.lessig.org/blog/archives/001993.shtml

23. "The problem is the public has little or no legal right to fair use," MIT's Henry Jenkins says. "Fair use is reserved for elite groups, like me and you. As an academic, I can make critical commentary for an academic work. You as a journalist enjoy a fair use right. But for fair use to kick in, you have to demonstrate that it's for certain sanctioned purposes such as criticism, comment, news reporting, teaching, scholarship, or research. And those purposes don't seem to include the kinds of things the public wants to do with media right now."

24. For example, Dutch security systems analyst Neils Ferguson discovered a flaw in an Intel video encryption system but removed all references to his research from his Web site for fear of prosecution under the DMCA.

25. Hiawatha Bray, "Cyber Chief Speaks on Data Network Security," *Boston Globe* (October 17, 2002). Also, at a conference of computer professionals, Clarke observed that most security holes in software are found not by software makers but by outsiders acting in good faith, and those efforts needed to be shielded from the legal wrath of companies upset at hackers who demonstrate the vulnerabilities of software and computer networks.

26. Peter Wayner, "Whose Intellectual Property Is It, Anyway? The Open Source War," *New York Times* (August 24, 2000).

27. Declan McCullagh, "Perspective: Will This Land Me in Jail?," News.com (December 23, 2002). Online at http://news.com.com/2010-1028-978636.html

28. A recent court decision declared that using a password someone gave you is not a violation of the DMCA, but it is only a district court decision, and law scholar Ernest Miller says the law is still uncertain in this area. See www.corante.com/importance/archives/002183.html

29. Jed Horovitz, interview with the author (July 1, 2003).

30. Maggie Shiels, "Unlocking the Copyright Culture," *BBC News Online* (June 24, 2002). Online at http://tinyurl.com/3b3t9

31. Andy Raskin, "Giving It Away (for Fun and Profit)," *Business 2.0* (May 2004), p. 112.

32. Some tech advocates have urged a Million Geek March on Washington to show their opposition to the digital clampdown. PBS.org tech writer Robert X. Cringely wrote a provocative column in 2002 that called on users to engage in "massive civil disobedience" to protest the DMCA. He offered a novel proposal: "Everyone who hates the DMCA has to illegally copy a movie or a song, and then tell both the Congress and the U.S. Copyright Office exactly what they did. We need 10 million or so confessed and unrepentant intellectual property pirates. That's too much illegal behavior to ignore." No one (at least publicly) took up Cringely on his idea. Robert X. Cringely, "Steal This Column," PBS.org (September 26, 2002). Online at www.pbs.org/cringely/pulpit/pulpit20020926.html

33. From the "Darknet" paper:

There is evidence that the darknet will continue to exist and provide low cost, high-quality service to a large group of consumers. This means that in many markets, the darknet will be a competitor to legal commerce. From the point of view of economic theory, this has profound implications for business strategy: for example, increased security (e.g. stronger DRM systems) may act as a disincentive to legal commerce. Consider an MP3 file sold on a web site: this costs money, but the purchased object is as useful as a version acquired from the darknet. However, a securely DRM-wrapped song is strictly less attractive: although the industry is striving for flexible licensing rules, customers will be restricted in their actions if the system is to provide meaningful security. This means that a vendor will probably make more money by selling unprotected objects than protected objects. In short, if you are competing with the darknet, you must compete on the darknet's own terms: that is convenience and low cost rather than additional security.

8 | Personal Broadcasting

1. I interviewed Raven on a number of occasions in 2003 and 2004.

2. Lisa Rein, interview with the author (July 23, 2003).

3. Warren Lieberfarb, interviews with the author (November 19 and 21, 2003). For a transcript, see Darknet.com.

4. Gregory L. Clayman, interview with the author (November 6, 2002).

5. Mike Ramsay, interview with the author (May 28, 2003). For a transcript, see Darknet.com.

6. Mark Pesce, "Redefining Television," *Mindjack* (May 17, 2004). Online at www.mindjack.com/feature/redefiningtv.html

9 | Edge TV

1. Devin Leonard, "This Is War," *Fortune* (May 27, 2002).

2. Ashley Highfield, interview with the author (November 12, 2003).

3. John S. Hendricks, interview with the author (April 15, 2003). For a complete transcript, see Darknet.com.

4. Crain Communications, "The PVR Revolution: Mere Myth or Nightmare to Come?" (November 18, 2002).

5. Mike Ramsay, interview with the author (May 28, 2003). For a complete transcript, see Darknet.com. In early 2005, Ramsay announced he would leave his CEO position but would continue as chairman of TiVo's board.

6. Howard Look, interview with the author (June 18, 2003).

7. Using a different technology, smaller companies such as Akimbo today deliver more than ten thousand video-on-demand programs.

8. Stewart Alsop, interview with the author (November 26, 2002). For a complete transcript, see Darknet.com.

9. Tom Watson and Jason Chervokas, "How the Net Could Nuke TV: Video File-Sharing," *[Inside]* (January 30, 2001).

10. Kyra Thompson, interview with the author (July 3, 2003).

11. The company rendered its name SONICblue.

12. Andy Wolfe, interview with the author (June 23, 2003).

13. Martin J. Yudkovitz, interview with the author (November 25, 2002).

14. Frank James, "FCC Chief Warns of Future Shock," *Chicago Tribune* (September 7, 2003).

15. The very idea of a network may change. Instead of linear programming that fills twenty-four hours a day, a network might put all its efforts into a handful of high-quality shows. New networks, staffed by two or three people, may spring up overnight, cobbling together footage from a variety of Internet sources. High-quality, cheap-to-produce niche programming will find an audience. New stars, programs, and themes will come from out of nowhere and attract a following.

16. John Battelle wrote eloquently on this issue in his *Business 2.0* column "Is TiVo NeXT?" (May 2003). Online at http://tinyurl.com/2apnr

17. For more information, see Christine Y. Chen, "I Want My iTV," *Fortune* (April 1, 2002). Online at http://tinyurl.com/347av

18. Highfield's speech was titled "TV's Tipping Point: Why the Digital Revolution Is Only Just Beginning." Online at http://tinyurl.com/24d3y

19. Rodney Books, "The Other Exponentials," *Technology Review* (November 2004).

20. Leslie Walker, "Media Giants Need to Learn to Sing a New Tune," *Washington Post* (March 25, 2004). Online at http://tinyurl.com/23vyz

21. Testimony by Jonathan Taplin, CEO, Intertainer Inc., before the Senate Judiciary Committee in a hearing titled "Competition, Innovation, and Public Policy in the Digital Age: Is the Marketplace Working to Protect Digital Creative Works?" (March 14, 2002).

10 | The Sound of Digital Music

1. Tony Abbott, interview with the author (November 20, 2003).

2. Erich Ringewald, interview with the author (January 4, 2004).

3. Kevin Kelly, "Where Music Will Be Coming From," *New York Times Magazine* (March 17, 2002).

4. Frank Ahrens, "Technology Repaves Road to Stardom," *Washington Post* (May 2, 2004).

5. Clay Shirky, "The Music Business and the Big Flip," Shirky.com (n.d.). Online at www.shirky.com/writings/music_flip.html

6. Rick Karr, "TechnoPop," NPR (September 20, 2002). Online at www.npr.org/programs/morning/features/2002/technopop/index.html

7. Roger McGuinn, interview with the author (February 3, 2004).

8. "Music on the Internet: Is There an Upside to Downloading?" Senate Judiciary Committee (July 11, 2000). Online at http://judiciary.senate.gov/hearing.cfm?id=195

9. Joy Lanzendorfer, "Filesharing Is Not the Enemy," AlterNet.org (May 14, 2004). Online at www.alternet.org/story/18698

10. Mike Sciullo, interview with the author (September 3, 2002).

11. Cary Sherman, interview with the author (March 2, 2003).

12. Neil Strauss, "Behind the Grammys, Revolt in the Industry," *New York Times* (February 24, 2002).

13. Steve Albini, "The Problem with Music," Negativland.com (n.d.). Online at www.negativland.com/albini.html

14. Courtney Love, "Courtney Love Does the Math," *Salon* (June 14, 2000). Online at http://tinyurl.com/2x25e

15. According to the Pew, the number of downloaders who say they don't care about copyright increased from 61 percent in July–August 2000 to 67 percent in March–May 2003.

16. Nathan Anderson, "Books & Culture's Book of the Week: Thou Shalt Not Swap," *Christianity Today Magazine* (May 24, 2004). Online at www.christianitytoday.com/ct/2004/121/13.0.html

17. James M. Burger, interview with the author (October 15, 2002).

18. Thirty-seven percent supported the industry's legal actions. Seven percent of those surveyed had no opinion. One thousand adults were surveyed, with results accurate to plus or minus 3 percent. Results available at http://company.findlaw.com/pr/2004/062904.musicpiracy.html

19. See Moby's entry at http://tinyurl.com/39xay

20. Janis Ian wrote about her experience online at www.janisian.com/article-internet_debacle.html and at www.janisian.com/article-fallout.html

21. Researchers at Harvard and the University of North Carolina tracked music downloads over seventeen weeks in 2002, matching data on file transfers with actual market performance of the songs and albums being downloaded. The study is online at http://tinyurl.com/yr5hf

Harvard Business School professor Felix Oberholzer-Gee, coauthor of the report, told *Rolling Stone*, "The Internet is more like radio than we thought. People listen to two or three songs, and if they like it, they go out and buy the CD." Damien Cave, "Don't Blame Kazaa," *Rolling Stone* (April 29, 2004).

Other credible research shows that the labels raised CD prices during a down economy and slashed the number of new releases by almost 25 percent over three years, and then measured sales losses not on lost sales but on fewer units shipped to retailers. See James K. Willcox, "Where Have All the CDs Gone?," *Sound & Vision* (June 2003). Online at http://tinyurl.com/3xqga

22. As the *Los Angeles Times* editorialized in August 2003, "Songs downloaded free deny artists and record companies their due. Even so, the recording industry has abetted the robbery with its own greed and ineptitude. . . . The digital revolution, like it or not, has transported the music industry to a place where it must thrive online. And the more the industry resists creating legal, easy and affordable ways to download all music—pleasing consumers, artists and entrepreneurs alike— the more it will achieve the opposite: making illegal sharing more entrenched and innovative." Editorial, "Tone-Deaf Music Industry," *Los Angeles Times* (August 4, 2003).

23. Editor in chief Chris Anderson wrote in the January 2004 issue of *Wired* magazine: "Unlike music labels, movie studios are not hated by consumer and artist alike. Labels are seen (not entirely unfairly) as gouging consumers, screwing musicians, and otherwise failing to earn their middleman markup. But the value of studios is clear. Movies are huge, expensive endeavors that can't be made in a garage or on a bedroom mixing board. Consumers are happier paying $10 for a special-effects extravaganza or an epic drama than they are $16 for a glorified mix tape. . . . Customers who feel they're getting their money's worth are less likely to turn into pirates. . . . Now the bad news: You're at risk of alienating your customers like the music industry did. The do-not-record 'broadcast flag' that the TV industry just pushed through the FCC will introduce new restrictions on programming, none of which benefit consumers. Proposed legislation that throws anyone caught with a prerelease movie on their hard drive into prison for three years is the sort of disproportionate response that gives the RIAA a bad name. The notorious Digital Millennium Copyright Act is Hollywood's fault. And extending copyright protection year after year so that the film and television archives stay shut isn't just bad law, it's depriving Americans of their cultural history."

24. Stewart Alsop, "My New Favorite Toy," *Fortune* (June 25, 2001).

25. For more on Bull's research, see Leander Kahney, "Bull Session with Professor IPod," *Wired News* (February 25, 2004). Online at http://tinyurl.com/2a8w8

26. Alex Salkever, "A Talk with iTunes' Conductor," *BusinessWeek Online* (May 7, 2003). Online at http://tinyurl.com/245zq

27. A beta release came in 1998. Bob Ohlweiler, Musicmatch's senior vice president of business development, said: "Before the jukebox, there was Winamp and some kludgey single-purpose players and the Real player, and early on there was an app called Audio Grabber that was just a ripper and encoder that would convert a CD into MP3. That was the classic combination: Audio Grabber for encoding and Winamp for playback, before Musicmatch became popular. The jukebox basically made a breakthrough in ease of use in one application where you could record, manage and play back your music from playlists you've created. In version 1.1 we added burning, so you had ability to burn and download music to portable devices."

28. Musicmatch Jukebox's widespread dissemination is because of bundling deals with all the major PC makers.

29. There are varying estimates for the size of the "music industry." The record industry sells $12 billion a year in the United States, mostly from the sale of CDs and other recordings. Sales worldwide total about $38 billion.

30. Dennis Mudd and other Musicmatch executives were interviewed by the author on August 22, 2002.

31. The DMCA can be found online at http://tinyurl.com/26q74

32. Under a deal with Apple, Musicmatch makes the software for PC-based iPods.

11 | Channeling Cole Porter

1. Jim Griffin, interview with the author (November 20, 2003).

2. I joined the Pho list in early 2003.

3. Bowie told the *New York Times*, "The absolute transformation of everything that we ever thought about music will take place within 10 years, and nothing is going to be able to stop it. I see absolutely no point in pretending that it's not going to happen. I'm fully confident that copyright, for instance, will no longer exist in 10 years, and authorship and intellectual property is in for such a bashing." Jon Pareles, "David Bowie, 21st-Century Entrepreneur," *New York Times* (June 9, 2002).

4. "*EW* Talks to David Bowie and Moby," *Entertainment Weekly* (August 19, 2002).

5. Cole Porter quotation, online at http://tinyurl.com/38fyo Incidentally, Sammy Cahn probably wasn't the first to use that expression.

6. William Fisher of Harvard and Neil Netanel of Texas are among those proposing compulsory licenses. Technorati principal engineer Kevin Marks dissected such licenses in this posting on Lawrence Lessig's blog:

> I strongly disagree—such proposals only benefit incumbent publishers, not creators. Here I explained this in detail:
>
> 1. By statutorily imposing a solution like this, it makes it much harder to establish a true marketplace for digital media—people are reluctant to pay twice. This will reduce overall spending on music.
> 2. Statistical measurement of a scale-free distribution like music (or the net) is hard to do well—because the central limit theorem does not apply, most sampling will count the large players accurately, but miss significant numbers of small players who may well predominate in aggregate. This kind of centralised scheme undoes the bottom-up formation and propagation of musical styles that the net can do, and puts us back into a top 20 world. I analysed movies, newspapers and weblogs scale-free distributions. If anyone has good data on music revenues by album or group, let me know.
> 3. Any centralised taxation-like scheme is highly prone to capture by a few interest groups—ASCAP and BMI are poorly regarded by independent musicians for this very reason.
> 4. By legitimating only non-commercial repurposing of existing copyright, it does nothing to cut through the thicket of rights and licensing that acts as dead weight on those who create; instead it pushes derived works into a second-class non-commercial status. My model in which derivative works pass through the cost of the source works is far more liberating.
>
> A far better idea is to establish a true marketplace for media that incorporates incentives for those who buy and sell within it to reward copyright holders.
>
> Posted by Kevin Marks on April 6, 2003. Online at http://tinyurl.com/35zhc

7. Hal R. Varian, "New Chips Can Keep a Tight Rein on Consumers," *New York Times* (July 4, 2002).

8. Pete Rojas, "Bootleg Culture," *Salon* (August 1, 2002). Online at http://archive.salon.com/tech/feature/2002/08/01/bootlegs/

9. "Q&A with R. U. Sirius, Don Joyce, Mark Hosler, and U2's the Edge," *Mondo 2000* (June 25, 1992).

10. Specifically, the irreverent notice on Negativland.com said: "Negativland's friends and lawyers who had seen 'The Mashin' of the Christ' had strongly advised against a public release ever occuring (the 'anti-circumvention' provision of the Digital Millennium Copyright Act says that doing this sort of decryption to make collage is illegal), but since God is said to see all secrets, only the public is left to be surprised by this unauthorized birth from Negativland. Voracious pirating of this work has spread across the Net and in the last few days high-resolution versions of 'Mashin'" have even been appearing on P2P networks disguised as a complete copy of 'The Passion of the Christ.'" Online at www.negativland.com/mashin/howto.htm

11. The *New York Times* reported: "Some of the world's biggest record companies, facing rampant online piracy, are quietly financing the development and testing of software programs that would sabotage the computers and Internet connections of people who download pirated music, industry executives say." Andrew Ross Sorkin, "Software Bullet Is Sought to Kill Music Piracy," *New York Times* (May 4, 2003).

12. Sam Diaz, "Genres Find Audience on Net Radio," *San Jose Mercury News* (April 30, 2004). Live365 gives users the Web-based tools and storage space to arrange playlists from music they enjoy. Amateur DJs upload their favorite music, then manage their playlists on the company's servers.

13. Raghav Gupta, interview with the author (May 26, 2004).

14. Ann Gabriel, interview with the author (June 15, 2004).

15. A list of AM and FM stations with HD radio technology can be found at www.ibiquity.com/hdradio/hdradio_hdstations.htm

16. Cheryl Leanza, interview with the author (May 4, 2004). The move to digital radio also raises a thorny public policy question: what is the difference between digital radio heard over a digital device (where no performance royalty is owed the artists) and Internet radio or wireless streaming music heard over the same digital device (where Congress imposed a performance fee)? None, really.

17. Brad King, "Music Biz Lament: Stealing Hurts," *Wired News* (September 26, 2002). Online at www.wired.com/news/mp3/0,1285,55393,00.html

18. Jennifer Ordoñez, "Pop Singer Fails to Strike a Chord Despite the Millions Spent by MCA," *Wall Street Journal* (February 26, 2002).

12 | Architects of Darknet

1. Seth Schiesel, "File Sharing's New Face," *New York Times* (February 12, 2004).

2. Amy Harmon, "File-Sharing Program Slips Out of AOL Offices," *New York Times* (June 2, 2003).

3. Saul Hansell, "Crackdown on Copyright Abuse May Send Music Traders into Software Underground," *New York Times* (September 15, 2003).

4. Powell Fraser, "Secret Networks Protect Music Swappers," CNN.com (July 30, 2003).

5. Benny Evangelista, "Firm Sleuths Out Illegal File Sharers," *San Francisco Chronicle* (July 21, 2003). Online at http://tinyurl.com/332no

6. Declan McCullagh, "Piracy and Peer-to-Peer," CNET News.com (July 7, 2003). Online at http://tinyurl.com/2p7f6

7. Ian Clarke, interview with the author (November 3, 2003). The full transcript of his interview is on Darknet.com.

8. "Case Studies: Info-Share," Groove Networks. Online at www.groove.net/default.cfm?pagename=CaseStudy_Infoshare

9. Spencer Reiss, "Dark Netizen," *Wired* (August 2004).

10. Alex Yalen, interview with the author (November 12, 2002).

11. Lauren Weinstein, interview with the author (December 8, 2003).

12. Heather Green, "The Underground Internet," *BusinessWeek Online* (September 15, 2003).

13. Clay Shirky, interview with the author (November 7, 2003).

14. Alex Salkever, "Big Music's Worst Move Yet," *BusinessWeek Online* (January 27, 2004).

15. Programming on cable and satellite is already protected through encryption. But surprisingly, up to 40 percent of all U.S. viewers still receive some television through an antenna, researchers have found.

16. Greenstein maintains that in-home use, such as home networks, should not be widely affected by the introduction of the broadcast flag. He says, "Many TVs use DTCP, including Mitsubishi and many other brands. Cable boxes are coming out using DTCP. When you acquire new source devices with 5C for IP, and new sink devices with 5C for IP, they should be able to communicate using today's wireless equipment between them. Also, there will be adapters that will wirelessly receive the digital video and audio and convert it for use in the analog inputs of existing TVs, VCRs, etc. So the broadcast flag should not be a significant impediment to in-home use. The real issue is the impact with respect to transmissions outside the home—some of which might be fair use, though others clearly would not be."

17. The FCC ruling has no effect outside the United States. There's nothing to stop viewers of American television programs in Europe, Australia, and elsewhere from recording and sharing HDTV shows if they so choose.

18. Zoe Lofgren, "FCC Rule Could Harm Tech Innovation," *San Jose Mercury News* op-ed page (November 17, 2003). Immediate casualties of the broadcast flag include open-source software technologies for digital TV, such as GNU Radio and dscaler. The FCC requires the software running in DTV receivers to be "robust"—that is, untamperable—and free software applications are built to be modified by end users.

19. This example is drawn from Cory Doctorow's essay at http://bpdg.blogs.eff.org/archives/000113.html

20. Greenstein notes: "Although [the entertainment companies] would like this, they currently are leaning toward a more technically feasible solution, known as CGMS-A, in which three bits signal five states: Copy Never, Copy One Generation, Copy No More (for the one-generation copy), Copy Freely, and Copy Freely but

protect against unauthorized distribution. There would still need to be a legislative component."

21. Robert X. Cringely, "I Told You So," PBS.org presents "I, Cringely: The Pulpit" (July 27, 2002). Online at www.pbs.org/cringely/pulpit/pulpit20020627.html

22. Ross Anderson, "'Trusted Computing' Frequently Asked Questions," University of Cambridge Computer Laboratory. Online at http://www.cl.cam.ac.uk/~rja14/tcpa-faq.html

23. Schoen's full paper, "Trusted Computing: Promise and Risk," is available on the EFF.org site at www.eff.org/Infrastructure/trusted_computing/20031001_tc.php

24. Clay Shirky, "Content Shifts to the Edges, Redux," Shirky.com (n.d.). Online at www.shirky.com/writings/content2.html

13 | Mod Squads: Can Gamers Show Us the Way?

1. Dean Takahashi, "'Embedded' in a Virtual World," *San Jose Mercury News* (April 26, 2004). Author's weblog is at http://secondlife.blogs.com/nwn/

2. David Kushner, author of *Masters of Doom*, profiled There Inc. and *Second Life* in "My Avatar, My Self" for the April 2004 issue of MIT's *Technology Review*. Online at www.technologyreview.com/articles/kushner0404.asp?p=1

3. "[B]uildings constructed in the U.S. after December 1, 1990, are protected under copyright law, and you might need permission to publish the picture," Derrick Story notes in *Digital Photography Hacks* (Sebastopol, Calif.: O'Reilly Media, 2004), p. 77.

4. The *Twelve Monkeys* episode is recounted in Lawrence Lessig's *The Future of Ideas* (New York: Random House, 2001), pp. 4–5. The *Simpsons* episode is recounted in his *Free Culture*, pp. 95–98.

5. See David Kushner's marvelous book *Masters of Doom* (New York: Random House, 2003) for details.

6. Estimate by the Consumer Electronics Association.

7. Estimate by IDC Research in Framingham, Massachusetts.

8. Geoff Keighley, "Game Development à la Mod," *Business 2.0* (October 2002). Online at http://tinyurl.com/ywefp

9. Hiawatha Bray, "'Mods' Squad Adds New Life to Old Games," *Boston Globe* (August 27, 2003).

10. The contest is online at www.makesomethingunreal.com.

11. Michael Marriott, "Games Made for Remaking," *New York Times* (December 4, 2003).

12. Phil Haymes, "Across the Pond with Phil Haymes, Part 3," *Gaming World* (n.d.). Online at http://tinyurl.com/2anrp

13. Seth Schiesel, "Some Xbox Fans Microsoft Didn't Aim For," *New York Times* (July 10, 2003).

14. Annalee Newitz, "The High-Tech Black Market," *San Francisco Bay Guardian* (December 10, 2003). Online at www.sfbg.com/38/11/cover_hightech.html

15. Schiesel, op cit.

16. Scarface answered my questions by e-mail on November 16, 2003. The full transcript of his interview is on Darknet.com.

17. Busts on the mod scene have not had an effect on the game release scene, but there have been separate busts on the games/apps/mp3 scene that have greatly affected access to releases because after those busts, sites have moved further underground.

18. Marriott, op cit.

19. See, for example, News Corp. chairman Peter Chernin's keynote speech at Comdex, analyzed by blogger Jonathan Peterson, "Breaking Down Peter Chernin's Comdex Keynote" (November 23, 2002). Online at www.way.nu/archives/000493.html

14 | Remixing the Digital Future

1. I interviewed Victor LaCour at the center on November 20, 2003, as well as by phone and e-mail.

2. Ulrich Neumann, interview with the author (February 13, 2004).

3. "Media and Entertainment 2010," an IBM Institute for Business Value Future Series report, 2004. The paper is online at http://tinyurl.com/2z36k

4. See the Center for Responsive Politics at www.opensecrets.org/industries/indus.asp?Ind=B02

5. Delaware, Illinois, Maryland, Michigan, Pennsylvania, Virginia, and Wyoming have already passed such laws. For details, see Tony Bradley, "Are You Breaking the Law?," About.com (n.d.). Online at http://tinyurl.com/2q42l

6. Glenn Reynolds, "Biden Alert," Instapundit.com (July 29, 2002).

7. John Schwartz, "Report Raises Questions about Fighting Online Piracy," *New York Times* (March 1, 2004). The full report is online at www.ced.org/docs/report/report_dcc.pdf

8. My view is that the power of global publishing brings with it responsibility. Camcording a film in a movie theater is wrong. Using P2P networks to get all your music cheats musicians and songwriters. Copyright holders should retain the sole opportunities for commercial exploitation of their work. But entertainment companies overreach when they insist on trying to control *all* uses of their works— an impossibility in an age of perfect copies and global distribution. We need to distinguish between commercial infringement by pirates and small-scale copying by individuals. When users do borrow prior works for personal, noncommercial projects, the original creator should receive due credit. Embedded metadata is one way to do so.

9. The law also should allow digital rights to expand and grow with the culture, and it should trump shrink-wrap licenses or fine-print contracts that seek to limit the public's rights. DigitalConsumer.org proposes a six-point Consumers' Bill of Rights, online at www.DigitalConsumer.org/bill.html

10. In the case of region coding, Yale's Ernest Miller tells me: "It depends on the device, actually, and how you get around the region coding. Region coding isn't an official part of the CSS encryption scheme in a sense. That is, you don't have to bypass CSS in order to change region coding on most devices (though one could possibly set it up that way, I believe). The region coding is actually tied to the CSS through contract. If you want to manufacturer a DVD player legally, you have to license CSS from the DVDCCA. When you license CSS, part of the contractual

obligation (according to reports) is that you enable region coding. Of course, if you are using a software DVD player and disable the region coding, even if you don't mess with CSS, you have likely violated the clickwrap contract for the software DVD player and you would be guilty of breaching your contract (though whether the contract is enforceable is another story). So the answer to your question is: Yes, they may be violating the law depending on how they get around the region coding."

11. In addition, the massive fines and prison time for DMCA violations and file trading should be reformed so that the penalty fits the offense. Finally, any reform of the DMCA should include disclosure requirements to warn customers when they are buying a device, CD, or other piece of media containing copy protections that result in less functionality.

12. Critics of Lawrence Lessig and other copyright reformers often seem exasperated by the paucity of realistic options available to those pushing to expand the public's digital rights. "[C]orporations spend vast sums in campaign contributions and lobbying to extend their property interests. It is hardly Lessig's fault, but it is hard to see how his side can compete," Adam Cohen wrote in a *New York Times* book review of *Free Culture*. Adam Cohen, "'Free Culture': The Intellectual Imperialists," *New York Times* Book Review (April 4, 2004).

While Lessig believes pushing digital culture underground so that "all the cool people will be playing the black market" will be ultimately destructive to the rule of law, I'm suggesting that when citizens are made to feel powerless, they are disposed to take up the tools at their disposal. They retreat to the Darknet only when sanctioned avenues are closed to them. (For the record, I also part ways with Lessig and others over the idea of a compulsory license for all-you-can-eat music downloading.) For more on Lessig's views on the subject of darknets, see Mego Lien, "Free Culture Advocate to Speak," the *Phoenix* (April 22, 2004). Online at http://phoenix.swarthmore.edu/2004-04-22/news/14033

13. Robert Bielby, "Digital Consumer Convergence Demands Reprogrammability," *Xcell Journal Online* (March 2, 2002). Online at http://tinyurl.com/yrtge

14. By 2008, three-quarters of U.S. homes will have at least one PC with entertainment functionality, and 30 million homes will have a data network. More factoids:

- In 1995, a four-megapixel digital camera cost $28,000. Today it costs less than $300.
- In 1997, a CD burner for the PC, with 2X recording speed, went for $469. Today a CD burner with 52X recording speed costs $32.
- In 1997, a 2.1-gigabyte hard drive sold for $179. Today a 200-gig hard drive—100 times bigger—costs $139.

Source for data network estimate: Parks Associates, a Dallas-based research firm.

15. In 1901 and 1906, the Victor Talking Machine Co. of Camden, New Jersey, bought the patents for the design of both the flat-disc phonograph and the phonograph cabinet.

Online Resources

In an endeavor of such wide scope, centering on a contentious, fast-moving subject, a single print book cannot compete with the Internet. For transcripts of interviews (with entertainment figures, technology chiefs, and pirates), additional background, reference sources, hyperlinked footnotes, pointers to grassroots media sites, and conversation around the topic of digital media, visit Darknet.com.